A History of Heavy Metal

A History of Heavy Metal

Andrew O'Neill

HEADLINE

First published in 2017
by HEADLINE PUBLISHING GROUP

1

Cataloguing in Publication Data is available from the British Library

Trade paperback ISBN 978 1 4722 4144 3

Ebook ISBN 978 1 4722 4146 7

Typeset in 11/14 pt Columbus MT by Jouve (UK), Milton Keynes

Printed and bound in Great Britain by Clays Ltd, St Ives plc

Headline's policy is to use papers that are natural, renewable and recyclable
products and made from wood grown in well-managed forests and other
controlled sources. The logging and manufacturing processes are expected
to conform to the environmental regulations of the country of origin.

HEADLINE PUBLISHING GROUP
An Hachette UK Company
Carmelite House
50 Victoria Embankment
London
EC4Y 0DZ

www.headline.co.uk
www.hachette.co.uk

For Charlie, John and Dave
and to the glory of Mercury

Contents

Acknowledgements

I am hugely grateful to all the dudes who helped me write this thing and those who help me bumble through life in general: my darling wife Stephanie, my editor Richard Roper, Nina Keen, Pete Dee, the hive mind of Alistair Fruish and John Higgs, Alastair Riddell for answering constant questions, Andy Heintz, Marc Burrows and Jez Miller of The Men That Will Not Be Blamed For Nothing, Frank Turner for sowing a seed, Simon Price for research leads. Jon Briley, Vivienne Clore and Bex Majors for getting me here.

All the bands I have ever loved, and all the bands I have ever hated.

And most of all Mercury/Hermes/Thoth. I hope I've done you proud.

....

FOR A PLAYLIST TO LISTEN TO
WHILE YOU READ THIS BOOK,
GO TO ANDREWONEILL.CO.UK

Introduction

What is Heavy Metal?

Before the dawn of mankind,
Before the birth of our own Sun,
Before the Universe itself, there was nothing but black.
Black. Black. Black.
Then came the Big Bang
The loudest riff ever heard[1] *. . .*
If you'd like to know what happened after the Big Bang
It's Planck time, particles and very, very hot.
The Universe expanded out and time itself began
Gravity switched on, and stars and planets came together

There are two types of people in the world: people who like heavy metal, and dicks. Don't worry too much if you fall into the latter category; I'm very persuasive.

Heavy metal is the most enduring of all modern musical genres. For nearly fifty years hairy men[2] with distorted guitars have made people bang their heads, expand their minds and form

---

1. Actually the Big Bang was virtually silent. Much as I hate to break the momentum this early in the book, it's important to get these things right. Otherwise we're starting off with you not trusting me and that's a fucking terrible relationship to have with a reader.

2. And a smaller but significant number of women.

lifelong friendships with like-minded people. While lesser musical styles come and go according to the vagaries of fashion, heavy
metal stands strong. It is a constant.[1]

Despite being a global phenomenon enjoyed by millions of
people, heavy metal remains somewhat misunderstood.[2] From
the very outset heavy metal positioned itself as outsider art and it
has been written off and derided by small-minded music critics
and the gatekeepers of 'acceptable' popular culture. Lester Bangs
of *Rolling Stone* described Black Sabbath's ground-breaking debut
album as sounding 'like Cream, but worse'. Metal is seen by many
outsiders as dumb, brash, unevolved, crass and even violent.

But that's fine. We don't need the squares and fuddy-duddies
of mainstream culture to dig it. We're having way too much fun
to give a shit what they think. *We* know what they're missing: the
single most expansive, vibrant, creative, intelligent, extreme,
hilarious and hedonistic subculture in the world.

Like Fenrir devouring the Sun, metal sprawls across all culture, swallowing influences and shitting out influence in its wake.
It can indeed be ham-fisted and crass, like Venom or Carnivore.
But it can also demonstrate immense virtuosity and musical
refinement like every guitar teacher's favourite band – Dream
Theater.[3] Metal can be hilarious, whether intentionally like the
gonzo comedy of Devin Townsend or unintentionally when its
affectations are po-faced and unsuccessful.[4]

1. Like Twiglets. Or piles.

2. Like a Russian substitute teacher with a severe speech impediment.

3. If you were to teleport any given Dream Theater gig to Sirius you would
kill three-quarters of the area's guitar teachers. Fact. Dream Theater are a band
who sound like they write their music on paper before picking up their guitars.
They are formed of ex-students of Berklee College of Music in Boston.

4. See the video for Immortal's 'Call of the Wintermoon'.

Metal can be uplifting and life-affirming like Judas Priest and Manowar or depressive like Warning and oppressive like Teitanblood. Metal at its best harnesses several of these elements – Pantera's incredible success is largely due to their tethering of Philip Anselmo's bonehead testosterone to Dimebag Darrell's graceful, soaring leads.

This defence having been made, heavy metal is experiencing something of a belated recognition in our post-post-modern media. And while it now enjoys a certain post-ironic broadsheet respectability, with reviews in the *Guardian* and academic theses written about it, heavy metal still has the power to shock and to confuse.

The history of heavy metal parallels the history of Western culture itself; a microcosm of the wider world. It is a fascinating story of larger-than-life characters living to excess, from the household names of Ozzy Osbourne and Lemmy to the brutal notoriety of the underground Norwegian black metal scene. It is the story of a worldwide network of rabid fans escaping everyday mundanity through music, of cut-throat corporate arseholes ripping off those fans and the bands they worship to line their pockets. The expansive pantheon of heavy metal musicians includes junkies, satanists and murderers, born-again Christians and teetotallers, stadium-touring billionaires and toilet-circuit journeymen. From its incubation in the steelworks and factories of the Midlands to festival stages across the world, from teenage bedrooms to the ashes of incinerated Norwegian churches, heavy metal has made its mark on every corner of the world.

To the uninitiated heavy metal can seem intimidating,[1] and while it is a natural home for outlaws and misfits, people on the fringes of society, it also manages to be a democratic, down-to-

---

1. Which is hilarious to us lot. There's nothing more reassuring to me than a large group of hairy metalheads.

earth subculture that embraces everyone. The term heavy metal is a broad umbrella. It incorporates chart-topping stadium acts like Iron Maiden and the genuinely nihilistic, ultra-underground denizens of metal's extreme fringes like Deiphago and Revenge.

At its most populist, metal reaches out to everyone. One of my favourite memories in twenty years as a metalhead was watching Metallica[1] convert thousands of Glastonbury revellers to the cause of heavy metal. It was the first time I'd been, having previously resisted the lure of that particular festival with significant ease, hearing it was now just a corporate shadow of its former counter-cultural self. I was amused by the idea of a thrash metal band[2] taking the headline slot more usually suited to the more anaemic end of indie pop. Metallica fucking owned it. Admittedly the people around me were somewhat disturbed by me screaming 'DIE! DIE! DIE!' at the top of my voice and were baffled by my constant headbanging, but after their blistering set the buzz was incredible, and shared by everyone. Dreadlocked trustafarians and mandied-up chavs joined wide-eyed festival virgins and the elite indie snobs in the visceral enjoyment of 'EAVY FUCKING METAL. A band who – even now – carry the torch of the extreme metal underground had entirely won over that most mainstream of music crowds. Metal is truly for the masses.[3]

Over the last three years I have performed my comedy show *Andrew O'Neill's History of Heavy Metal* to a huge range of audiences, from the teenage metalheads of the Download festival to the broadsheet-reading theatre-goers of the Edinburgh Fringe to comedy-and-heavy-metal-literate Scandinavian comedy crowds.

1. Unashamedly my favourite metal band. Well, somewhat ashamedly. See Chapter 6.

2. A contentious description, perhaps, but they still play their thrash stuff live.

3. Just like witches at black masses . . .

This is a story is for everyone, and this book allows me the opportunity to flesh it out and to dig deeper into the history of the music, the subculture and the characters who shaped it.

Before we dive headlong into the blackened realm of chaos that is the History of Heavy Metal I should probably first define what heavy metal is (and more importantly what it *isn't*). Metal's boundaries are scarred by the sort of constant war depicted in the Doctor Who story *Genesis of the Daleks*. Across the globe battles rage day and night about whether a particular band is metal or not, in gigs, rock bars, and most vehemently in the blasted wastelands of online comment sections.

Take, for example, the wise words of 'Blackadder367' under the official video for 'Ace of Spades':

> Music industry dont care about you, or Motorhead, or anyone, they care only about profit. *Allowing them to shape your brain about genre stuff or anything else is disaster.* Acctualy, music industry propaganda doing this, for bussines selling reasons and organization of market. [sic. Obviously. Emphasis mine.]

To be fair to Blackadder367 (and his 366 ancestors), Lemmy denied the label of heavy metal until his dying day, claiming that Motörhead were 'a rock'n'roll band, like The Beatles'. (Which is bollocks.) Nevertheless, the first uses of the term 'heavy metal' were entirely negative. It was a term of criticism, and these negative associations stayed with the old-school bands.[1] Even Lars

---

1. Ed Tudor-Pole off of Tenpole Tudor once admonished my band The Men That Will Not be Blamed for Nothing for describing ourselves as punk. 'You're not punk – you're better than that!' What? Better than Black Flag and Crass? I don't fucking think so.

Ulrich of Metallica went through a phase of saying 'hard rock' instead of 'heavy metal' in interviews. 'There are no adults in hard rock,' he once told Jools Holland. Mate, you've got the word metal IN THE NAME OF YOUR BAND. His eye was on the bottom line, not wanting to alienate potential paying punters[1] with the brutish associations of heavy metal. Hanging out with Guns N' Roses and U2 instead of with Slayer and Exodus was clearly fucking with his mind.[2]

This need to escape the perceived limitations of heavy metal is brilliantly depicted in the excellent comedy film *Bad News*:

> Vim: 'I think you're really starting out from the wrong
>   point of view, 'cause . . . we're not basically a heavy
>   metal band. Er . . . we're a bit more subtle than that.
>   Aren't we, Colin?'
> Colin: 'What?'
> Vim: 'We're a bit more subtle than that.'
> Colin: 'Yeah, we're subtle . . . but basically . . . we're
>   heavy metal, aren't we?'
> Spider: 'Yeah, Colin's right, Den. If we made a record it'd
>   be so heavy you couldn't get it off the turntable!'
> Vim: 'Yeah. I know that. I know. But what I'm saying is
>   we're not . . . simple heavy metal.'
> Den: [Indignant] 'I thought we were heavy metal?!'
> Vim: 'Yeah, I know we've got heavy roots . . . and I
>   mean . . . what I'm trying to say is we're trying to
>   progress a bit, trying to break a few barriers.'
> Den: 'Are we?'
> Vim: 'Yeah.'

1. PPPs
2. Let us never forget the white biker jacket.

[One and a half hours later.]
Vim: 'LOOK! We are not just another stupid heavy
    metal band.'
[Den pulls the van over.]
Den: 'I'm not going any further until I hear Alan say that
    we're heavy metal.'

Of course, this three-times-before-the-cock-crows denial of heavy metal is anathema[1] to metal fans. We take enormous pride in not just liking metal, but BEING metal. Metal is not just a musical genre – it is a whole subculture, a way of life. A mode of being. Heavy metal has a distinct style of dress. Cherry-picked from biker culture, punk, fetish wear, army surplus, Vikings . . . it's a synthesis of all the stuff metal music has taken influences from.

Not all metal fans have this attitude. It's entirely possible to love heavy metal while still dressing like a – whisper it – *normal* person. But why the fuck would you want to do that? Given the choice between dressing like a bloke in a Topman advert and dressing like Erik from Watain, I'll go for the latter, thanks. Ever since Judas Priest went all gay-biker-y, clothing has been an essential part of the metal subculture.

There's a weird paradox here – while some bands still eschew the label and some fans of the music think the dressing-up bit is a bit lame, straight culture has repeatedly stolen the tropes of heavy metal clothing and tried to adopt it into fashion.

Every couple of years a new outrage is committed by a pop star or inane TV presenter, whether it's David Beckham wearing an Exodus shirt or Kanye West in a Megadeth shirt or that knob

1. Not to be confused with the band Anathema, to whom this denial would also be anathema.**
** If you keep saying 'anathema' it starts to sound weird. Anathema. Anathema. Go on. Do it out loud. Anathema.

off the Jonas Brothers wearing a biker jacket and playing the worst guitar solo ever at the country music awards.

It's a subtle act of cultural appropriation. An attempt to tap into metal's outsider edge. It's also bullshit.

I used to work in a shop in a student union. One of my student customers regularly wore a T-shirt with a picture of Ozzy Osbourne and the word METAL on it in a Teutonic font. I noticed he didn't do *the nod*,[1] despite the fact that I was always listening to metal on the radio, I had long hair (still have, obviously) and I practically lived in an oversized Marduk T-shirt. So I asked him, all friendly like, 'Hey, man, what metal bands you into?' 'Oh,' he replied, 'I don't like metal.' After this things get a little bit hazy. I vaguely heard him say, 'I just like the shirt,' as everything turned dark and I passed out with a sort of ringing in my ears.

To us, it seems bizarre for *them* to appropriate something that has given us no cred, no cultural currency, and that occasionally gets us beaten up. Metal shores itself up against the non-metal because we have typically been rejected by the non-metal. It's seldom our choice. Metal relishes its status as the underdog. And so we are amused (and some are occasionally offended) when the people with all the cultural power try to appropriate that edge. Because – and this is key – we don't dress like this to be different from the mainstream. We dress like this to be *the same* as our heavy metal heroes and friends. It's a symbol of belonging as much as an act of rejection. It's an expression of who we are more than who we are not.

1. The nod is a subtle but important acknowledgement of another metalhead. The same thing is shared between bikers and drivers of VW camper vans. It's our equivalent of a masonic handshake. Where it is absent (say, in London or between poseurs) it signifies BULLSHIT.

Idiots often mistake a categorisation of 'metal' for some kind of validation. Plenty of terrible bands are definitely metal, and many great bands are definitely not. It's like when people deny something is a comedy if it fails to make them laugh. Instead of saying 'It's shit comedy' they say 'It's not comedy.' Or art. Or sex. What?

There is a heaviness inflation within metal which affects these categories. Retrospectively the earliest uses of terms like 'heavy metal' or 'death metal' can seem a bad fit for pioneers of the genres after bands have self-consciously picked up the genre and developed it. Sonically a band like Aborted has very little in common with a band like Possessed, but both are death metal. Without appreciating the development of the genre between the two it's hard to recognise that the former would possibly not have existed without the latter.

For this reason the entry standard for 'heavy metal' has definitely changed over the years. Led Zeppelin were seen as a definitive heavy metal band back in the day. But after Judas Priest and the New Wave of British Heavy Metal bands developed the genre into something much more distinctive, Led Zeppelin no longer fitted quite so easily. To my sensibility they're an overdriven blues band, not a heavy metal band.

The early seventies saw the term thrown about with reckless abandon.[1] Aerosmith, Alice Cooper, AC/DC, Queen, even Grand Funk Railroad were called heavy metal.[2]

There is a very simple reason for this. Heavy metal didn't exist as a genre in its early days. The bands who played metal then were on their own. Pioneers in a musical Wild West.

Nowadays we are totally spoiled with a wide range of

1. Yep, I've checked and there is a band called Reckless Abandon.
2. Grand Funk Railroad are not a heavy metal band.

specialised metal magazines like *Kerrang!*, *Metal Hammer*, *Terrorizer*, *Zero Tolerance* and *Decibel*, and websites like Blabbermouth and Metal Sucks, so it's easy to forget that up until the late 1980s heavy metal bands competed with pop and rock acts for exposure in the more mainstream music press. The British music paper *Sounds* played a huge part in coalescing metal into its own scene. Its coverage of the NWOBHM solidified that movement and the magazine's heavy metal pullout, *Kerrang!*, became its own entity and is still going strong today, while *Rolling Stone*, the *NME*, and even *Smash Hits* featured metal bands throughout metal's early years. So when a band was casually referred to as 'heavy metal' it was from a position of ignorance, from the OUTSIDE, not from a position of genre pride. In much the same way Slayer are called 'death metal' by ignorant journalists and Iron Maiden are called 'thrash' by twats, Aerosmith were called heavy metal by just about everyone and they really, really aren't.

It reminds me of a piece of stand-up comedy by Liam Mullone about his nephew not being accepted as gay by his local LGBT community:

> the gay community of Melton Mowbray said that he wasn't really gay because he hadn't committed to it. Which made me think that the entry requirement for being gay must have really gone up.
>
> When I was at school, just turning up with a sky-blue lunchbox was considered more than sufficient to earn that title, and to keep it for 18 years . . .

It wasn't until the mid-seventies that Judas Priest began to accept the label of heavy metal and drop the blues influence that umbilically attached early bands to the rock and roll sound of the sixties.

Retrospectively there seems a definite division between such definitely metal bands as Black Sabbath, Judas Priest, Slayer and

Cannibal Corpse, and the softer, more melodic, less doomy or aggressive acts like UFO, Alice Cooper and even, dare I say, Deep Purple and Led Zeppelin. This is not to deny the huge influence of these bands. And while proto-metal is a useful term for bands such as Cream who preceded and influenced metal, we need a term, I think, for bands considered heavy metal at the time but not now. Hard rock relegatories? Sub-metal? Light metal?

In the early eighties heavy metal subdivided like an amoeba into several sub-genres. Now metal geeks could argue on even smaller points. Yes, a band might be definitely heavy metal, but are they black metal? Thrash metal? Death metal? Doom? Cross-over? Power metal? Grindcore? Is grindcore even metal? Who are you and why are you asking me all these questions?

Then those sub-genres divided again. Yes they're heavy metal, yes they're death metal, but are they brutal death metal? Technical death metal? Melodic death metal? Swedish death metal? Blackened death? Death-thrash? The level of detail is pretty much fractal.

Ultimately, genre labels are unimportant. The map is not the territory. They exist as a descriptive guide, but the boundaries between genres are all porous. There is no such thing as a national accent. Every country has dialects which shift across the terrain of that country. Dialects along national borders tend to sound like a cross between both countries' accents. This is because national borders are an artificial human construct. The Liverpool accent is a cross between North Wales and Manchester. The Alsatian dialect is half French, half German.[1]

An easy way of defining the boundary is by clearing up what heavy metal ISN'T.

---

1. And this combination of French sensitivity and German rigour is what makes them such good guard dogs.

Here's a handy cut-out-and-keep list. Keep it in your wallet and deploy it whenever you need back-up in an argument.

THINGS THAT ARE NOT HEAVY METAL

(a) Any album that came out before
    Black Sabbath by Black Sabbath
(b) Goth*
(c) Guns N' Roses
(d) *Stomp*[1]
(e) *Some Kind of Monster*
(f) Late-nineties Prodigy
(g) Punk
(h) Nickelback
(i) Your band

In contrast, here is a list of things that *are* heavy metal which aren't even music:

(a) Tanks
(b) Satan
(c) Headbanging
(d) Denim
(e) Leather
(f) Denim and leather
(g) Brought us all together

---

1. A mistake made by my nan. One day we were watching telly, and *Stomp* was on, and my nan asked, 'Andrew, is this heavy metal?' You can see where she's coming from. They've got bins. She was very literal-minded, my nan. She was very disappointed by *Zoo* magazine. She only started buying single cream after my grandad died.

(h) It was you that set the spirit free

(i) Siege weaponry

(j) Goats

(k) Skulls

(l) Goat skulls

(m) Birmingham

(n) Your mum

*Some things are both goth *and* metal, though:

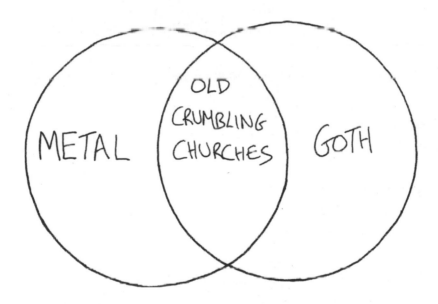

This account of heavy metal is a deeply personal, opinionated one. Metal is a huge subject and whole books could easily be written about each and every band mentioned herein. So tracing a line through the history is a matter of editing. Every key band could be substituted for another. While this book makes no claim to be comprehensive, this is *my* history of heavy metal. I hope you dig it.

Our taste in music is usually based on arbitrary decisions we made during adolescence, based often on what our friends and older siblings were listening to, and then a sort of confirmation bias that grows out from there. In this book I have tried to apply some objectivity when it comes to the stuff I have decided I think is shit, but I'm probably still going to offend you. Please don't fall for thinking that I am 'wrong'. Try to think more along the lines that views are subjective.

And that it's you that's wrong.

1

Roots, Bloody Roots
c.40,000 BCE–1969

The urge to make rhythmic noise is a fundamental part of human nature. Humans are hard-wired to find pleasure in making loud sounds. If you are in any doubt about this fact, furnish a child with a drum kit. Then sit back and enjoy the delighted look on its parents' faces, knowing the racket *will not stop*. The ubiquity of organised noise-making, from tribal drumming to football chants, from the archaeological evidence of prehistoric percussion instruments, to the baffling international success of *Stomp*, tells us that it is a human need, and a human trait.

Long before the electric guitar or the spandex trouser, the history of heavy metal begins with the first humans to bash rocks with sticks, and continues every time a teenager's synapses are fired by their first taste of heavy metal's primal roar. Metal is an expression of an essential part of humanity. This is why it continues to be such a massively popular musical form in spite of the total lack of support from mainstream radio and television.

A few years ago a cave in southern Germany gave up its ancient secrets to archaeologists. Two small flutes, carved out of bird bone and ivory approximately 42,000 years ago, turned out to be the oldest surviving instruments ever discovered. *Homo sapiens* have only been around for about 200,000 years, so we now know that for at least the last fifth of the existence of our species we have been manufacturing musical instruments. In all likelihood humans had been making music for thousands of years before this. Ethnographic studies of existing hunter-gatherer societies suggest that Palaeolithic humans most likely made music using voices and percussion instruments 'made of organic materials, and thus unlikely to leave an archaeological trace', according to 'The Evolutionary Origins and Archaeology of Music' by Iain Morley of Cambridge University. Plus there was lots of clapping, slapping and stamping. Think Bobby McFerrin.[1] Mainstream thought is that our Stone Age ancestors were singing, hitting things with sticks and making a racket in the echoing, acoustically satisfying environment of a cave as far back as they existed. The more you think about hairy monosyllabic cavemen smashing stuff up to make a pleasing racket, the less I'm convinced there is further argument to be made; that's a perfectly serviceable working definition of heavy metal.

Most accounts seem to suggest that music is hard-wired,[2] much like language. It's just something that humans do; behaviour that emerges out of our brain-wiring. Like falling in love. Or lying. Or breaking someone's heart.[3]

Music has measurable and predictable effects on the brain. Strong beats produce synchronised patterns in brain activity. Mainstream science suggests music can aid memory recovery, help heal brain damage and overcome addiction. The more, let's

1. When in doubt, ALWAYS think of Bobby McFerrin.

2. Researching this topic of 'Is music hard-wired' online is tricky ever since Metallica announced the release of their album *Hard-Wired to Self Destruct*.

3. Or genocide. Or being jealous of those who are younger than you and so poisoning their drinks when they come round to watch reruns of *Doctor Who* in your flat. But gently so they never realise.

say, *unscientific* areas of the internet make even bolder claims. Their 'binaural' beats can apparently open your third eye, release kundalini, align your chakras and claim compensation for mis-sold PPI.

Most of the music said to 'increase IQ' or 'improve spatial awareness' is classical. So what does heavy metal do to the brain? Well, based on observation I'd argue that heavy metal:

(1) Increases your capacity for alcohol
(2) Makes you sexier
(3) Makes you think everything was better in the past

Heavy metal is capable of immense complexity and sophistication. It operates partly on an intellectual level; its ideas, lyrical themes and dazzling virtuosity tickle the highest parts of the brain. But let's be frank – heavy metal also operates on a very primitive level. All right, it *mainly* operates on a very primitive level. Heavy metal is loud. It has a very strong beat. It is emotionally strong – often aggressive. Heavy metal is visceral.

Music makes people happy. It stimulates the reward centres of the brain. According to boffins:

> Music involves subtle violations of timing and, because we know through experience that music is not threatening, these violations are ultimately identified by the frontal lobes as a source of pleasure. The expectation builds anticipation, which, when met, results in the reward reaction. – Malini Mohana, 'Music and How It Impacts Your Brain, Emotions', www.psychcentral.com

According to the same article, when we are born we are unable to differentiate between senses – a form of total synaesthesia. We swiftly learn to distinguish between sight, sound, smell, feel . . . In a similar way, extreme metal can sound like a wall of

incomprehensible noise to the newbie. The different elements are
unpacked once we learn what we are listening to. Extreme music
is an acquired taste – to the uninitiated it can sound unpleasant,
like noise. But to those who get it and learn its subtle variations,
the extremity provides more visceral pleasure than normal music
does to normal people. Basically, a Morbid Angel fan gets more
out of one of their gigs than a Coldplay fan does at theirs; metalheads are better than the rest of the population. And that's
SCIENCE.

Heavy metal is not like other popular music. It serves different functions, and some functions that are the same, but it goes
about it in a different way. When it makes us happy it is not by
talking about happy things; rather it provides a stimulation
through contact with its extremity.

A friend of mine described her first live experience of grindcore as 'invigorating. Like standing under a waterfall.' Metal is
more like the masochistic experience of horror films or thrillers
than the relaxing experience of soul or Classic FM's brand of
Soothing Sounds for Stressed People. There is something about
heavy metal that taps into the brain's primal circuits. All music is
an emotional experience, bypassing the conscious mind.

Making noise is incredibly and provably therapeutic. Primal
scream therapy is notably effective and incredibly popular.

> the patient recalls and reenacts a particularly disturbing
> past experience usually occurring early in life and
> expresses normally repressed anger or frustration *especially*
> *through spontaneous and unrestrained screams, hysteria, or*
> *violence* – Merriam-Webster dictionary [emphasis mine]

The inventor Arthur Janov suggests that talking therapies are
limited because they focus on the cerebral cortex and higher rea-
soning areas of the brain, and do not access the more basic parts

of the central nervous system, which are the root of the pain. Holy Moses, that's a really good explanation of why heavy metal makes me feel so good! It has been proven in studies that shouting, screaming and even swearing are effective at increasing the body's capacity to withstand pain.[1]

Heavy metal makes people feel really, really good. There are two obvious parallels with drugs: (1) heavy metal is addictive, and (2) heavy metal encourages escalation as sensitivity decreases through contact.

Metal is addictive because its extremity produces an extreme physiological response. A heavy metal concert is a visceral experience. At a live show fans enjoy the feeling of drums thudding in their chest, lights piercing through smoke to dazzle their eyes, the sweat and heat of other bodies. Heavy metal shows can be a full-contact sport, with stage-divers raining down like sweaty bombs and crowd surfers clambering overhead and the frenetic near-violence of the mosh pit. It's no wonder that metal imagery so often harks back to the ages of Viking raiders and medieval battles. Metal is physical as much as audible. The experience of heavy metal is the shamanistic magic of sensory overload.[2] It fires adrenaline, endorphins and serotonin, biochemicals that are pleasurable and addictive. Metal is so addictive, in fact, that in 2015 a Swedish man by the name of Roger Tullgren was declared eligible for disability benefits because his addiction to heavy metal concerts prevented him holding down a job.

The evidence for escalation is everywhere. The history of

1. I know this cos I once saw a programme where Stephen Fry and Brian Blessed put their hands in icy water and did loads of swearing. It was awesome.

2. Heavy metal has taken its toll on my body. I have tinnitus, two broken front teeth and a neck so disproportionately thick for my skinny body that I cannot find shirts that fit me.

heavy metal is a never-ending quest for a heavier sound. Most metal fans will feel a progressive need for something even more intense to provide the same rush as the first *oh my God that's heavy*.

(Heaviness in musical terms is a hard concept to pin down. The term comes from hippy slang, meaning 'profound' or 'deep'. Musically it can refer to a harshness of sound, volume, distortion, but more often it's more metaphorical – it refers to the 'downer' effect on the listener. I'll discuss this in more depth when we get on to death metal. The REALLY heavy stuff!)

So how did we get from hairy pre-civilised humans, bashing things with sticks and making a load of pleasant noise in caves to hairy semi-civilised humans bashing things with sticks and making a load of pleasant noise in music venues?

Tracking the development of any musical style is an inexact process. Styles blend into each other, they take two steps forward and one back. They do not evolve in anything like a steady way or in a linear fashion. We have to track trends, rather than direct lines. Determining when rhythm and blues became rock and roll or when the New Wave of British Heavy Metal became thrash metal is like determining when late night turns into early morning. It appears different depending on which end you're looking from. Often it's necessary to use prefixes like 'proto-' or 'post-' to situate a band relative to a genre. There is a strong case to be made that heavy metal is the sum of everything that had come before. It has tribal drumming. It has the multi-octave vocal range of opera. It has the rootsy storytelling of folk and the bardic tradition. It uses the musical palette of the blues and the dynamics of Russian orchestral music. Metal is such a huge and diverse category that there is literally no aspect of music it hasn't cherry-picked from. Nevertheless, a thread can be traced along its main path.

*

Before we go any further, I would like to throw in a warning.

As a general rule, never move back in with your parents. As another general rule, beware of anyone making bold statements about the origins or provenance of genres. A friend recently told me about a talk by two 'expert' speakers who'd 'been there' at the birth of punk. They both claimed that Malcolm McLaren and Vivienne Westwood were solely responsible for the creation of punk. This is, of course, total bollocks. Alas, my chum was naive to the realities of the punk rock nostalgia movement and said with no irony, 'Apparently everyone else claimed credit but it was just those two.' It turns out the speakers weren't so much punks at the time as hangers-on and, unsurprisingly, mates with 'those two'. The showbiz dazzle of McLaren and Westwood apparently blinded them to the reality of punk's birth in late-sixties Detroit and early-seventies New York. So much for authority.

The roots of heavy metal are in the percussion and vocalisations used by the earliest humans. Tribal drumming is the earliest historical ancestor of the heavy metal sound. (The Brazilian metal band Sepultura incorporated tribal drumming into their mix on two albums in the mid-nineties to brilliant effect.) Humans have always been drummers. This is evident not only from archaeological and ethnographic evidence but also from the fact that even drummers can drum. Drummers. The simplest of all life forms. Only truly happy when hitting things with sticks. Or, in the case of Keith Moon, blowing up toilets.

Rhythm is innate to human beings, but while it is easy to imagine drumming to be the part of heavy metal with the longest unchanged history, the modern drum kit is a relatively recent innovation. Drumming as we know it today (using a multi-drum set), came together slowly over the course of the nineteenth and early twentieth centuries. Between pre-history and the Middle Ages, drumming had evolved from simple tribal drumming with organic, local objects to organised military use with more complex drums. Such use is recorded as far back as Genghis Khan.[1] By the 1800s military marching bands were a popular source of musical entertainment. Simultaneously, drumming developed within orchestras. In both cases, percussionists would specialise – using only one drum each. Around 1870 military-style percussionists began combining the contrasting sound of two drums, a technique known as double drumming.[2] Slowly more contraptions were added to this arrangement and drumming became more complex and expressive. Foot pedals were developed, snares were invented. The hi-hat was back-engineered from a crashed flying saucer. Slowly but surely, percussionists became drummers. Familiar drummer-like traits began to emerge, such as van ownership, sarcasm and grumpiness. As soon as the drummer evolved out of the primordial soup, the drummer jokes started . . .[3]

At the same time as the modern drummer was evolving, guitars were taking an increasingly prominent place in popular music. If the foundation of heavy metal is drumming, the walls are built of guitars.[4]

1. You don't get anyone called Genghis any more, do you?

2. Brilliant, eh? What a clever name.

3. There are loads of great drummer jokes: 'What's rubbish?' – 'A DRUMMER!'; 'Who is the member of the band most commonly derided?' – 'THE DRUMMER!'; 'Which member of the band feels a bit left out socially but tries to put on a brave front despite the whole experience triggering horrible memories of an awkward childhood?' – 'THE DRUMMER!' Hahahahaha! Brilliant.

4. Or, at the very least, walls of Marshall stacks . . .

Before the Second World War the guitar was mainly a backing instrument; a team player in jazz ensembles, orchestras and big bands. The guitar's expressive beauty and huge versatility were buried behind its bitter rival – the piano.[1]

It was African-American music that first brought the guitar to the fore as a lead instrument, most importantly in the blues. The blues is the earliest recognisable ancestor to heavy metal. Blues was an American original – the product of slave culture, dragging forcibly uprooted African rhythms and harnessing them to American folk instruments.

The tribal music of Africa is often used as a lazy and somewhat prejudiced shorthand for 'primitive' music. In reality there's nothing primitive about it, especially compared to the pop music shit you listen to, you racist. The egalitarian tribal cultures of pre-colonial West Africa had their own distinctive and complex music forms. It's an error to link relatively recent tribal cultures too closely with that of palaeolithic ones, or indeed those that maintain a gatherer-hunter existence in the modern world.

African tribal music evolved into the more advanced West African music which was transported across the Atlantic with the slave trade. Over time, these African sounds evolved into distinct African-American sounds, via work songs, spirituals that merged African rhythms with European-influenced Christian music.

This transporting of a musical style across the Atlantic will become a familiar motif in the development of metal. Blues originated as a purely vocal musical form. A simplistic but incredibly expressive form of music which reflected the situation of America's rural black population, still living under the cloud of slavery

---

1. Much like how Geri Halliwell's true genius was only fully revealed after the Spice Girls split up and she went solo, showing a musical talent comparable in its breathtaking complexity to Bach and Rachmaninov.

and the reality of racial oppression – working for minimal pay in the same back-breaking jobs they had been made to do under slavery, only now being paid just enough to subsist, to rent hous- ing from white landlords who had previously been slave owners. There is a bitter irony in the fact that blues is now predominantly played by middle-class white dudes. There's nothing inherently wrong in that – at least it is being celebrated. It's just a bit weird; beautifully illustrated in the film *Ghost World* when a fictional Delta blues legend is supporting a horrific dude-bro blues-rock band called Blues Hammer.

Of course, without white dudes playing blues there'd be no heavy metal . . . so my criticism isn't exactly vehement.

Blues developed into a wide variety of styles, varying accord- ing to geography. Rural styles differed from those that emerged in the urban environs of Chicago, Detroit and Memphis. Early blues singers were almost exclusively women. (Male black per- formers were still forced into 'unthreatening' clown roles.) Bessie Smith was the first blues superstar: in the twenties and thirties she commanded up to a thousand dollars per show.

Early recordings of blues artists are haunting. Recorded in the 1920s, Blind Lemon Jefferson's[1] eerie, high vocals influenced the histrionics of Led Zeppelin's Robert Plant and thus every metal band who followed. The most celebrated early blues player was Robert Johnson, a genius said to have sold his soul to the devil in exchange for supernatural playing skills – a myth he perpetuated himself with the songs 'Hellhound on My Trail', 'Me and the Devil Blues' and 'Crossroad Blues'. His voice is transporting – so utterly evocative of another time and place. He is a mysterious

1. The bit of research that made me laugh the most in the course of writing this book? 'I wonder what Blind Lemon Jefferson's real name was? Oh. Lemon Jefferson. Right.'

figure, about whom little is known.[1] He recorded in 1936 and 1937 and died the following year at the age of twenty-seven, probably poisoned. While Johnson has a diabolical reputation, in truth all secular music was colloquially called 'the devil's music' in the culture Johnson grew up in.

It is Howlin' Wolf who most influenced metal's vocal style. Howlin Wolf's voice is like no other. Deep, thick, gravelly and resonant, it sparkles with wit and intelligence. His personality shines through in his recordings. In 1970 a group of musicians including Eric Clapton and Charlie Watts brought Howlin' Wolf to London to collaborate on a recording. He turned out to be an arsehole. Arrogant, bad-tempered and pretty much impossible to work with. Perfect. The result is brilliant, Wolf's haggard vocals adding grit and guts to the sixties white-guy blues sound.

Howlin' Wolf is truly heavy. His song 'Killing Floor' has been covered by Hendrix and Led Zeppelin and countless others. He is the most direct link between the old blues and the emergence of heavy metal.

Blues mixed with other black American musical forms such as gospel and jazz to produce *rhythm and blues*. Originally coined to replaced the bluntly offensive term 'race music', rhythm and blues is an amorphous category which stretches to accommodate whatever music of African-American origin various people want to fit inside it. Early R&B artists such as Sister Rosetta Tharpe sang earnest, powerful Christian songs and evolved the form towards what became increasingly recognisable as rock and roll, a style of music that has distinctly un-Christian associations:

> He would sing to draw people to the local town prophet
> and spiritualist, Doctor Nubilio, who wore a turban and a

---

1. Apart from that he definitely sold his soul to the devil. Definitely.

colorful cape, carried a black stick and exhibited something
he called 'the devil's child' – the dried-up body of a baby
with claw feet like a bird and horns on its head.

. . . and that is why you'll never be as cool as Little Richard. This
hoodoo, folk-magic feel combined with an alien queerness to
make rock and roll legend Little Richard utterly unique. His vocal
style took the aggression of Howlin' Wolf and added a massive
boost of energy. His piano playing style and vocal gymnastics
are like those of a man possessed. He was the ultimate showman.
It's impossible to listen to 'Long Tall Sally' or 'Tutti Frutti' and
remain still. Another high-energy piano player was the very
sweaty Jerry Lee Lewis. Watching footage of Jerry Lee playing
back in the fifties it's surprising that his style of energised, outlaw
piano playing never took off. He just looks so fucking cool.
(Apart from the whole thirteen-year-old wife business . . .) Instead
it's the guitar that became the instrument of choice for rock and roll.

It was Chuck Berry who took rock and roll piano playing
and transposed it to the newly electrified guitar – an entirely new
approach to the instrument. Practically every rock and roll band
from the Beatles to Status Quo (especially Status Quo) directly
copied Berry's playing style. Meanwhile Bo Diddley took a different path, developing his own uniquely primal and rhythmic
style of rock and roll. But in racially segregated America it was
nearly impossible for a black artist on their own to cross over into
mainstream acceptance.

Meanwhile, rural white America was documenting its own
mythology in country and western music. It was this that combined with the emerging R&B to produce rock and roll as we
now know it. Basically people took black music and racist music
and mixed them together to make millions of dollars for the
white men who owned the record labels. Sam Phillips, the

producer who first recorded Elvis Presley, explicitly stated this intention to rip off black music and flog it to a white market. Marion Keisker, receptionist at Sun Records, says:

> Over and over I remember Sam saying, 'If I could find a white man who had the Negro sound and the Negro feel, I could make a billion dollars.' James Miller, *Flowers in the Dustbin: The Rise of Rock and Roll, 1947–1977*

Elvis was the catalyst for rock and roll going global. He took the rockabilly sound of the Maddox Brothers and Carl Perkins and added a fluid sexuality and an incredible voice. Early TV appearances were controversial. Elvis's body language was seen as so explicitly sexual that on his third appearance on the *Ed Sullivan Show* (America's biggest TV programme, with an audience share of 86 per cent) he was filmed from the waist up. Despite the censorship, these appearances made him a megastar. Chuck Berry and Bo Diddley had scored hits, but Elvis took rock and roll to the masses. His commercialised take on it went worldwide – opening up the British audience to American roots music. Everyone wanted to be Elvis. Second only to the Beatles in terms of direct influence over the architects of heavy metal, Elvis was a hero to most.[1] Following his path, blues and R&B came back over the Atlantic and fell into the hands of music obsessives like John Lennon and Keith Richards.

Rock and roll is typified by a backbeat – a snare hit on every second beat – ONE *TWO* THREE *FOUR*. Think of the verse of 'Rock Around the Clock'. Or every single Status Quo song. It is energetic

1. 'but he never meant shit to me, he's straight up racist the sucker was, simple and plain – motherfuck him and John Wayne!' – Chuck D, Public Enemy

and hugely, innately danceable. Rock and roll is like the product of alchemy. It is perfect music. And it was perfectly expressive for a generation that was just beginning to find its own identity.

Teenagers didn't exist before the 1950s; the term hadn't been coined. Kids sublimed into adulthood without an intermediate stage. In the 1950s economic circumstances changed – teenagers had money to spend on clothes and entertainment. And the seven-inch vinyl single was the perfect item to encapsulate their new purchasing power.

This teenage identity posed a threat to the existing order. It was bound up in notions of rebellion, and rock and roll provided a soundtrack to that rebellion. It was popular music with a hint of menace. It appealed to outlaws and bikers, as much as to the teen gangs and the rebels. So subversive was rock and roll seen to be by the establishment that the instrumental track 'Rumble' by Link Wray was banned by radio stations in America because of its implication of juvenile delinquency.

As ridiculous as that sounds in the twenty-first century, there was a precedent for rock and roll music as the seed of violence. The stand-out is the reaction to the 1955 American film *Blackboard Jungle*. The film was significant for its revolutionary-for-the-time portrayal of inner-city violence and discontent. It featured 'Rock Around the Clock' by Bill Haley and the Comets three times over the course of the movie, although its use in the opening credits was cut by film censors. The song, heard with unprecedented clarity and volume through state-of-the-art cinema speakers, caused riots. Kids tore up and slashed seats and started fights. In the buttoned-up, conservative post-war era, rock and roll represented the sound of freedom. It represented rebellion – a world bigger than that of their parents. Suddenly, anything seemed possible. Music was an engine of transformation.

Unfortunately, rather than tearing down existing systems and building a Utopia in its ruins, the teenagers of the fifties spent all their spare money on clothes, becoming the first conspicuous consumers. The fleet-footedness of capitalism took their rebellion and sold it back to them.

It would be another fifteen years before teenagers truly attempted the rebellion hinted at by rock and roll, but that was a whole different era, and an awful lot would change before then. Rock and roll got watered down and rendered safe through commercial engines. Record companies removed its menace and sexuality and churned out parentally approved 'teen idols' like Bobby Rydell. It seemed as though the flame had died.

But on the other side of the Atlantic several youngsters were poised, like human growbags, to take the seeds shed by American rock and roll and nurture them into something even more powerful, and considerably heavier. In a dreary post-war Britain, shipping was to be the key to the rock explosion. Obsessive young fans such as Paul McCartney and John Lennon in Liverpool and Mick Jagger and Keith Richards in London bought records directly off the transatlantic ships that docked in their local ports.

But while the sixties rock giants were still at school the UK had quickly developed its own rock and roll. These late-fifties bands lacked the primal urgency of the early American sound. Though Cliff Richard was initially surprisingly good, with a genuine Elvis-like feeling of danger, his subsequent conversion to Christianity took away his grit and his later work with The Shadows sounds distinctly safe; music you'd take home to meet your mother. They were joined by Tin Pan Alley boy stars such as Tommy Steele, Marty Wilde and Billy Fury, who sounded anaemic compared to the full-blood rock and roll of Little Richard and Bo Diddley. There were exceptions – Johnny Kidd and the Pirates' song 'Shaking All Over' remains peerless.

There was another crucial element to the British mix that

would change all this – skiffle. The sound of post-war austerity may have a distinctly un-rebellious, cardigans-and-wholesomeness image, but it was the punk rock of its time. Almost single-handedly inspired by Lonnie Donegan and his version of Lead Belly's 'Rock Island Line' it was a grass-roots method of playing involving ad-hoc instruments such as the washboard (played with thimbles) and the tea-chest bass. It invigorated the teenagers of a depressing pre-technicolour Britain with a DIY, here's-a-chord, here's-another, now-form-a-band mentality. It led to an explosion of creativity. The Beatles, The Rolling Stones, The Who, The Kinks, The Troggs, The Animals, the Yardbirds; they all took what the Americans had started and made it their own. Everyone started a band. The British Invasion was about to begin.

It is with the electrification of the guitar that heavy metal's roots begin to resemble what we know today. Acoustic guitars are a relatively quiet instrument compared with the volume produced by brass instruments and pianos. Attempts were made to use microphones to pick up the noise coming from the sound hole and put the signal through the venue's PA system, but this was prone to feedback – the guitar picking up the sound from the speakers and the signal being amplified over and over again in a feedback loop, creating a painful high-pitched squeal. With electrification, guitars could compete for audibility within bands while avoiding the problems of feedback associated with using microphones. Guitar pickups produce current when the vibration of a steel string interacts with the pickup's magnetic field. It was Gibson who released the first electric guitar we would recognise today with the ES-150 (named for 'Electric Spanish' and the $150 package it was sold in[1]).

1. Keep saying package and it sounds weird.

Acoustic guitars with pickups also suffer problems with feedback, but the way pickups work means that guitars could be solid-bodied – the sound is produced mainly by the interaction of the string and the pickup so the acoustic amplification isn't necessary.

Leo Fender produced the first solid-body guitar, the Broadcaster (later renamed the Telecaster) in 1950. Gibson followed in 1952 with the Les Paul, named after one of the most popular guitarists of the day, who had a hand in its development. Fender's next model, the Stratocaster (1954) is an ergonomic delight (unless you have boobs, mind).

The solid design made it possible to shape the body of the electric guitar in any way you wanted. As such, Gibson's next two were POINTY! The Explorer (a sort of stretched rhombus shape) and the Flying V (a v-shape, apparently originally called 'The Flying Arrow' and commissioned for a 'Red Indian Duo', back when that was an acceptable thing to say) came out in 1958 and are still go-to guitars for metal bands who want something with a bit of edge; the Flying V in particular has now become the ultimate symbol of heavy metal. The idea was taken a step further with Jackson's Randy Rhoads, which possibly the first guitar pointy enough to make it a viable stabbing weapon. Since then the company BC Rich have cornered the market in guitars you'd struggle to get through airport security. It's my opinion that Gibson's next significant model, the SG (solid guitar) of 1961 is the best guitar ever made, played by Sister Rosetta Tharpe, Angus Young and, er, me.

It's remarkable how little the design of electric guitars has changed since these early models. They are design classics and still staples of rock and roll.

Electric guitars require amplification. The first guitar amplifiers were meek. Early Fender models were polite in the extreme and early British amps fared no better – those like the Watkins

Westminster (10 watts of feeble power!) and the various amps made by Elpico (which would later become a key component in the development of distortion, but not without the addition of good old-fashioned vandalism) were about as loud as a laptop. Enough to wake up a light sleeper on a quiet afternoon, nothing like enough to get over the noise of a busy pub, and if you're playing a hall – forget it.

The British company Vox developed the 15-watt AC15 in 1958 and followed it up with the double-powered AC30 the following year after demands were made by The Shadows – Cliff Richard's backing band. These amplifiers could fill a theatre . . . but you needed a few of them. Vox amps were subsequently adopted by the Beatles, and though the company upgraded the power as much as possible, the Beatles stopped performing live because their audiences were louder than their backline. The Vox AC30 became the standard amp of the 'British Invasion' bands such as The Kinks, the Stones and (initially) The Who. Vox amplifiers were the power behind the transformation of rock and roll into rock music, but it was Jim Marshall, a drummer turned drum teacher turned drum shop owner who developed the amplification that would power the transition of British rock music into heavy metal. His close relationship with his students and with the customers in his shop allowed him and his team of engineers to develop the sort of amp the kids were all craving; something louder than the 'make-do' amps and with a more satisfying distortion.

Marshall and engineer Ken Bran took a Fender Bassman apart and noted its circuitry. Some of the Bassman's Septic[1] components were unavailable so they substituted valves and

1. Septic tank = Yank = American. Lesson one in Cockney rhyming slang. Look out for more over the course of the book.

components that were 'near enough', leading to a different sound. But it still wasn't loud enough. Several tweaks later and the 45-watt JTM45 was unleashed in 1963 (or '64 – historians are divided . . .). Tethered to a separate speaker cabinet, it kicked out a louder sound than the Fender Bassman, and it was cheaper than the imported amps. Endorsement deals with The Who and Jimi Hendrix (and later Led Zeppelin) made the Marshall the amp synonymous with the power of stadium rock and proto-metal. It's just a shame the Beatles didn't get their hands on them – they might still be a live act.

The Beatles are the most successful and most influential band ever. Part of their influence is down purely to the scale of their success and their ubiquity in the 1960s, but their relentless experimentation and testosterone-fuelled internal competitiveness led to them being at the very cutting edge of music throughout their surprisingly short career.

The boot camp of marathon sets in Hamburg led to them being a ferocious live unit, and careful management softened their hard edges (they were all leather suits, amphetamines and whores in Hamburg before Brian Epstein turned them into a singularly marketable act). But it was the songs that sold them. Tight harmonies, combined with staggeringly inventive chord soundings (they competed to be the first to learn new chords).

In fact, you know, sometimes we'd travel the whole of Liverpool just to go to someone who knew a chord we didn't know. I remember once hearing about a bloke who knew B7. Now, we knew E and we knew A, that was quite easy, but we didn't know B7, that was kind of the missing part, the link, the other chord, the lost chord. So on we got, on the bus, trooped across Liverpool. Changed a couple of buses, found this fella, and he showed us – dum, dum, dum, dum, dum dum B7 and we learned it, off him, got back on the bus, went home to our mates and went ZZZZZING! GOT IT! – Paul McCartney

The Beatles cracked America and opened a market for other British rock bands. If they'd stopped there they would still be a significant part of this narrative. But they continued to forge ahead, sucking in influences from London's buzzing avant-garde art scene and spewing them out in the most experimental, technically innovative and brilliant pop music anyone had ever heard. And importantly *everyone* heard it. Their unprecedented and unmatched size is the biggest factor in their influence. Thank fuck they were good.

The Beatles' only real rival for the position of biggest band in the world in the 1960s was a very different outfit. The Rolling Stones started as a blues band. Contrary to the Beatles' artistic restlessness, the Stones remained fairly traditional for most of their career. But while the Beatles were pitched by their management as cheeky lovable lads,[1] the Stones cultivated a more sinister, rebellious image. While the Beatles were singing 'I Wanna Hold Your Hand', the Stones demanded, 'Let's Spend the Night Together'. There was something more grown-up about the Stones. They were less obviously pop. They also made it big in America. This 'British Invasion' paved the way for heavy metal to follow later.

For all the success of these two titans in America, and the exporting of Englishness as a commodity, for my money the most British of all the British Invasion bands was the one that never quite broke over the Atlantic – The Kinks.

1. Much to John Lennon's stated disgust.

While the Beatles were singing endless permutations of 'I think it is a good idea if you and I go out with each other' and the Stones were singing endless permutations of 'I think it is a good idea if you and I have sexual intercourse,' The Kinks were painting vivid pictures of parochial English life. They hold the distinction of having written the single greatest pop song of all time – 'Waterloo Sunset'. And, quite possibly, the first heavy metal song.

Dave Davies was an angry young man. His relationship with his brother Ray, frontman and vocalist of The Kinks, was violent. Ray comes across as a bully, an egotist genius, a thug poet. But Dave had a temper too. Dave was quiet, sensitive, but driven by a fraternal competitiveness more organic and real than that of Lennon and McCartney. Dave had a sound in his head. He was deeply unsatisfied with the polite, clean, shimmery Shadows-type sound produced by English amplification. He wanted his guitar to roar. He took a razor blade to his little Elpico amp, slashing the paper speaker cone and produced the startling, barking sound heard on 'You Really Got Me':

BA-DA-DA BA-DA!
BA-DA-DA BA-DA!

The riff slashes through the mix like Dave's razor blade. Listening on headphones you can actually hear the rattle of the broken speaker. The guitar urges Ray on to a more aggressive vocal delivery. Then the key change creates a sense of euphoria in the listener, firing off the brain's ecstatic hormones, and by the point of the solo Ray screams orgasmically, 'OH NO, NO!' And we are off. Heavy metal has an antecedent. The dial has finally been turned to eleven.

Alas, The Kinks never rubbed along with America. Their first tour in the States was marred by on-stage fights, arguments with union officials and ultimately blacklisting by the American Federation of Television and Recording Artists. The ban meant they missed out on the peak of interest in British rock and roll and, according to Ray Davies, America missed the band at their live peak. But it wasn't all bad. The American market being cut off they focused on a more uniquely English sound. Their divine album *The Village Green Preservation Society* went against the rock and roll grain in favour of a much more interesting, parochial storytelling style. But with their early blasts of power chord rock they had set a standard which all the other bands would attempt to attain.

True rock and roll heaviness – the transition into rock music, then hard rock – emerged from London. The Kinks directly influenced The Who, the band who most consistently wielded a real sonic heft in the mid-sixties.

The Who were a strange combination of art school sensitivity (Townshend) and street thug aggression (the rest of them). That blueprint carries on through the development of heavy metal and punk rock, possibly best exemplified by the expressed desire of Black Flag's Henry Rollins to be seen as a 'warrior poet'.

The riff for 'My Generation' is worth a book in itself. It is huge. Colossal. Far bigger than it deserves to be. And then there's the bass break. The guitars over that still sound like the Beatles. But it's Roger Daltrey's incredibly aggressive, sneering vocal delivery that really elevates the song in terms of its heaviness. It's an anger that wouldn't be heard in mainstream music until punk broke in 1977.

But the real story of the early Who was amphetamines. The stuttering delivery in 'My Generation' is said to be an impression of a mod on speed. According to Pete Townshend, 'I Can't Explain' is:

a song, written by some 18-year-old kid, about the fact that
he can't tell his girlfriend he loves her because he's taken

too many Dexedrine tablets . . . I really didn't like working with that band at all. What we produced was not something I wanted any part of, particularly. The Who didn't make the kind of music that I wanted to make, they weren't the kind of band I wanted to be in, and it was just one of those things where I just happened to be there and you put us together, we went off in this particular direction. If we'd been robbing banks I'd have had as little control in whether or not I was a part of it. I always felt uncomfortable. I always felt ill at ease. And my wife, for example, it drove her nuts! I would come back from a tour and she'd say 'what was it like?' and I'd say 'it was hell' and she'd say 'well why do you do it?' and I'd say 'because I don't have a choice' and she'd say 'well you do have a choice' and I'd say 'I don't have a choice! I DON'T HAVE A CHOICE!' I felt trapped. I felt imprisoned. But I also felt that as a band we were performing a function. In other words, I'd got a commission. This was the interesting point. I wrote the first song for The Who called 'I Can't Explain' which was a hit here. And I felt that that had connected with the audience. What I'd felt had happened was that the band, the record company, the managers and the audience were all saying to me 'we really like this song you wrote. Write some more.' And I thought 'Ah!', you know, 'I'm an artist – I've got a commission.' And that has sustained me all my life.

What was awful was getting up to the point where I'm going to leave art college and go off with this fucking horrible band of yobbos. People with whom I had absolutely nothing in common, whatsoever. Nothing. Next thing I knew I'm breaking up guitars at gigs, saying 'I am destroying the instrument of my bourgeois childhood longing.' 'It's not an act! It's auto-destructive art!' That's where I still am.

Pete Townshend in The Who is like the subtle controls of a spaceship tethered to the power of the enormous explosive power of its rockets. The Who were pushing the boundaries of heaviness, which was met with a reaction from an unexpected quarter, bringing everything full circle:

> I was in Scotland and I read in *Melody Maker* that Pete Townshend had said: 'We've just made the raunchiest, loudest, most ridiculous rock'n'roll record you've ever heard,' says Paul McCartney. 'I never actually found out what track it was that The Who had made, but that got me going; just hearing him talk about it. So I said to the guys, 'I think we should do a song like that; something really wild.' And I wrote 'Helter Skelter'. You can hear the voices cracking, and we played it so long and so often that by the end of it you can hear Ringo saying, 'I've got blisters on my fingers. 'We just tried to get it louder: 'Can't we make the drums sound louder?' That was really all I wanted to do – to make a very loud, raunchy rock'n'roll record with the Beatles. And I think it's a pretty good one.

While 'I Can See for Miles' isn't particularly heavy by the standards of The Who ('My Generation' packs much more of a punch), 'Helter Skelter' is fucking brutal. The guitar is distorted and harsh. The bass is pounding and rounded. Ringo is hitting the drums harder than he's ever hit them before,[1] and his swinging rhythm drives the song along in a manner approaching doom metal. The song is just barely within melody, and the bent guitar notes foreshadow later metal solos. It's a brilliant, crushing piece of garage metal. And it's written by the guy who also wrote 'The

---

1. No wonder he had blisters on his fingers!

Frog Chorus'.[1] Unexpectedly, the Beatles had written the heaviest song yet.

But while all the British invasion bands – the Beatles, The Who, The Kinks, The Troggs, The Animals – wrote occasional heavy songs, one band was pushing heaviness with such consistency that they became the benchmark against which all of the later emerging heavy metal bands would be measured. That band was Cream.

Eric Clapton[2] had risen to prominence in the Yardbirds[3] and John Mayall and the Bluesbreakers. His style was trad blues with a hint of English rock. He teamed up with (drum genius and notorious arsehole) Ginger Baker and (bassist and apparently reasonably good bloke) Jack Bruce. Cream played a harder-edged, considerably heavier version of the blues-rock that was all the fashion, with psychedelic elements that would soon be ubiquitous among British rock bands.

Cream also played at an incredibly high volume, driven by the new Marshall amplifiers that had been developed to meet players' demands for theatre-filling power. Ginger Baker complains that his hearing was permanently damaged by the volume Cream generated.

They only lasted four years, but with banging tunes like 'Sunshine of Your Love' and 'Tales of Brave Ulysses' they left a bold and heavy mark on the musical landscape. Their legacy was soon carried on by the first generation of bands that would attract the derisory name 'heavy metal'.

1. The song's actually called 'We All Stand Together' but let's not pretend it's worth giving a shit . . .

2. Guitar genius and outspoken opponent of immigration.

3. . . . of whom more later – they basically became Led Zeppelin, innit.

Meanwhile, developments in technology helped to develop the sound even further.

Amplifier distortion – later to become a key part of the heavy metal guitar sound – was initially engineered *out* of these early machines. But, as we've seen above, artists such as Dave Davies realised that distortion could add even more power to their playing. Aware of this new desire for distortion, engineers modified their designs to allow the amps to overdrive.

Loud volumes and distorted sound called for a new approach to the guitar. Jangly open chords would get lost in the fuzz, so riffs were written which could cut through the mud. Riffs like The Who's 'My Generation', the Beatles' 'Day Tripper' and Cream's 'Sunshine of Your Love' were the engine of a heavier sound.

As heavy as Cream were, this competition for heaviness between the big British bands was overshadowed by the arrival in London of someone just that much heavier than anyone else.

Jimi Hendrix was born in Seattle in 1943, and after serving in the US Air Force (he broke his leg in a parachute jump) he spent several years honing his guitar chops on the 'Chitlin Circuit', the predominantly black live music circuit. He played every day, for hours, constantly having to learn new songs, always having to deliver with no mistakes. It was a relatively thankless existence, and he dreamed of making it on his own, as a solo artist.

> *I know you'd probably call him a tramp*
> *but I know it goes a little deeper than that*
> *he's a –*
> *BIWM! Bi-bi-bi-biwn . . .*
> *Highway Chile.*

Jimi ended up forming his own group – Jimmy James and the Blue Flames – and secured a residency at New York's Cafe

Wha? It was there that Chas Chandler, bassist for The Animals, saw him, and offered to bring him to London to make him a star. It was necessary for Hendrix to be airdropped into the swinging London music scene for his talents to be fully appreciated. In the bitter winter of 1966 he was introduced to the British musical elite. His first show in the UK was in front of Eric Clapton and Paul McCartney. He was soon a star in his own right.

Hendrix's style was an incendiary take on the blues. He utilised screaming feedback, stage gimmicks he'd developed backing (and upstaging) such acts as Little Richard, and a fluency that was more expressive than any guitarist before him – tapping directly into his soul.

Pete Townshend claims that he and Eric Clapton struck up a friendship based on their shared awe of Jimi Hendrix.[1] The Cream song 'Sunshine of Your Love' was written by Jack Bruce immediately after seeing Hendrix for the first time: 'after the gig he went home and came up with the riff. It was strictly a dedication to Jimi. And then we wrote a song on top of it,' Clapton told *Rolling Stone* in 1988. Hendrix then paid the compliment back on hearing news of Cream's split, playing the song on the TV show *Happening for Lulu* and dedicating it to the band.

Townshend was also pissed off that Hendrix seemed to copy his gimmick of smashing up guitars on stage. Townshend had adopted this violent manoeuvre in a brilliant act of what Brian Eno's 'Oblique Strategies' suggest as 'honour thy error as a hidden intention'. In September 1964, The Who played the Railway Tavern in Harrow. Townshend was already a frenetic stage

---

1. Before Jimi they were rivals. 'Fuck you!' 'No, fuck you.' Then Jimi came along . . . 'Fuck *HIM*!' Like the end of *Watchmen*.

presence, and he accidentally smashed the headstock of his guitar into the venue's low ceiling:

> I was expecting everybody to go, 'Wow, he's broken his guitar, he's broken his guitar,' but nobody did anything, which made me kind of angry in a way. And determined to get this precious event noticed by the audience. I proceeded to make a big thing of breaking the guitar. I bounced all over the stage with it and I threw the bits on the stage and I picked up my spare guitar and carried on as though I really had meant to do it. – interview with Jann Wenner, *Rolling Stone*, 1968

It might even be put down to petulance, but expensive petulance for a musician who had yet to make any serious money. This gimmick got repeated throughout Townshend's career, so when he saw Hendrix doing it . . . he had to up the game and smash up all the instruments on the stage. This rivalry came to a head at the Monterey Festival in 1967. Contrary to today's convention of the more prestigious act going on last, Townshend and Hendrix argued over *not* wanting to follow the other. The story is best told by Townshend in the 1973 documentary *Jimi Hendrix*:

> I said to Jimi well, fuck it, man we're not gonna follow you on. So he said 'Well, I'm not gonna follow you on', so I said 'Listen: we are not gonna follow you on and that is it. You know. As far as I'm concerned we're here, ready to go on now, our gear's gonna be there, that's the end of it.' And . . . there was a certain look up in his eye and he got on a chair and he played some amazing guitar just standing on the chair in the dressing room . . . Janis Joplin was there and . . . Brian Jones, Eric and me and a few other people just standing round. And then he got down

off the chair and just said . . . turned round to me and just said, 'If I'm gonna follow you, I'm gonna pull ALL the stops.'

Then in September 1970 Hendrix committed the ultimate act of auto-destruction by dying. Whether Townshend's caution for downloading child porn was a belated attempt to have the last laugh is anybody's guess . . .[1]

Hendrix was that much heavier, and he inspired a new heaviness in everyone who saw him. Hendrix became a part of a tendency within the British rock and roll scene of revisiting the origins of blues – seeking out influence from a purer form, before it can morph into rock and roll. The Rolling Stones started off as a blues covers band. The Yardbirds stood out as the foremost English blues band. (They would later morph into Led Zeppelin.)

There is an irony that white English bands went back to America and re-popularised a black, American musical style which had by that point fallen out of favour. Legend tells of the Stones discovering Howlin' Wolf so down on his luck that he had resorted to painting the ceiling of his record label to make up for the financial shortfall his stalled career had created.

So by the end of the sixties there was a significant clutch of bands playing heavy rock with doomy riffs and distorted guitars. Cream and Led Zeppelin and Blue Cheer and Iron Butterfly and Steppenwolf . . . We now call this music 'proto-metal'. A retrospective category, proto-metal includes such diverse acts as Vanilla Fudge, The Crazy World of Arthur Brown, Jethro Tull, King Crimson, Grand Funk Railroad. I would even include Led Zeppelin

---

1. The under-reported explanation for Townshend's child porn thing is that it was part of a large credit card scam, and he didn't so much as look at, let alone download, any images. At last a rock star hero whose dodgy reputation can be proved false! All is well in the world!

and Deep Purple. Many of them share lots of common elements with Black Sabbath, some inspired and influenced them, but they were precursors. Missing links. Humans with big skulls found preserved in bogs. The proto-metal of the late sixties was the primordial soup from which heavy metal was born. It consisted of all the right amino acids and long molecule chains – elements that are recognisable as the constituent parts of heavy metal, but it had yet to be infused with the demonic spark of life that gave rise to the beast we know as heavy metal.

With the passing of the 1960s into the 1970s a change came over the counter-culture. The Beatles split up. The rivalry between Lennon and McCartney that had been the engine of their creativity finally tore them apart. The Stones flirted with occultism through the genius avant-garde film-maker Kenneth Anger and things seemed to start going wrong. Unnerved by such phenomena as a locked bedroom door being painted gold on the inside, and a string of bad luck including a drug bust, the band distanced themselves from Anger, and Jagger 'burned all his occult books'. But their bad luck was only just beginning. In May 1969 their guitarist Brian Jones fell victim to drug addiction and left the band, drowning in his swimming pool only weeks later. At a free concert in Hyde Park they planned to commemorate Brian Jones with the release of white cabbage butterflies. When the boxes opened, most of them were dead. In December 1969 a festival at the Altamont Speedway in California provided a disastrous full stop to the sixties dream. A group of Hell's Angels had been brought in to provide security. It was the worst idea ever. Entirely at odds with the peace-and-love sentiment of the audience, they beat people with steel poles, and a fan – Meredith Hunter – was beaten and stabbed to death.

The trip was going bad. And one band in particular was on

hand to document that feeling. Black Sabbath were the lightning in the primordial soup. The spark of life that brought Frankenstein's monster to life. The half-brick that started the riot.

The hippies tried with peace and love and it didn't work out. Now we gotta tell the truth, and . . .
. . . it's ugly.
– Max Cavalera, Sepultura

2

Black Sabbath

In 2011 a rumour circulated that the UK government census was open to abuse. Should a certain (undefined) number of citizens state some particular thing as their religion, the rumour ran, the government would be forced to recognise it as an 'official religion'. This was, of course, complete bollocks. Nevertheless, as a result 6,242 people stated their religion as 'heavy metal'. Although the rumour was false,[1] the idea of heavy metal as a religion was here to stay.

Every religion has its own creation myth, and the religion that is heavy metal has Black Sabbath.

> *And lo it did come to pass, among the blasted furnaces of the Blackest Country, three wise men and a holy Fool did find their paths entwined.*
>
> *In the beginning was the word. The word was Blues. And the Earth was without form and void. And actually it turned out the name Earth was taken. But they managed to get a few gigs on the pub circuit . . .*

If you were a teenager in 1970 with a few quid in your pocket you could, if you wanted, buy the album *Elton John*, by Elton

---

1. Death to false metal rumours! Like the rumour that chips make you run faster.

John. Or, if you had better taste and an eye for a creepy album cover, you could have bought the album *Black Sabbath* by Black Sabbath.[1] Of course, if you'd bought the Elton John album, you would have been wrong. Black Sabbath were the first heavy metal band. Not Led Zeppelin, not Deep Purple, definitely not Grand Funk Railroad.[2] Heavy metal's date of birth is Friday, 13 February 1970: the release of Black Sabbath's self-titled debut album. Everything that came before this point was proto-metal. *Black Sabbath* was Heavy Metal.

So, what made Sabbath different to the glut of doomy, heavy rock that was being written and recorded at the start of this new decade? What made this album Heavy Metal? Well, before they even formed a band these four individuals were already pretty metal. For a start they grew up in Birmingham. Birmingham is metal. If it only spawned Black Sabbath it could claim credit as the birthplace of heavy metal, but Sabbath are merely the tip of the iceberg.

An incredible number of truly seminal metal and hard rock bands come from Brum and its surrounding towns and cities – Black Sabbath, Judas Priest, Robert Plant and John Bonham of Led Zeppelin, Deep Purple, Diamond Head, Napalm Death, Jethro Tull, Slade, Wizzard, Godflesh, Anaal Nathrakh, Doom, Sacrilege, Benediction, Mistress, Funeral Throne. It's the ground

1. Not a brilliant year for album titles, 1970. 'What shall we call the album?' 'Just call it whatever the artist is called.' Other unimaginative album titles from 1970 include *John B. Sebastian* by John Sebastian, *Hello, I'm Johnny Cash* by Johnny Cash, and *The Great Songs of Roy Orbison* by – you guessed it – Martha and the Vandellas. *The Great Songs of Roy Orbison* was a much more commercially successful record than the previous year's *The Mediocre Songs of Roy Orbison*, but nothing like as popular as the following year's surprise hit, *Seriously, on This One Roy Orbison is Really Just Phoning It In*.

2. Grand Funk Railroad are not a heavy metal band.

zero of heavy metal. The secondary evidence is found at every major heavy metal festival in the country, and on every major heavy metal tour in the world. You WILL find at least one Brummie or Black Country bloke working on the crew. Lights, sound, rig, whatever. Listen out for the accent. We trained everyone there. It's like the *Top Gun* of heavy metal.[1]

Before forming Black Sabbath the four members had various heavy metal jobs. Guitarist Tony Iommi worked in a sheet metal factory. Drummer Bill Ward worked in an *iron foundry*. Vocalist Ozzy Osbourne, after his brief prison term for theft, worked in a slaughterhouse. And bassist Geezer Butler was . . . well . . . he was an accountant. You can't have everything. (Although an accountant in a *metal* factory!)[2]

The four grew up in close proximity in Aston, a brutal working-class area of a brutal working-class city. Poverty and violence were endemic. To these four young lads the future promised a life of hard work in factories, hard drinking in local pubs and not a great deal else. Music was a release. An escape from the mundane. A hint of something exotic and a possible way out of life on a production line. (Fittingly, heavy metal has become a blissful form of escapism – the perfect musical diversion from exactly that sort of background.)

The four members of Black Sabbath were born between February 1948 (Tony) and July 1949 (Geezer). The country in which they spent their childhood was totally dominated by the shadow of the Second World War. That war is the fulcrum around which any history of the twentieth century must pivot. Within the

1. Fun fact: Judas Priest were originally lined up to provide the soundtrack to *Top Gun* but they turned it down.

2. I was introduced to Black Sabbath by a Midlands factory worker. Which feels so much like a torch being passed on . . .

history of heavy metal it is a recurring feature. For the young
men who went on to invent and then develop heavy metal, the
Second World War shaped the economy, the society and the
physical topography of their childhood, as well as the musical
counter-culture in which they would eventually flourish. For
many born long after its conclusion, it remains a subject of fascin-
ation.[1] Lemmy collected Second World War memorabilia. Bands
like Hail of Bullets, Eastern Front and Marduk have made careers
out of it.

For Britain, the Second World War was a total war. Every
possible resource was consumed in the pursuit of victory, from
the physical bodies of conscripted young men to the churchyard
iron railings that were removed and turned into weapons of war.
Politically Britain transformed itself into a sort of benign totalitarian state. Close control and surveillance of its population were
widely accepted as necessary for home defence. Industries were
co-opted for the war effort.

Most of Britain's current identity, from nationalism to social-
ism, harks back nostalgically to this time when society and state
were intertwined in the pursuit of what was for most a noble
goal. This buys into a myth of a unified country pulling together –
a myth which massively overreaches the facts. Robbery, burglary
and rape all flourished in the blackout. The black market was
huge. The right wing believe Britain was better in the past, the
left believes the state can fix its problems. The shift to the left
after the war has been variously attributed to people talking in
barracks and bomb shelters, to the working class demanding it
be rewarded by the state for whom it sacrificed so much. Another
often-overlooked factor is the notion that the state, given enough
power, can restructure society for a common good.

1. I used to work in the Cabinet War Rooms and Churchill Museum . . .

Right up until the 1970s Britain's government and society were dominated by people who had fought in the war. Many figures of authority had been in the armed forces. As a result, Britain was socially conservative, still essentially a militarised society. For fifteen years after the war ended National Service required all healthy men between the ages of seventeen and twenty-one to serve in the military for a period of eighteen months. Homosexuality was illegal and still being prosecuted up until 1967. The death penalty was still being imposed in Britain's jails until 1964.

In stark contrast to the general trend of an increased conservatism in British and American society following on from the militarisation of its population was the birth of the Hell's Angels – a rebel motorcycle club formed by ex-Second World War soldiers who found post-war home life distinctly boring in comparison to the adventure and camaraderie they'd experienced in the war. Proudly outlaw, the Hell's Angels and other outsider motorcycle clubs typify many of heavy metal culture's ideals. Although the two things are not the same, bikers and metalheads share an aesthetic and a mentality. The Hell's Angels and biker culture in general have a close relationship with heavy metal. The Swedish black metal band Watain style themselves as a bike gang. The Rolling Stones employed the Angels as security in their ill-fated Altamont gig. The Angels stabbed a man to death. The concert is commonly seen as the painful death of sixties idealism and the birth of the cynical age out of which heavy metal would be born. Shortly afterwards, Black Sabbath toured the United States and received a visit from the Hell's Angels' president. As Geezer remembers, 'He told us who he was, says I'm from whatever chapter of the Hell's Angels and I give you my approval.' Peter Grant, manager of Led Zeppelin, utilised them at the Bath festival in 1970: 'We had to get the Hell's Angels to help

us get them on site. I'd made a contact with the American Hell's
Angels in Cleveland with the Yardbirds, so we had no bother
with them.'

Conservatism aside, the main legacy of the war in the UK
was a dreariness. Between 1945 and 1963 Britain was a distinctly
bleak place to live. Britain's economy was severely damaged by
the cost of fighting a total war. For the first two years it had
fought alone,[1] while the United States remained neutral, and
profited from both sides – selling arms and equipment to the UK
and cars, soft drink and computer systems to the Germans. Which
is a bit like seeing a mate getting mugged and then selling your
mate and the mugger a knife each. Britain only recently finished
paying off its war debt to America. So much for our special
relationship.

The country's resources were chronically depleted. For the
first few years of Black Sabbath's lives food rationing was still in
effect, only ending in 1954. The city was physically broken. As a
major manufacturing city, Birmingham had been heavily tar-
geted by German air raids and there was no money to fix the
damage. Kids played in bombed-out buildings and craters.

To depressing post-war Britain, American culture was a shining beacon. Despite that country's own social conservatism and
red-scare paranoia, the economic boom afforded by the country
taking full commercial advantage of a world war which it only
committed to fighting in the final years meant that a lifestyle
revolution could take place.

In Britain, that revolution took a little longer to arrive. It is
commonly said that Britain turned from black-and-white to colour in the sixties.

1. Completely un-aided. Except for the involvement of Canada, Australia,
New Zealand, South Africa, India . . .

It seems now that the Beatles mark a point in British history when the world turned from black-and-white into colour, and then into DayGlo, that tilting point from post-war austerity to 'you've never had it so good' affluence. Their provincialism, their jokey, unapologetically working-class manner, allied to musical genius, changed the face of what was socially and culturally acceptable at a stroke. They were an explicit act of revolt against the barriers of age, class and the division between popular and high culture – a force that nobody could afford to ignore. – Mick Brown, *Daily Telegraph*

The Beatles were a pop culture challenge to the morals and mores of post-war Britain. Even their hair length was seen as subversive. The military-standard short-back-and-sides was the hairstyle of choice for the buttoned-up conformist, whereas long hair meant rebellion against straight society. More to the point, it meant: 'I am not in the army.'[1] The later emergence of opposition to America's war in Vietnam (and the UK's support of that war) made that statement even more relevant.

The Beatles changed everything. It is no overstatement to suggest that without the Beatles heavy metal would probably never have existed. Every single musician involved in the first decade of heavy metal's existence was directly influenced by the Beatles – musically, visually, and by the simple notion of writing original songs. Later, the Beatles' commitment to innovation, experimentation and their signal-boosting of avant-garde art provided a second wave of influence. The Beatles revolutionised

1. And remember that in the early sixties *every* adult man had been in the armed forces. Much like how in the 2010s every adult man has owned a copy of *(What's the Story) Morning Glory*. (No such counter-cultural explanation is available for the current trend of the 'man-bun' so beloved by hipsters.)

the music industry. They showed rock and roll to be a possible means of escape from a life of working-class graft; that music could be a path to incredible wealth and fame. They normalised many behaviours that had been seen as part of the extreme counter-culture, from drug use to esoteric spirituality.

This counter-culture turned into the hippy movement – a subculture that prized free love and peace as solutions to the ills of the world. The empathy-increasing effects of LSD and mushrooms push people to seek community and love. But LSD has a flipside – the bad trip. A terrifying paranoid nightmare – a horrific out-of-control ride that you cannot stop. Acid trips last for up to eight hours and a bad trip can seem to last for weeks as the acid fucks with your capacity to track time. A bad acid trip can permanently debilitate. Sabbath's life in the depressing industrial town of Aston was the bad acid trip to the hippy movement.

Geezer, Tony and Bill were blues freaks. In common with many of the significant musicians of the 1960s they were music geeks, digging for rare vinyl in backstreet record shops, dreaming of one day making it in their own band. They each played in various outfits, Tony even joining Jethro Tull for a brief television appearance.

The defining artistic influence in the late 1960s was psychedelia. It spawned the Summer of Love, and the Beatles' masterpiece, *Sgt. Pepper's Lonely Hearts Club Band*. It was fuelled by experimentations with hallucinogenic drugs, most notably the artificially synthesised LSD that caused hallucinations, visual patterns and a reduction of activity in the brain's 'default mode network', which is 'primarily responsible for our ego or sense of self', according to Daniel Miller in the *Washington Post*. 'With the ego out of commission, the boundaries between self and world, subject and object dissolve.' The effect? Mystical experiences, hallucinations, a feeling of expanding horizons and increased empathy. Peace and love, basically. LSD had many advocates in the late sixties, and seemingly every musician experimented with it. The hippy movement combined these pharmaceutical epiphanies with Eastern mysticism to create a positive, optimistic, youth-orientated counter-culture. Musicians then fed back into that by creating music which reflected their psychedelic experiences and the culture around them. It all seemed remarkably positive.

But psychedelia has a dark side. The flower power optimism that seemed to lie on the surface of the late sixties covered a dark underbelly. Vietnam, poverty, civil disobedience and state violence, the very real threat posed by a nuclear war of total annihilation . . . To most people living in Aston the Summer of Love seemed like a piss-take.

Acid has two sides, and bad trips were part of the deal. Black Sabbath were the expression of the bad trip. The Averse Sefira. From their very beginnings Black Sabbath were making music as outsider art. Never confident enough in themselves to be explicitly political (or indeed explicitly satanic . . .) they nonetheless expressed ideas that desperately needed expression. They were the lodestone for the dream turned sour. As the sixties turned into the seventies, the party was over and the ground was littered with wrinkled balloons, used condoms and sick. Sabbath were the sound of the sixties hangover. It was no longer groovy. It was dark, depressing and sometimes even frightening.

Ozzy and Tony had been at school together, the older guitarist bullying the diminutive Ozzy – a power dynamic that would carry on throughout their working life. As teenagers they all played in bands – Ozzy had blagged his way into his first singing role in a band called Approach and took the unusual step of buying his own public address system. The ownership of such a rare and precious item came in particularly useful when he wanted out of Approach and put an ad in a shop window looking for a new band. The magic words 'has own PA' caught the eye of Geezer,

who was looking for a new singer to be in his eclectic band, The
Rare Breed. They played covers of soul and rock and roll songs
and made themselves look as freaky as possible.

Meanwhile, Tony Iommi had been playing in several local
bands. And was about to take his first step as a full-time musician.
At the age of seventeen he was on his way out of Aston. He had
secured a job with a band, The Birds & the Bees, who had been
booked for a tour of West Germany. 'The day I was leaving, actually, to turn professional . . . the old "turn professional" one,' he
was persuaded by his mother to complete his duty to the sheet metal
factory that employed him as a welder. On this day he was forced to
use a machine he had never used, which cut the sheet metal he
would then weld. Its operator was absent and Tony received no
training. The Euro-fascists who impose ludicrous health-and-safety
legislation on us weren't yet a thing (it's political correctness gone
mad).[1] 'I was pressing this piece of metal and the press just came
straight down on me, and of course as you pulled it back I pulled
the ends of my fingers off.' The fingers were the second and third
on his right hand – as a left-handed guitarist these were the fingertips
that did most of the work. On the eve of his first professional tour
this was a disaster. His career as a musician was clearly over. He fell
into a deep depression. Then a friend came over and played him
some Django Reinhardt, the virtuoso jazz guitarist who played
with only two fingers, the rest having been paralysed in a fire.
Iommi was inspired; he was only missing the ends! He made pros-
thetic fingertips from plastic melted from a washing-up-liquid

1. It's no coincidence that since Britain joined the Common Market we have
lost our place as the centre of the heavy metal world. Thanks to Brexit, factory
owners can go back to ignoring their workers' welfare and Britain can once
more produce innovative bands through the gift of horrific workplace
accidents.

bottle, and glued leather to them for grip. He downtuned his guitar to lessen the tension in the strings and developed a distinctively deliberate fingering style. 'I had to work on how hard to press down on the strings. Because I couldn't feel anything – apart from pain.'

After his rehabilitation Tony played in various groups, finally finding himself in a band with the drummer Bill Ward – The Rest. The two bands found themselves on bills together, playing similar cover songs but never being particularly enamoured of each other. Tony jumped ship to join Mythology and Bill followed. That band was busted for marijuana possession and broke up. At the same time The Rare Breed disbanded due to general low morale after some terrible gigs. Ozzy stuck his ad up again and with an air of inevitability the four found themselves playing together. Drawn together by a gravity not of this world. Or a coincidence entirely of this world. Whichever you prefer, really.

Initially called The Polka Tulk Blues Band and later changing their name to Earth, they played heavy, blues-based downer rock. Tony quit for a chance to play in the already-successful Jethro Tull, but felt it wasn't right and returned to the fold. His experience with Tull gave him a new determination. Regular rehearsals and more gigs followed. They recorded several demos and eventually got themselves a manager.

Like any good religious text, there are contradictions in the genesis story of Black Sabbath. There are several versions of how they got the name.[1]

---

1. One of the reasons I haven't pursued contemporary interviews for this book is that bands' origin stories become mythologised through repeated re-telling over the years. I can barely remember the details of where my band recorded our first record and that was less than a decade ago. It's unlikely Sabbath can actually remember what happened in 1969 because: (a) it was a long time ago, (b) memories get rewritten and thus change every time you access them, and (c) they have done an absolute shitload of drugs.

One suggests that Earth rehearsed opposite a cinema and one day Geezer noticed a large queue for the horror film *Black Sabbath*. Two things struck him: number one, horror films were big business in the late 1960s. For over a decade British cinema had dominated the horror landscape, with Hammer Films making gory Eastman Color horror a worldwide phenomenon. If they wrote songs about the same subjects they might be on to something – death, depression, possession, Satan, murder . . . And, number two, Black Sabbath is a better name than Earth, and also there's a load of other bands called Earth. Let's change the name to Black Sabbath!

A slightly different version told by Geezer in recent interviews is that the name had been floating around for years ever since his brother saw the film. And Tony takes credit for the horror theme idea himself in an interview for the BBC: 'We really liked horror films,' he says 'and it was just that feeling you got of being frightened, I thought it would be good to be able to do that – to do that in music.'

No matter whose idea it was or where it came from, clearly a change was in the air. They'd already been playing 'heavy' psychedelic blues, but the change of name signalled a new approach. They wrote their first proper original song, based on a tritone riff 'borrowed' from Holst's *The Planets*. The lyrics came from a terrifying experience Geezer had recently had. Geezer was very interested in occultism[1] (he was an accountant, he could afford the books). After a particularly intense night of reading occult books he woke up to see a malevolent black figure at the foot of his bed.

---

1. Although he now denies he actually did any rituals, this strikes me as bullshit. Like saying you smoked weed but didn't inhale. Geezer's complete disavowal of occultism is in my opinion born out of fear of what actually happened to him rather than a sudden rationalism.

Everything suddenly came together. The planets aligned (pun intended). Tony's guitar tone, Ozzy's soulful, plaintive voice. Demonic possession and the occult were the perfect subject material for such a dour sound.

Sabbath had struck upon something big – writing songs about the dark side of life. Not just in a blues way; this was far more than 'My baby left me'. Partly a direct response to the peace'n'love hippy movement that alienated them, partly just as an expression of themselves, their circumstances and their depressive minds. Lyrically, Sabbath dealt with everything the hippy movement was ignoring in its hopelessly naive attempt to get the world to hold hands and love each other, man. Sabbath talked about war. About death raining from the skies and your children's futures being the battlefield and the grave. They talked about depression and isolation. About corrupt governments and pollution. About the threat of atomic annihilation. THAT is what made them heavy metal. Plus of course the fact that (although considerably less often than they are credited with) they talked about Satan.

A large aspect of Sabbath's appeal was their expression of the occult. Over the years they have muddied the waters in terms of their exact involvement. Bill Ward now says that dark things happened – that they got in out of their depth. Geezer has at times hinted at genuine occult practice, although he dismisses it as 'all that cobblers'. Which may be because Geezer is a Catholic.

The fact that they all shit themselves soon after the release of their first album and suddenly began wearing crucifixes on stage suggests that some shit did go down. No one believes in Satan quite as much as Christians.[1] Of course, Christianity has

1. Except, perhaps, Muslims.

inspired some of the greatest art mankind has ever produced; from the ceiling of the Sistine Chapel to the music of Bach, from the paintings of Hieronymus Bosch to the song 'Mistletoe and Wine' by Sir Cliff Richard. It's said that Satan has the best tunes – Sabbath certainly prove that when they try to talk about Christianity. The song 'After Forever' was supposed to provide some clarity to their position. Musically it's perfectly fine, slightly proggy with a nice catchy stomp. Lyrically, it's dogshit. The rhymes are forced and the content is like bad sixth-form poetry.

At the very least, their seminal song 'Black Sabbath' was very definitely based on an experience Geezer Butler had after what he states VERY CLEARLY definitely WASN'T a night of occult experimentation. However much he may disavow black magic in his later years, if it wasn't for his 'interest' in the late sixties, Sabbath would never have achieved quite the same level of success.

They released their first album to considerable commercial success and immediate critical disdain. From its very outset, heavy metal was outsider art. Lester Bangs of *Rolling Stone* described them as sounding 'like Cream, but worse'. But it didn't matter. The horse had bolted. Heavy metal now had its starting point. Everything before Friday, 13 February 1970, was proto-metal. This was the first heavy metal record.

The cover is perfect. A witchy-looking young woman stands in front of a disused mill – a landscape that evokes the era when witch hunts and the Industrial Revolution pulled English society in two conflicting directions. The inside of the gatefold depicts an inverted cross – it was the record company's idea and it apparently annoyed the band but, fuck it, it was a spark of genius.

The first song is worth the price of admission alone. After an atmospheric tolling church bell heard through a thunderstorm, that opening riff, borrowed from Holst's *The Planets*, is a deceptively simple three-note arrangement. Doomy, deep, bassy, atmospheric and scary. Then Ozzy's crystal-clear voice, tremulous with fear, floats over the top of it. It's a horror story straight out of Dennis Wheatley. They manage to avoid it being cheesy. It's a perfect song.

'The Wizard' is either a Tolkienesque fantasy or a metaphor for a drug dealer. Starting with a harmonica it's more of a throwback to the club blues of Earth, though Bill Ward's pounding drums give it a weight that is beyond anything else of that type. Completing a trilogy of literary references, 'Behind the Wall of Sleep' takes its cue from H. P. Lovecraft and is a trippy psychedelic workout. The next track takes the Satanic metal of 'Black Sabbath' and constructs a more personal narrative. Told in the first person, it's Satan seducing a potential lost soul. The second half is closed by an instrumental workout and two covers that they totally make their own – the original three-minute version of 'Warning' is expanded in Sabbath's hands to over ten!

The album was a huge success. Sabbath toured extensively. A huge launch took place in America with a bizarre parade featuring the Church of Satan's Anton LaVey.

It's easy to overstate the case for Sabbath's first album, and indeed their first song, as being the be-all-and-end-all of the creation of heavy metal as a genre of music, but it was with their second album that Black Sabbath built upon what they had created and really set the game up for the rest of us.

Paranoid was conceived and released incredibly swiftly, coming out only seven months later. With that album they pushed further into darkness. 'War Pigs' is possibly Sabbath's heaviest song. Geezer had been deeply affected by the Vietnam veterans he'd encountered on their US dates, and wrote a horrifying protest song – one that unflinchingly stared the problem in the eye.[1] He also rhymed 'masses' with 'masses', which is a bold move. The rest of the album builds on this solid foundation. 'Planet Caravan' is pure psychedelia, 'Iron Man' another tale of horror. 'Electric Funeral' and 'Hand of Doom' both deal with the reality of conflict, the first about nuclear war, the second about drug addiction among Vietnam veterans. The album closes with 'Fairies Wear Boots', a story of Ozzy's fight with some skinheads.

With these two albums, Black Sabbath invented heavy metal. They were more consistently hard, heavy, pessimistic and fucking REAL than anyone else around.

Two more perfect albums followed – *Master of Reality* and *Volume 4* continue in much the same vein. Sabbath toured internationally and began to change the minds of their early detractors. Even Lester Bangs got on board.

The rest of the seventies for Sabbath saw an eventual decline in quality, a decline in interpersonal relationships and a decline into substance abuse for all of them. Bill Ward drank. Tony took heroic amounts of cocaine. Ozzy did absolutely anything and everything. Geezer was vegan.

Eventually Ozzy was kicked out for doing *even more drugs than everyone else* and Ronnie James Dio was drafted in to replace him. Two amazing albums, *Heaven and Hell* (1980) and *Mob Rules* (1981) revitalised Black Sabbath artistically but the personalities never gelled and it was short-lived.

Ozzy Osbourne went on to have a remarkably successful solo

1. 'No wonder we never got any chicks at our gigs,' moaned Ozzy in his autobiography.

career, while Black Sabbath's fortunes waned. They never made a truly great album again. Tony Iommi remained the sole original member, going through a revolving-door line-up of vocalists, including Deep Purple's Ian Gillan and the second-longest-serving singer, Tony Martin.

A one-off reunion with Ozzy for Live Aid in 1985 was disappointing, and Tony kept churning out albums of varying quality. Another one-off collaboration with Ozzy took place in 1992, which sowed the seed for a full reunion. In 1997 Ozzy, Geezer and Tony reunited to headline Ozzy's own festival tour, the Ozzfest. And it was glorious. A live album recorded at the Birmingham NEC was a commercial success and they recorded two new songs.

Bizarrely, Ozzy became a reality TV star in the early 2000s with the show *The Osbournes*. Tony and Geezer reunited with Dio to form the contractually specific band Heaven and Hell for a worldwide tour and a new album. The live show they put on blew poor Ozzy out of the water, Dio being one of the most powerful and enigmatic frontmen of all time.

Ronnie James Dio died of stomach cancer in May 2010. Two years later Iommi was diagnosed with lymphoma and has successfully undergone treatment. Considering the substance abuse the original line-up of Black Sabbath put their bodies through, it's remarkable that any of them are still about, let alone managing to tour.

In June 2013 Black Sabbath released the album *13*, recorded by Tony, Geezer, Ozzy and Rage Against the Machine's drummer, Brad Wilk. Festival appearances followed and, as I write, Sabbath have just completed a farewell tour called *The End*, sadly without Bill Ward on drums. Despite the lack of the drummer who contributed so much to the sound that started heavy metal, it is satisfying that at the end of their career, Black Sabbath were back on form, and filling arenas. Heavy metal has never been healthier and its originators are enjoying the fruits of their labour.

They're so rich now that Geezer probably actually does have a butler.

3

The Golden Age of Heavy Metal

Black Sabbath were the first heavy metal band. Led Zeppelin had paved the way, Deep Purple contributed to pushing things heavier and Grand Funk Railroad were ... erm ... making some music.[1] But the term 'heavy metal' was thrown around with gleeful imprecision in the late sixties and early seventies and a ton of bands were described as heavy metal when to modern ears they are clearly something else. Something not-quite-metal. The meaning of the term has since shifted.

The band that changed the rules on what is considered 'true' heavy metal and what is just hard rock/proto-metal/electric blues was Judas Priest. On their second album, 1976's *Sad Wings of Destiny*, Judas Priest redefined the meaning of the term. They coalesced everything that had made Black Sabbath different from their hard rock peers and then they placed a rocket under it. They stripped down and turbo-powered their sound. Black Sabbath's sound was rooted in their blues past, but Judas Priest created

---

1. Grand Funk Railroad are not a heavy metal band. Americans seem to think Grand Funk Railroad were the first heavy metal band. They were not a heavy metal band. They are wrong. So wrong. I mean, fundamentally and hugely wrong. They're not even important to the story. Stop it.

something that stood alone. Heavy metal was now a genre of its own.

Before *Sad Wings of Destiny* hard rock classification was like the Wild West. Any dude with a gun[1] could shoot[2] any other dude[3] without warning.[4] The explosion of hard rock that took place in the late sixties and early seventies was a vibrant, amorphous, genre-less morass of sounds and styles produced by a vast number of bands. The music journalists who had emerged along with this music achieved a status which was previously unheard of among critics of pop culture. As a result they were incredibly self-important. It was their job to make sure rock music was taken *seriously, man* in order to bolster their pseudo-intellectual bollocks. They acted as gatekeepers and sneered at anything they deemed beneath them. Wielded by them, the term heavy metal was an insult, and in their war against music that sullied their notion of what-should-be they splashed the derogatory term heavy metal about in a manner that now looks like the work of a deeply uncool stepdad.[5]

The term was first used in literature in 1962 by William Burroughs in his novel *The Soft Machine*, which includes a character known as 'Uranian Willy, the Heavy Metal Kid'. His 1964 novel *Nova Express* describes the 'Heavy Metal People of Uranus wrapped in cool blue mist of vaporized bank notes – And the Insect People of Minraud with metal music'. In 1968 Steppenwolf were the first to use it in a song – 'Born to be Wild' talks of the 'heavy metal thunder' of motorbikes.

1. pen

2. describe

3. band

4. as heavy metal

5. 'Oh hey, kids, I love this heavy metal you're listening to. It's got a groovy beat.' 'Actually – Brian – it's grunge. God, you're so embarrassing.'

However, not quite fitting the modern notion of heavy metal does not take away from the importance of these other seventies hard rock, not-quite-metal bands. Without them metal would certainly not be what it is today, and at the time they helped build the edifice of heavy metal which would later bear such rich fruit. Yeah, that's a terrible mixed metaphor. Fucking sue me.

After the mega-sales of the Beatles and the global fame of the other British Invasion bands came a new era of massive live performances. In his rejection of the Beatles in the early sixties an executive at Decca records famously said, 'Guitar bands are on the way out.' He could not have been more wrong.[1] Guitar bands were in the ascendant and by the early seventies guitar-based heavy rock bands had become arena-filling, globe-trotting behemoths. One band in particular stood head and shoulders above the rest, smashing attendance records and defining the rock and roll lifestyle for all time.

No band represented the new era of arena rock like Led Zeppelin. They stand apart, untouchable and totally legendary. While Sabbath's legacy has been watered down by sub-par albums and Ozzy's gradual evolution into a reality TV clown, Led Zeppelin have managed to remain aloof and inaccessible, retaining the image of true rock gods. They sold more records, filled bigger arenas and at least one of them fucked much, much younger girls than any of the other bands.

Led Zeppelin's origins are in the factory production line of London's swinging pop scene. Jimmy Page had been a prolific

1. It was the wrongest prediction in history since Henry VIII declared, 'This one's a keeper.' A music industry mistake only topped by the time Ozzy's manager said, '*I don't care if he hasn't had breakfast, give him the dove and get him in the press conference.*' The biggest pop music blunder up until the time a mate of Pete Townshend's said, '*You should get on the internet.*'

session guitarist, playing on an eclectic range of records such as
'The Last Time' by The Rolling Stones, 'With a Little Help
from My Friends' by Joe Cocker, 'Downtown' by Petula Clark,
'It's Not Unusual' by Tom Jones, and 'Hi Ho Silver Lining' by Jeff
Beck. Page wanted a band of his own. He joined the blues band
the Yardbirds – a group who at one point had included guitar
god and semi-professional racist Eric Clapton. The Yardbirds
already had success in the United States and Page jumped on
board just as they were embarking on a huge US tour. After the
Yardbirds split he started a new band, which he called the New
Yardbirds, partly due to commercial concerns – the Yardbirds had
a considerable following – and partly due to contractual
obligations.[1]

Page assembled a band with John Paul Jones, a bass player he
knew from the London session scene, a singer from the Midlands
called Robert Plant, who had been recommended by Terry Reid,
and a drummer called John Bonham, who had in turn been suggested by Plant.

The first rehearsal the four had was incredible. They clicked
musically in a way none of them had ever experienced. They
went straight on the road – first as the New Yardbirds and then
as Led Zeppelin, a name coined by The Who's John Entwistle for
a previous collaboration between him, Keith Moon and Jimmy
Page that had never materialised. Within a few weeks of forming,
Led Zeppelin were in the studio recording their first album.

Led Zeppelin broke in America first. They signed a massive
deal with Atlantic records and toured extensively in the US before
making any real impression in their home country. The head start
afforded by the Yardbirds obviously helped, as did the music

1. Also, *This is Spinal Tap* hadn't yet made all variant-band names look
inherently ridiculous.

industry *nous* Page had acquired in his years spent as a session guitarist.

Another large factor in their early success was their manager, Peter Grant. Grant was notoriously intimidating. An enormous bear of a man,[1] he was a former bouncer and professional wrestler, known for using force when verbal persuasion didn't work. Grant and tour manager Richard Cole were extremely close to the band – both were fans, which is surprisingly rare in the music industry. They formed a protective cordon around the band, keeping them safe from hassling fans (through the medium of splitting open their jaws, where needed) and they kept them amused and occupied when on the road.

Grant changed the landscape of live music. Instead of settling for the usual split in favour of the venue, Grant began demanding 90 per cent of ticket sales. He had an instinct for a rip-off and more than once discovered hidden ticket stubs – where venues had sold more tickets than they declared. He actively prevented bootlegging by destroying recording equipment and popping into record shops to confiscate unauthorised releases.

When Led Zeppelin's deal with Atlantic came up for renewal, the executive complained, 'You've ruined me!'

Led Zeppelin became the biggest band in the world, outselling label mates The Rolling Stones on vinyl and in arenas, though for most of their career they were either ignored or rejected by the music press. Again – heavy metal (as they were seen by the press) is outsider art. The mainstream music industry and music press, those gatekeepers of cool, never really understood it. Their biographer Stephen Davis puts this down to the youth of their audience.

'Already Led Zeppelin was in trouble because it was the younger kids, the little brothers and sisters of the great sixties

---

1. Not a real bear.

generation, who loved Led Zeppelin the most. For this, Led Zeppelin would never be forgiven by the rock establishment.'

This rock establishment is still in force – *Rolling Stone* magazine's 'Top 100 Artists of All Time' includes no extreme metal.[1] It
also misses out Queen and places the Beatles, The Rolling Stones
and Bob Dylan in an unassailable top position, as though that decision of canonicity was made in 1969 and can never be changed.[2]

Led Zeppelin's music was sublime. It's not heavy metal. It is,
however, a direct and distinct progenitor of heavy metal and they
are very much one of the bands who inspired the more widespread and regular use of the term.[3] Led Zeppelin's sound was
much more a blend of turbo charged blues and folk.

While definitely pioneers in terms of sound and feel, they
wear their influences so explicitly they have been described as an
early form of mash-up; sampling and borrowing riffs freely and
sometimes covering whole songs with minor changes like, say,
the title (in the case of 'The Lemon Song', which is essentially
Howlin' Wolf's 'Killing Floor'), or just covering the song without
credit in the case of 'Dazed and Confused', which is very, very
similar to a song by Jake Holmes called . . . 'Dazed and Confused'.
Some celebrate this creative use of influence, some call it plagiarism. Some have gone further. A certain school of thought sees
Led Zeppelin as nothing more than a gilded covers band.

Led Zeppelin definitely had an ambivalent attitude towards
influence, but then so did the scene they came from. It was
unusual even as late as 1969 for rock and roll bands to generate

1. And if you think U2 are better than Metallica you are reading the wrong
book. The book you should be reading is *All Your Opinions are Suspect and Your
Friends Think You're a Knob* by Ivor Twatbrain.

2. They have changed their mind about Led Zeppelin though.

3. Their name evokes it! Led Zeppelin! Lead is a heavy metal!

entirely original material. Elvis Presley didn't write a single song. The Beatles changed that practice, inventing what *Rolling Stone* called 'the idea of the self-contained rock band' which excluded external writers and session musicians. But even the Beatles took their time to go fully original. Their first album, *Please Please Me*, contained six covers, as did *With the Beatles*. It was only by *A Hard Day's Night* that they were doing all of their own stuff. The Stones took until their fourth album to stop relying almost entirely on covers. Even Hendrix began his solo career with a cover – 'Hey Joe'.

Going further back – even more than rock and roll, blues bands relied on standards to fill their repertoire. The Yardbirds – the band Led Zeppelin evolved from – were mainly a blues standards band. So it's not surprising that Led Zeppelin leaned heavily towards incorporating their favourite songs into their own recordings. The problem comes with the lack of credit. To be fair to Led Zeppelin, it seems mainly to come down to a generally lax attitude to attribution rather than anything more counterfeit. However, after Zeppelin made such huge amounts of money, the original songwriters seemed to feel that credit, and the money associated with that credit, was due to them and a number of legal actions were taken. Zeppelin tended to settle out of court, and over the course of their career reissues of their records have started to include the names of people who have 'influenced' the writing of songs.

A high-profile case was resolved only a few months before the time of writing. In purely legal terms, Led Zeppelin were vindicated over allegations of outright theft. In June 2016 a jury cleared them of allegations that the iconic opening to 'Stairway to Heaven' was ripped off from the song 'Taurus' by the American band Spirit. Listening to the track it's hard not to see the similarities. The riffs sound so similar, in fact, that they were not deemed admissible as evidence in court; the legal position being not whether or not they are similar, but whether or not that was the result of plagiarism or coincidence. It was assumed the jury would see the resemblance as proof. However, according to the BBC news website:

> The plaintiff's lawyers had argued Led Zeppelin became familiar with Spirit's song after the two bands played on the same bill at a club in Plant's hometown in Birmingham in 1970, a year before 'Stairway to Heaven' was released in 1971.

Insanely, Page says he had a car crash on the night of the gig which 'may have' affected his memory.[1] Yeah, okay, mate. Also,

---

1. Accusations of plagiarism are all too common in the world of stand-up comedy. My first ever gig involved a joke about zebras being unable to work in supermarkets, because every time they tried to put something through the till they'd scan themselves. At my second ever gig the comedian on before me said 'They should sell zebras in supermarkets. You wouldn't need a barcode,' which is an INFERIOR joke but still meant I couldn't do mine and I dropped it due to its obvious lack of originality. There was no way he could have seen my joke at the only other gig I'd ever done and then have the brass neck to perform a shit version of it in front of me. In stark contrast, a few years ago a fan told me someone he kind of knew was doing an entire routine of mine and passing it off as his own. He even went so far as to post a video of it on YouTube. I set my dogs on him and now he is dead. On the flipside, I recently dropped one of the best jokes I've ever written because someone else was doing the same joke. 'As the old vegan proverb goes – you can't make an omlette.' Although I think I came up with it independently I can't be sure I hadn't seen him do it and then remembered rather than created it. SO I dropped it. And that makes me better than Led Zeppelin. Vim Fuego in the amazing spoof metal film *Bad News*: 'I could play "Stairway to Heaven" when I was twelve. Jimmy Page didn't actually write it until he was twenty-two. I think that says quite a lot.'

my dog ate my homework, this isn't what it looks like and it was like that when I got here.

Lack of credit aside, what Zeppelin did with their influences and 'borrows' was transformative. An act of alchemy. Their first album – simply called *Led Zeppelin*[1] – opens with a colossal, pounding riff. Bonzo's drums are huge. But then . . . sweetness! The combination of darkness and light makes them sound controlled. The light serves to make the heaviness sound even heavier – the end of 'Babe, I'm Gonna Leave You' stomps like a motherfucker. 'You Shook Me' is true British blues.

Over their career they took their influences and made them more extreme. They increased the contrast between heavy and folky. Drummer John Bonham was a big influence on the way in which metal would use drums. His sound was huge, his attack brutal. Influenced by Carmine Appice from Vanilla Fudge, he was an early exponent of the extensive drum kit. Unlike Keith Moon, whose flamboyant style lacked accuracy, Bonzo was metronomic as well as adventurous. Like Keith Moon, he was also a massive pisshead with a love of life that bordered, when drunk, on the psychotic. Moon and Bonzo were partners in crime.

Led Zeppelin's excesses were legendary. Renting out whole floors of hotels was de rigueur for bands ever since The Rolling Stones set the precedent. They would take the whole top floor of the Regency Hyatt on Sunset Boulevard, taking televisions from one side of the hotel and throwing them out the windows on the

---

1. Another brilliant leap of imagination for the album-naming committee there. They went on to shatter all conventions with the unusually titled *Led Zeppelin II*, the outside-the-box *Led Zeppelin III*, and exactly what the enemy would expect us to do, and therefore exactly what we shan't do, *Led Zeppelin IV*, which officially didn't even bother with a title at all, but people like patterns.

other side to create plausible deniability when the horrified staff arrived to remonstrate with them.[1]

They had their own branded plane, which was so big it had a fucking FIREPLACE in it.

Their sexual exploits were just as excessive. Page was reputedly into whipping girls. One story stands out as much fishier than the rest. I swear to Cod it's true, though. They fucked a girl with a fish. More accurately, they reportedly 'pleasured' a fan with a freshly caught red snapper. Or possibly a mudshark. Or maybe it wasn't them and it was Vanilla Fudge who did it while they looked on. Whatever. It's still kind of horrific.

Did this obsession of combining sex and food stem from the deprivations of an upbringing in a UK which still had rationing? Robert Plant was said to have made very specific dining plans one night and kicked off on being told that it would not be possible to fill a lady with that particular food, because none of the late-night shops sold cream cakes.

Jimmy Page was a big fan of the Edwardian occultist Aleister Crowley. He went as far as to buy Boleskine, the house on the banks of Loch Ness in which Crowley had performed an aborted Abramelin ritual. In typical sixties/seventies style Page seemed to take Crowley's mantra of *Do As Thou Wilt Shall be the Whole of the Law* at face value and pursued a sex life that in any attentive system would have attracted the attentions of the police. It's common knowledge that he pursued a sexual relationship with fourteen-year-old groupie, Lori Maddox. He even 'shared' her with David

---

1. I have often wondered if the current trend for hotel windows having limited openings for 'safety' is what led to flat-screen TVs . . . I'm not suggesting a conspiracy between television manufacturers and rock bands, but YOU CAN'T DENY THE EVIDENCE. I'm no stranger to trashing hotel rooms myself. I once cooked instant noodles in a hotel kettle and made only a cursory attempt to clean it afterwards.

Bowie. While Maddox herself talks in fond terms of her dalli-
ances with the rock elite, it's highly likely that a sure way to raise
Page's heart rate is to mention Operation Yewtree.

After eleven years, nine studio albums, thousands of women
and one fish, Led Zeppelin came to an abrupt halt with the death
of John Bonham in September 1980. He had been drinking heavily and choked on his own vomit. A few reunions have happened
sporadically since then, but Bonzo's death effectively ended the
band.

Though an undeniably significant influence on all heavy
metal, Led Zeppelin fought against the label themselves – 'It's a
bastard term to us. I can't relate that to us because the thing that
comes to mind when people say heavy metal is riff-bashing, and
I don't think we ever just did riff-bashing at any point. It was
always inner dynamics, light and shade, drama and versatility
that we were going for.' Whatever, Jimmy. Fuck you.

To be fair to Page, while Led Zeppelin were certainly
loud, certainly heavy, certainly interested in black magic, they are
not a heavy metal band. They simply don't have the doom of
Black Sabbath. Their lyrics deal too much with hope and escape
and love and not enough with death and Armageddon and
paranoia and being a man made out of iron. Led Zeppelin have
too much sweetness, too much of a delicate touch and too much
folk. Way, way too much folk. I mean, the folk stuff is good but
it is not heavy metal[1]. Heavy metal songs do not make you a
heavy metal band. Any more than telling jokes makes you a
comedian.

So why are Led Zeppelin considered heavy metal?

In truth Led Zeppelin were no heavier than Cream or Jimi

---

1. Of course, now we have folk metal, but that has more of an explicit metal
content than Led Zeppelin ever had.

Hendrix – they just operated in a time when the term 'heavy metal' had become a descriptor of hard rock, and were the biggest band of its type. It was when they played, not what they played, that made them one of the 'big three originators' of heavy metal. Much like Jesus Christ was not a Christian.

The other of those 'big three originators' is Deep Purple. Not having either the occult trappings of Led Zeppelin, the existential angst and paranoia of Black Sabbath, or the heaviness of either, Deep Purple are a strange pick for the role.

Their first album, *Shades of Deep Purple*, is very mid-sixties-sounding psychedelic rock. Some of the tunes would fit perfectly on the soundtrack for an Austin Powers movie, such is the dominance of the keyboard and the very English-sounding psych pop sound. You can smell the go-go dancers. The single 'Hush' was a hit in the States, though the album sank in the UK. (What did the Yanks know that we didn't when it came to heavy bands in the late sixties?) The follow-up, *The Book of Taliesyn*, is way too keyboard-based to be metal. It's still too *groovy, baby*. Their third, self-titled, album has fucking harpsichord on it.[1] The song 'Bird Has Flown' stands out with a delicious stomp. But it's still not there. No.

It wasn't until the band's fourth record, June 1970's *In Rock*, that they began to crank up the heaviness and become a contender for the accolade of being an actual heavy metal band, though, like Jimmy Page, organ player Jon Lord[2] denied the term. Which is oddly fitting because it's the contribution of John Lord that to me

1. What is this, the fucking Tudor era? Eh? Bloody Henry VIII, is it? Greensleeves? Is it? Is that what this is? *A Man for All Seasons*, is it? I thought this was a metal band, not the bloody Hampton Court house players.

2. 'Lord Organ' is what you call yourself when you were trying to flirt with people on the internet.

mostly rules them out from being a metal band.[1] (Plus, compared to
Black Sabbath, which had come out four months earlier, it's distinctly lacking in doom.) It was the influence of Led Zeppelin on
guitarist Richie Blackmore that provided the catalyst for the
change. During Deep Purple's career, Blackmore would struggle to
steer the band into the darker waters he wanted, which eventually
led to him decamping and forming his own actual heavy metal
band, Rainbow, with Ronnie James Dio – who would later front an
incarnation of Black Sabbath and become an icon of heavy metal.

    Deep Purple In Rock has a very literal cover. It depicts the band
as Mount Rushmore.[2] It begins with a statement of intent – a blast
of Hendrix-derived guitar histrionics which very firmly sets out
Blackmore's stall. This is going to be a record that rocks. The
sound is still rooted in the sixties and the lyrics hark back to the
glory days of rock and roll with their quoting of Little Richard,
but the song has a pace and driving attitude that are new for Deep
Purple. 'Bloodsucker' takes its template from Led Zeppelin. 'Child
in Time' is self-consciously epic, opening like something Judas
Priest might do five years later. The organ tethers it to prog. Just
as it starts to get going it tails off into guitar noodling. 2/5. Can
do better. 'Flight of the Rat' is all about the solos. Guitar, then
keys, then guitar, then keys. Go, boys! 'Living Wreck' has a
garage-y fuzz. And to finish it off in the manner the record started
in, 'Hard Lovin' Man' is Blackmore's best Hendrix impression.

1. Also, I'm not saying John Lord was pretentious but he kept a bust of
Beethoven on his piano. Which is straight out of a bit by the parody 'versatile
singer-songwriter from Sheffield, South Yorkshire', John Shuttleworth. 'I've got
a bust of Beethoven. Cos he did music, didn't he? Course he did.' Of course, it's
possible that Jon Lord has heard that bit and is referencing it, ironically.

2.   Geddit? IN ROCK. They are IN some ROCK. Well, technically they
were made OUT OF rock. But you see what they're doing.

The success of this new direction made Deep Purple synonymous with hard rock, and the insulting phrase 'heavy metal'
was thrown at them by journalists. They joined Black Sabbath
and Led Zeppelin among the heaviest bands around. But it wasn't
until 1972 that they released the album that counts as their most
significant contribution to heavy metal. *Machine Head* still doesn't
match Sabbath for heaviness, but it's the sound of a band coming
into their own. Opener 'Highway Star' is focused and stomping.
But then 'Maybe I'm a Leo' goes all electro-funk . . . It kind of
reminds me of the Grange Hill theme tune . . . 'Pictures of Home' is
less heavy than half of Hendrix's output . . . I'm really struggling
to see why this band is constantly namechecked as an orginator of
heavy metal . . . It's good enough, but it just isn't metal!

Anyway, all of this pales into insignificance next to the opening riff of 'Smoke on the Water':

> *DUN, DUN, DAAAAAA!*
> *DUN, DUN, DA-NAAAAAAA!*
> *DUN, DUN, DAAAAA, DU-DAN, DAAAAAA!*

And, blimey, with a riff that good, how good must the rest of the
song be?![1]

Deep Purple suffered from terrible interpersonal relationships. Richie Blackmore quit, then rejoined, then fired people.
They got through vocalists like Donald Trump gets through his
out-of-court-settlement fund.

Like Led Zeppelin, Deep Purple are a progenitor. Not proto-
metal, but not quite metal either to modern ears. They remain

---

1. Not very. It starts off amazing and then peters out . . . It's very much the
Saving Private Ryan of classic rock songs.

seminal. They remain important. They are one of the foundation stones of the heavy metal sound.

In complete contrast to the way in which Deep Purple and Led Zeppelin rejected the term 'heavy metal', the mid-seventies saw the emergence of a band who were so metal they took the name 'heavy metal' and proudly applied it to themselves.

Judas Priest emerged from the same thriving Midlands music scene that produced Black Sabbath and half of Led Zeppelin. Both those bands had a significant hand in directing the young band towards a heavier sound. Priest's original line-up was entirely different to that which would record their first album, *Rocka Rolla*. Bassist Bruno Staplehill coined the name on the instructions of vocalist Alan John Atkins,[1] who asked him to 'think of a name similar to Black Sabbath'.

After several false starts and considerable line-up changes, the familiar front row of Rob Halford, Alan Hill, and the duel guitars of K. K. Downing and Glenn Tipton were joined by the first of several drummers. Hailing from the Black Country (not to be confused with Birmingham: they are different, apparently, and it's important, apparently), not far from where Black Sabbath grew up, Priest were forged in the same industrial furnaces as their countrymen and were heavily influenced by them.

Priest's take on heavy metal was a step forward from the first wave of bands. They stripped back the obvious blues influence that typifies Sabbath and (more particularly) Led Zeppelin in favour of a sound that is closer to what modern ears recognise as heavy metal. Glenn and K. K.'s guitars intertwined and danced with each other and Rob Halford's vocals had a focus and

1. Not to be confused with John Atkins, who is my oldest friend and the founder member of the sludge-noise legends Palehorse. I mean, you're unlikely to know him but I just thought I'd mention him here cos he's nice.

four-octave range that at times comes over like an air-raid siren. A perfect complement to the guitars.

Priest increased the tempos, added a shred-tastic virtuosity to the guitars and generally added technique to the mix.

Sad Wings of Destiny changes the game. It has a focus, a sense of the importance of economy, to offset the epic, and a feeling of power that raises the bar for heavy metal. In subject matter they were the first true successors to Black Sabbath, with songs about murder, oppression and genocide. Musically Judas Priest severed heavy metal from its blues roots and made it its own thing. And they were not ashamed to embrace the label. They didn't stop there, constantly experimenting and getting heavier through their career, peaking with the extraordinary thrash metal of *Painkiller*. Priest's approach moved heavy metal on, inspiring a whole new generation to reinvigorate the genre with the massive explosion of creativity that came in the form of the New Wave of British Heavy Metal. They also gifted heavy metal a distinctive image that set it apart from its hippy roots.

A significant by-product of Judas Priest's incredible metal career is the fact that Rob Halford conducted most of it while dressed as a cartoon version of a gay man, while keeping his homosexuality a secret. He single-handedly introduced an image taken from the gay underground. Heavy metal culture embraced the leather-daddy BDSM leather and spikes look, thinking it was the most masculine look possible. Which, in a way, it totally is. They were unaware of the massively obvious homo-erotic subtext to the uniform. It's the greatest ever example of hiding in plain sight. When Halford came out in 1998 the metal community was bafflingly shocked,[1] and homophobic metalheads realised they'd been dressing kind of gay the whole time. What a total hero.

---

1.   Other revelations that have surprised the metal community include the religion of the Pope and the toilet habits of bears.

Priest's stripped-down, energetic but distinctly working-class approach to heavy metal set them apart from the proggy self-indulgence that was besmirching much of the rest of rock music in the 1970s. They wrote what are essentially super-powered pop songs with choruses, riffs and hooks. Later in their career they would embrace the stadium format with anthems such as 'United' which are almost football chants.

Judas Priest changed the meaning of the phrase 'heavy metal'.

At this point, metal was still in its infancy. While Sabbath were pushing their sound heavier and Priest were taking metal to its next step, hard rock continued to develop and progress alongside metal, all the while feeding into heavy metal's gene pool – seeding what would later explode into a dozen different sub-genres in the eighties, and all the while being consistently mislabelled (to modern ears) as heavy metal.

WHAT? MISLABELLED?!

Yep. While as late as 1989 *Kerrang!* magazine included such bands as Queen, Bad Company, The Jimi Hendrix Experience and the Sex Pistols in their list of the '100 Greatest Heavy Metal Albums of All Time', seemingly mistaking the category 'heavy metal' with the category 'guitar-based', in the 2010s we see things differently. In the seventies and eighties all hard rock was also called heavy metal. There was no distinction between the two terms. Since then us metal taxonomists and nerds have argued the point to death. Hell is other people. Purgatory is a room full of metalheads who have been told they can't pass through until they all agree on whether an infinite list of bands is metal or not. It's worth reiterating that the classification of 'heavy metal' should not be taken as comment on the worth of any given band. Booker T. & the M. G.s are better than Megadeth in my opinion, but Megadeth are very definitely metal and Booker T. & the M. G.'s are very definitely an R&B/funk band. I think.

So . . .

At the same time the world of hard rock was filling up with new bands who exhibited a leaner, harder, more modern sound. UFO from the UK and Scorpions from Germany had both formed in the sixties. UFO began in North London with a fairly unremarkable late-sixties-rock approach, with a little dash of space rock, to limited success. After a tour with Scorpions they stole the Germans' guitarist, Michael Schenker, and wrote some banging hard rock. Scorpions got a replacement and also wrote some banging hard rock. Win/win.

Though Scorpions went terrible and glam and made 'Rock You Like a Hurricane' and then, worse, 'Wind of Change', their seventies stuff is good. Particularly the song 'Robot Man', which sounds like he's saying 'Robert man', which is funny. Less funny is their album cover for *Virgin Killers*. Oof. You wouldn't believe me if I told you. And don't Google it unless you want to get banned from going near schools.

Both bands straddled the line between hard rock and heavy metal, adding a further virtuosity while maintaining a down-to-earth, working-class feel.

Emerging from the turmoil of Deep Purple, guitarist Richie Blackmore founded the band Rainbow, essentially hijacking Ronnie James Dio's band Elf, and recorded the egotistically titled album *Ritchie Blackmore Rainbow* in 1975. Blackmore subsequently fired the rest of the band for the subsequent tour and began to develop a sound that to my judgemental ears fulfils all the requirements to be characterised as heavy metal. The 1976 album, *Rising*, is a fucking classic and you should put this book down, fire up the internet and listen to it.

Getting through more members than a hungry German cannibal, Blackmore parted company with Dio, and Rainbow descended into pop-rock mediocrity, scoring such father's-day-compilation-CD-worthy hits as 'All Night Long' and 'Since You've been Gone'.

AC/DC are probably the band who most often get incorrectly called heavy metal. One of the biggest bands in the world, they play a uniquely[1] accessible brand of hard rock with a sound so stripped down it's practically custom-made as example music for guitar teachers. They emerged from an Australian pub-rock scene that produced very little else of international note and represented a distillation of blue-collar life the like of which Bruce Springsteen can only dream. The name comes from a label on a vacuum cleaner.[2] They are obsessed with balls, with the songs 'She's Got Balls', 'Ballbreaker' and the Oscar Wildean 'Big Balls'. The Wikipedia entry for this is worth quoting, saying that 'Big Balls' 'finds [original singer Bonn] Scott, a deceptively clever lyricist, using double entendres by using ballroom and costume parties to obviously reference his own testicles'. Let's examine the lyrics, which make reference to 'big balls', 'dirty big balls' and 'biggest balls of them all'.

Yep. Deceptively clever. A noted hedonist, Bonn Scott died an alcohol-related death in 1980 and was replaced by flat-cap-wearing Brian Johnson. (Notably, Noddy Holder of Slade was approached first but turned the offer down.) The first album with Johnson, *Back in Black*, was an enormous success, though fans have been divided ever since over their preference for each respective era.

Peculiarly, AC/DC's diminutive guitarist, Angus Young, dresses like a schoolboy and literally no one knows why.[3] In

1. If you don't count Airbourne, or any of the thousands of other clones.

2. Other names considered by AC/DC included 'Hoover', 'No User Serviceable Parts Inside' and 'For Best Results Change Bag Regularly'.

3. Literally. No one.

recent years Brian Johnson has suffered hearing difficulties and been replaced on tour by Axl Rose from Guns N' Roses. A gateway drug to hundreds of raving metalheads, AC/DC are enormous fun . . . but not heavy metal.

Boston's Aerosmith have two distinct phases. One good, one fucking terrible. They were at one time unassailable in their dominance of the hard rock landscape, playing a blues-rock style heavily influenced by The Rolling Stones. This first era was a significant influence on Nirvana's Kurt Cobain and Metallica's James Hetfield. Then drug addiction and squabbling took them down hard. They lost the guitarist and songwriter Joe Perry and their popularity waned . . . then they did a collaboration with Run-D.M.C. and rose like a phoenix from the heroin spoon. Alas, the stuff they wrote in this renaissance era is really rubbish pop-rock like 'I Don't Want to Miss a Thing' and 'Love in an Elevator'.

Thin Lizzy are definitely not metal but they're really, really, really good and they influenced every band that uses dual guitars. And 'Cowboy Song' is probably in the top five songs ever written, I reckon. Yep.

Alice Cooper's influence on the aesthetic of heavy metal cannot be overstated. His make-up hints at the corpse paint of the black metal lads, his onstage horror show is like a Fisher Price version of what death metal and black metal bands would later go on to do with REAL blood, not the ketchup-y fake stuff. His stadium anthems of rebellion and the dark side of life led many people onto a darker path and heavy metal patch jackets worldwide are adorned with his logo alongside that of the heavy metal greats . . . But he's not heavy metal.

Without KISS there would be no Pantera, no Norwegian metal scene, no corpse paint, probably no pyro at big shows.

They were true rock gods and gave heavy metal much of its swagger. They even outdid the most vehemently gross gore metal bands by taking *off* their make-up and showing their terrifying, distorted, inhuman real faces. But they are not heavy metal.

Whitesnake can fuck off.

One of the most experimental and adventurous rock bands of the 1970s was the hugely successful Queen. Among the incredibly eclectic mix of styles produced by Queen over the years, a good few songs stand up as verifiable heavy metal classics. Indeed, listened to selectively it's possible to put together a Queen mix-tape that's almost as heavy as a late-seventies Sabbath record. Tunes like 'Stone Cold Crazy' (later covered by Metallica and even played with Tony Iommi and James Hetfield at the Freddie Mercury tribute concert in 1992 . . .), 'Keep Yourself Alive', 'Liar', 'Brighton Rock' . . . all are hard rock. But not heavy metal.

Whitesnake can fuck off. Again.

Whether metal or not, all of these bands have had a huge influence on the metal we have today. Modern heavy metal is not simply a direct unblemished descendant of Sabbath – it's a mix of influences that got picked up along the way, including punk, hardcore and all of this seventies hard rock. I'd go as far as to argue that metal would have emerged out of this lot anyway even without Sabbath – the hard-wired human need for heavy is irresistible.

The other band that was really pushing the heaviness in the mid-seventies was Motörhead. Combining the snotty aggression and speed of punk with heavy metal's volume and musical fluency, Motörhead were more straightforward and stripped-down than Priest but just as heavy.

Motörhead formed after Lemmy was kicked out of Hawkwind for doing too many drugs.[1] He had been around the music scene for years, roadying for Hendrix and providing vocals for Hawkwind's 'Silver Machine', and decided to start a band that combined his two favourite things – rock and roll and the sound of wars. They were initially called 'Bastard', but that name was vetoed by management and Lemmy went for 'Motörhead' instead. In an early interview for *Sounds*, he hinted at their vile power saying 'if Motörhead moved next door your lawn would die.'

Lemmy always denied that Motörhead were a metal band, claiming instead, 'No, we're just a rock'n'roll band, like the Beatles.' This is bullshit. Lemmy – just cos your favourite band is the Beatles, it doesn't mean you play the same music as the Beatles. There is clearly a big difference between 'Orgasmatron' and 'Roll Over Beethoven'. If Motörhead are just a rock and roll band,[2] then they are the heaviest rock and roll band ever.

Lemmy's bourbon-ravaged vocal rasp was strikingly different from the baleful whine of Ozzy and the air-raid siren histrionics of Rob Halford and Ian Gillan. Coupled with the band's down-to-earth image (or lack of image), it meant that Motörhead's audience came as much from the exploding punk movement as the metalheads. In fact, several tracks on their debut album are just as much punk as they are metal, taking a lead from MC5.

---

1. How the fuck?! In reality it was the *wrong type of drugs*. He was busted in Canada for possession of cocaine, though it turned out to be speed, while the rest of the band favoured hallucinogens.

2. They're not. They're heavy metal.

They truly crossed over, helping break down the barriers between metal and punk, as Jamey Jasta from Hatebreed told me: 'We wouldn't exist without Motörhead. They did this first.'

Motörhead's broad appeal and their high profile in television and radio meant that they transcended the metal/punk/hard rock subcultures, being briefly the heaviest band with popular appeal. Lemmy's growing status as a rock icon meant that he became bigger than Motörhead. The outpouring of sentiment after he died came from all quarters. People who'd never bought a Motörhead record in their life felt a real sense of loss. I was initially pretty fucking sceptical about this, but then I realised that, indeed, Lemmy wasn't just ours. He was an icon for everyone.

Their biggest song is one of the most recognisable in all of hard rock history. As a result there are millions of people who can sing along to 'Ace of Spades' without being able to name one single other Motörhead song. One of their stand-out appearances was on the revolutionary British sitcom *The Young Ones*. The show was perfectly suited to an appearance by a down-and-dirty metal band. *The Young Ones* was anarchic, gross, violent and surreal, and it represented a sea change in British comedy, represented best by the iconic scene in which the violent metal/punk Vyvyan[1] smashes through a screen that is showing the cosy family sitcom *The Good Life*:

> No! No! NO! NO! We're not watching the bloody *Good Life*! Bloody bloody bloody! I hate it! It's so bloody nice!

1. Played by Adrian Edmonson, the creator of the excellent spoof metal band documentary *Bad News*. A man who I once managed to piss off while drunk and banging on about how *Bottom* never received the full appreciation it deserved. The phrase 'never meet your heroes' is sometimes true, but 'never allow your heroes to meet you' was more apposite in this case.

Felicity 'Treacle' Kendall and Richard 'Sugar-Flavoured-Snot' Briars! What do they do now? Chocolate bloody button ads, that's what! They're nothing but a couple of reactionary stereotypes, confirming the myth that everyone in Britain is a lovable, middle-class eccentric – and I – HATE – THEM!

The Young Ones featured a different band each week because the producers realised they would get more funding for the show due to a weird quirk of BBC finances. Motörhead also appear in another 'alternative comedy' show – *Eat the Rich*, made by *The Comic Strip*.

Motörhead have had a tremendous impact on the trappings and image of heavy metal. Lemmy popularised the wearing of bullet belts – stemming from his love of militaria, particularly that of the Second World War. Lemmy's bullshit-free attitude is the template for all heavy metal heroes. He was hilariously straightforward. Asked about his commitment to a particular brand of amplifier for a BBC documentary he said: 'I like Marshall amps, so I use them.' His was an almost monastic devotion to the rock and roll lifestyle. A simple formula: keep making records and keep touring in support of them. Drinking Jack Daniels and smoking and taking so much speed his doctor told him that if he stopped his heart would too.

Motörhead's playing style helped revitalise the whole genre. Drummer Phil 'Philthy Animal' Taylor introduced two distinctive techniques. The song 'Overkill' introduced the double-bass drum to heavy metal, changing metal drumming for ever. Also influential was what became known as the d-beat drum style, which was adopted by eighties punk bands – so named because it came to define the highly influential Discharge and was then adopted by a hundred bands who all began with the letter D!

Surprisingly Motörhead have only sold around 15 million records. In influence they punch above their weight, and when Lemmy died at the end of 2015 the grief expressed for the loss of such an iconic figure came from all quarters. He was irreplaceable.

The success of Judas Priest and Motörhead helped revitalise heavy metal, and in their wake a whole new scene erupted.

The *New Wave of British Heavy Metal.*

4

The New Wave of British Heavy Metal

The New Wave of British Heavy Metal (or NWOBHM as no one should say out loud) is the single most important movement in the history of metal. What came before it was amorphous, incoherent and only rarely describable as 'real' heavy metal. It wasn't a scene – bands were adrift in the wider ocean of pop music. What came after was the emergence of heavy metal as a subculture. The vast majority of bands that made up the NWOBHM never enjoyed anything like mainstream success. Theirs is a story of grass-roots passion that influences heavy metal to this day.

In 1977 the landscape of popular music changed significantly, and heavy metal was directly affected. The controversy that arose around the Sex Pistols and the subsequent release of their album *Never Mind the Bollocks . . . Here's the Sex Pistols* led to an explosion of the punk rock movement. Joined by bands such as The Damned, The Adverts and The Clash they helped strip rock music back to its component parts and added politics and a genuine air of rebellion. In addition a DIY ethic sprang up – no longer did bands need to seek the approval of a major record label in order to produce a record: they went straight to the manufacturers and did it themselves. For a short while punk was huge.

The degree to which punk bands and artists exhibited these

'punk rock' qualities varied wildly – The Damned offered little in the way of social critique and, far from being DIY, the Sex Pistols were something of a manufactured, corporate product – but punk as a movement and as an idea was far more significant than any one band (despite what the Punk Nostalgia Industry might try to tell you).

Punk was the product of its time and of its environment. An onslaught of angry, youthful disaffection, it perfectly encapsulated the sentiments of the time in a way that most hard rock and heavy metal bands could not. Furthermore, punk was a musical reaction *against* the virtuosity and detached rock-god status of the stadium rock bands like Led Zeppelin. It was aimed at the street. It was immediate and seemed to be the obvious way to express oneself through the guitar/bass/drums/vocals format of rock and roll. It harked back to some of the progenitors of heavy metal and in some ways exhibited metal's core attributes better than metal did.

Punk rock originated as more of an attitude than a distinct musical style. Its roots stretch back to the garage rock of the 1960s, through Detroit's MC5 and the Stooges and then to New York, where bands such as Suicide and Television were disparate sonically but had a commitment to a certain approach – non-commercial and direct. It was the New York Dolls and the Ramones who inspired impresario and pathological credit-taker Malcolm McLaren to return to England and replicate what he saw as a movement with a vast potential. He put together the Sex Pistols, punk's first manufactured band, whose notoriety led to them becoming a lightning rod for all of the punk that was to follow. Some believe the Pistols to be the absolute pinnacle of punk, others that they ruined it for everyone else.

The Pistols created a tremendous national scandal. A sweary television appearance led to shocked tabloid headlines. On 4 June

1976 they played at Manchester Free Trade Hall to four and a
half million people.[1] In that audience were The Smiths, Mick
Hucknall of Simply Red, Oasis, the entire 1994 Manchester
United squad and Russell Brand.

On 22 October 1976 The Damned released 'New Rose', their
debut single and officially the first ever British punk seven-inch.
Very quickly punk bands sprang up nationwide. The pervading
attitude of punk rock was that 'anyone can do it'. The magazine
Sniffin' Glue . . . and other rock'n'roll habits popularised a graphic
that had first appeared in *Sideburns* magazine – a picture of three
chord shapes with the legend: 'Here's a chord. Here's another.
Here's a third. Now form a band.' The gap between the audience
and those on stage was narrowed to the point that thousands of
aspiring punk rockers felt they could do it too. There was no
need to be a virtuoso – anyone could be in a band.

This celebration of amateurism within punk[2] has become a
sticking point within heavy metal. While it was a revelation that
it was no longer necessary to be a virtuoso musician to be in a
band – *I couldn't play guitar like Jimmy Page, but I could play guitar like
them* – metalheads who really *could* play were pissed off that they
were being eclipsed by those who couldn't – especially Iron
Maiden, who in 1977 were struggling to get signed and being
told to adopt a punk image. They've been pretty bitter about it
ever since.

But in truth heavy metal was in need of a kick up the arse.

1. . . . if you are to believe what people say. In reality, there were very few
people there, but, as the legend goes, everyone who was there started a band.
That gig led to the formation of The Smiths, the Buzzocks, Joy Division and –
bizarrely – Simply Red.

2. Which was not always the case. The Pistols were perfectly good musicians,
for example. Well, until Sid Vicious joined . . .

Releases by The Damned, The Clash, the Sex Pistols and The Adverts made most hard rock acts look like dinosaurs. The sort of dad rock that Alan Partridge or Jeremy Clarkson would like. The youth of the punk movement made most of the bands whose roots stretched back to the 1960s seem old[1] and old hat.[2] Punk was anti-establishment and rock music had become the sound of the establishment, its progenitors buying up mansions and living abroad for tax reasons while Britain suffered an economic meltdown.

Punk had two immediate effects on heavy metal. Firstly it shifted rock and roll's focus away from virtuosity and complexity, away from the unassailable rock gods like Led Zeppelin and the overblown, self-indulgent progressive acts like Yes and Emerson Lake & Palmer and shifted it towards bands who were more accessible, more street-level. Newer bands like Judas Priest survived by adapting and adopting. Motörhead were embraced by punk rock kids partly because they sounded kind of punk and partly because unlike all the other metal bands they seemed pretty down to earth. Motörhead in particular destroyed barriers between the genres. Even so, sniffy journalists of the type who had never had a good word to say about Sabbath and Led Zeppelin creamed themselves over punk with its art school rebellion. They derided the continuation of metal, hoping it would somehow just fuck off.

But it didn't . . . because the second effect of punk on heavy metal was considerably more positive.

Punk thrived on a DIY ethic. Independent record labels sprang up like daffodils in spring as people realised that the major labels were not the be-all and end-all and it was in fact possible for *anyone* to record a band and manufacture records. DIY record production is an incredibly simple idea. Rather than

1. Literally.
2. Metaphorically.

trying to get a record deal with a record label who then basically lend you the money to make an album, you just record the album and then get in touch with the record plants who make records and press them up yourself. It cuts out the middleman. In the age of MP3s, streaming, Bandcamp,[1] and all, it is now a totally standard way of operating. My band, for example, is its own record label. We make our records ourselves and are not beholden to anyone else. We can make exactly the music we want and any profits get ploughed back into running the band. This enduring story of punk – its continuation through American hardcore, UK82/anarcho-punk and their various offshoots – is oddly lacking in the Grand Narrative of punk. The above-ground effect of the Pistols and The Clash was extremely short-lived and fundamentally absorbed into capitalist culture anyway.[2] Mainstream punk was quickly de-clawed, turning into New Wave and a revitalisation of British pop music, but the popularly held notion that punk died when the Sex Pistols split is a bullshit and elitist idea entirely opposing the punk rock ethic. Punk has never gone away and its DIY, anti-establishment approach to rock music is alive and well in a rich variety of forms all around the world.

Parallel to the development of punk, a new movement was stirring in the UK. It centred on a few independent labels: Neat

---

1. Welcome to the part of the book that will seem really dated in no time at all! 'What's Bandcamp?' cry the readers of the future. 'I think it's something they had during the war.'

2. Eternal icon of rebellion Johnny Rotten now makes his money through investment in the property market. Ever feel like you've been cheated? Conversely, metal never rejected capitalist culture and yet is seen as an outsider thing by the mainstream press even to this day.

in Newcastle, Guardian Records in Durham, Ebony in Hull and Heavy Metal Records in the balmy climes further south of Wolverhampton. Some truly DIY bands started up their own labels to self-release their records. Another focal point of this new movement was a peculiar phenomenon in the north of London – the heavy rock disco. From 1975 to 1980 charismatic DJ Neal Kaye[1] ran The Bandwagon Heavy Metal Soundhouse[2], a metal club night that attracted an enormous following. His titanic sound system played not only from his extensive collection of rock and metal LPs but also featured demos by bands who were friends of the Bandwagon such as Iron Maiden. The phenomenon of air guitar – or, to be more precise, *cardboard* guitar – was popularised here. Featured in a brilliant BBC documentary narrated by Danny Baker (and lampooned expertly by the peerless Bob Mills in *In Bed with Me Dinner*), Rob Loonhouse explains that he simply hasn't the time to become a really good guitarist, so he makes do with pretending,[3] possibly the ultimate extension of punk's 'anyone can do it' ethos.

1.   Whose Wikipedia page is currently a hilarious autohagiography: 'He was a great rebel rousing DJ, who had a special sense of duty and commitment for his crusade to help establish heavy metal music as a real major force in the international music world and, he was very professional in presentation and delivery when behind the decks, combining his vast knowledge of the music he loved, with a great sense of fun and sheer lunacy, he helped to create the Soundhouse legend, followed and supported by his loyal Wagon fans wherever he went to appear on stages large and small.' I wonder who wrote that.

2.   . . . or TBHMS, as no one ever called it.

3.   Rob Loonhouse: 'I tend to practise at home, I tend to like to know where the chord changes are, where the solos come in. I tend to like to make it look as if I am actually playing: I do know what I'm doing.' Bob Mills: 'Yeah, well, you don't just wanna look like a wanker, do you?'

A live gig at the Bandwagon by Samson, Iron Maiden and Angel Witch drew the attention of a *Sounds* journalist, Geoff Barton, whose double-page spread on the gig was the defining moment of what the editor, Alan Lewis, described in his subtitle as the 'New Wave of British Heavy Metal'. *Sounds* began a heavy metal chart, based on what Kaye played and had requested at the Soundhouse.[1]

This high-profile highlighting of new metal bands in a national music paper was a huge boost for the resurgence in heavy metal. The New Wave of British Heavy Metal was nothing short of a rebirth. It was an astonishing outburst of activity and creativity which led to literally hundreds of bands emerging throughout the UK and (despite the suggested geographical limitations of the name) abroad. Finally a movement existed that was proud to be associated with the name heavy metal. The attitude of 'I can do that' which stemmed from punk led to some of the greatest and most influential bands of all time, who influence heavy metal right up to the present day.

The names associated with NWOBHM give an indication of the imagination and creative energy that abounded, names like Dumpy's Rusty Nuts, Bashful Alley, the Monty-Python-inspired Ethel the Frog, the animal-based Tygers of Pan Tang (a reference to work by the fantasy writer Michael Moorcock), Def Leppard, Tysondog, Praying Mantis, Quartz, Virtue, the more occult-flavoured Angel Witch, Witchfynde, Witchfinder General, Cloven Hoof, Satanic Rites, Satan . . .

The bigger bands of the era signed to major labels: Iron Maiden to EMI (as did Saxon, eventually), Def Leppard to Vertigo – but it was an independent label that came to truly define the New Wave of British Heavy Metal. Always something of a

---

1. Barton would go on to start *Kerrang!* magazine.

shambolic operation, Neat Records grew out of a recording studio. Owned by Benny Hill lookalike David Wood, Impulse
Studio was built into the green room of an old theatre in Wallsend,
the north-eastern town most famous for producing rainforest
campaigner and sex guru Sting. Largely funded by money made
from running a mobile disco, Wood began to release records by
bands recording in Impulse. Jazz went out on a label he named
Wudwink (with a few notable non-jazz exceptions, including
local punks the Angelic Upstarts), folk on a label called Rubber
Records. He also released live recordings of comedians. Sting's
early groups Last Exit and Newcastle Big Band both had releases
on Wood's labels, as much later did A Tribe of Toffs, whose novelty song 'John Kettley is a Weatherman' was released by Wood's
Completely Different Records imprint and got to number 21 in
the UK charts in 1988.

Back in 1979 the Whitley Bay band Tygers of Pan Tang
recorded two demos at Impulse Studio, one of which got sent to
Geoff Barton at *Sounds.* He loved it, and the positive reaction the
tape received there and in other music papers led to Wood offer-
ing them a deal for a single on the newly minted Neat Records.
But metal was new to David Wood, and so (according to the
interview he gave for the incredibly detailed book *Neat & Tidy:
The Story of Neat Records*), 'I sent someone out to the record shop
to ask about rock/heavy metal stuff.'

'Don't Touch Me There' was a modest success and so Neat
continued in the same heavy metal vein with Fist's 'Name, Rank
and Serial Number/You'll Never Get Me Up (In One of Those)'
and White Spirit's 'Back to the Grind/Cheetah'. Wood then
struck a deal with major label MCA for these three bands. Ultimately the deal fell flat, much to the detriment of everyone.

Next came Raven and Venom. Both stayed with Neat for
album releases and both flourished in their own way. Raven

toured the States several times, even moving over there for a while. As for Venom . . . well, that's another story.[1]

There is an odd whiff of 'also-ran' around the vast majority of NWOBHM bands. They were caught in the middle of two contrasting approaches to being a metal band. Up until the early eighties bands all operated within a music industry model. Even with the DIY influence of punk rock, bands still aspired to being signed by a record label, becoming famous, selling loads of records and appearing on *Top of the Pops*. Def Leppard's self-released EP was a means to an end, not an end in itself. They were not championing a new way of doing things; they were trying to get into the system. There was not yet an 'underground' in which bands could play to the highest standard while not necessarily doing it for a living. Today even seminal bands like Neurosis have day jobs to make ends meet – particularly in the post-record-sales era. But back in the early eighties it was commercial success or obscurity. Most NWOBHM bands fell into the latter camp . . .

The pattern seemed to be a repeated story of initial success, major-label interference and a slide into relative obscurity. But three bands reached escape velocity and went stratospheric.

Saxon enjoyed enormous success in the early eighties. Even more anthemic than Judas Priest, but with more of a grass-rooted lyrical basis, they were possibly the first heavy metal band to sing about being a heavy metal band. Saxon are truly made up of US LOT. 'Heavy Metal Thunder' from their second album, *Strong Arm of the Law*, talks in veiled terms about the metal scene, but the song 'Denim and Leather' was the point at which heavy metal became self-conscious. Never before had a band talked in these terms – about the grass-roots experience of being a metal fan, of having to

1. See the black metal chapter.

strive to find the music you love. Saxon are the opposite of the grandstanding stadium-colossus bands. They have a true under-dog spirit, unmatched since early Black Sabbath.

Def Leppard began sounding like most NWOBHM and then took a turn towards the commercial. And it worked a treat. For them. I mean, they sounded awful but they sold a lot of records, conquering America and selling out stadiums worldwide. Their self-released debut EP is actually pretty good. But then they went totally pony.

In 1984, Def Leppard's drummer, Rick Allen, lost his left arm after being involved in a car crash. In a show of incredible loyalty and all-round-good-bloke-ness the band kept him on as their drummer. He developed a way of triggering drums with several foot pedals and continues to be a genuinely impressive drummer. Def Leppard's enormous success in the States is what the other NWOBHM bands were aiming for, though none went for it with quite the same ferocity, plus of course they quite possibly lacked the shark-eyed commercial killer instinct and pop chops to write the sorts of songs that millions of people want to hear. Bear in mind that most humans are awful, and so if millions of people want to buy your art . . . it's probably not good art.

Notable for their success and musical ability but more often noted for their 100 per cent absence of penises, all-female London band Girlschool enjoyed huge success in the glory days of NWOBHM, at a time when female metal bands were pretty much non-existent. Proving themselves on their own terms they headlined the Reading Festival in 1981. Forever associated with Motörhead, they toured with Lemmy and co. several times and formed the collaboration 'Headgirl', recording an EP featuring a cover of Johnny Kidd and the Pirates' 'Please Don't Touch' and covers of each other's songs. Girlschool are still together and touring.

Iron Maiden formed on Christmas Day 1975, the same year as Motörhead, but like Judas Priest took half a decade to release an official album. Their demo – *The Soundhouse Tapes* – made them big even before they were signed. They grew frustrated with record labels telling them to cut their hair and embrace a punk image, explaining the hostile attitude to punk they've had ever since. (Despite their antipathy to the movement, their early songs show influence from punk and even glitter rock.)

After replacing their original singer, Paul Di'Anno, with the more trained operatic-style vocals of Bruce Dickinson they attained an international level of success only previously matched by Led Zeppelin. So astonishing was their early success that Dickinson experienced a bout of depression after their first world tour, having so thoroughly achieved all his ambitions, like Alexander the Great weeping when he saw the breadth of his domain 'for there were no more lands to conquer'[1]. The only option available was to do it all again, only bigger and better. This sentiment of 'been there, done that' may be what led him to learning to fly commercial planes and becoming Iron Maiden's pilot, which is a bit like having a drummer who's got a van . . .

In sound, Maiden were very much along the lines of Judas Priest: stripped back, eschewing the blues for Pure Fucking Metal. Lyrically their early output was dark – dealing with depression, urban decay, isolation. Later they expanded to more epic, mythical and historical themes.[2]

Today, Maiden still play arenas and stadiums worldwide. Like Motörhead, they have a rabid following which goes way beyond

1. Which sounds like an impressive reference until I remember I got it from *Die Hard*. (The benefits of a classical education.)

2. As yet, I haven't been able to confirm my theory that a childhood friendship with Suggs was the inspiration for the song 'Can I Play with Madness'.

just metal fans. They are a brand, selling more T-shirts than Topman, and they even have their own branded beer, Trooper, which is nice and also vegan.

Despite their titanic success, Maiden are still seen as uncool. There is something cosily reassuring about this, though. The satirical spoof-news website The Daily Mash hit the nail on the head with its article 'Iron Maiden fans somehow immune to self-consciousness epidemic':

> They just like their thing for what it is, their hairy backs aren't a statement and when they wear double denim with a bumbag it's in no way ironic. The rest of us will never achieve that level of enjoyment of anything, because our stupid aspirations have made us into dicks.

Maiden are consistently overlooked by the music press. Which is fine by us. They can review Coldplay at Glastonbury – we'll read about Maiden in *Metal Hammer* . . . They will forever be a sort of massively successful underdog. The elephant in the room of the music industry. They'll never be sexy, they'll never be truly cool. But they will always be ours.

And while Maiden would break right through to the mainstream and keep the sound of the NWOBHM alive throughout the 1980s, the New Wave of British Heavy Metal would soon evolve once more into distinct sub-genres like speed metal and thrash. As a distinct movement, NWOBHM went out with a whimper. Shifting tastes meant that British audiences were drawn to the heavier thrash bands that were coming out in America. It had done its job, and it could die.

There is a resurgence of interest in NWOBHM bands at the time I'm writing this. Partly it's a reaction against the more 'plastic'-sounding commercial metal, very much helped along by the unwilling black metal superstar Fenriz from Darkthrone, whose band of the week blog is massively influential in the metal underground and has helped spearhead a movement against over-produced bands with triggered drums in favour of an organic, early-eighties sound. Mainly, though, it is part of the twenty-first-century, post-post-modern trend of young people claiming cool points by being into uncool, old shit.[1]

The true influence of this bunch of bands, geographically predominantly limited to Britain and historically limited to the period 1979–85, was twofold. Firstly, it saw heavy metal become its own thing. While the end of the 1960s provided the primordial soup necessary for the birth of heavy metal, the end of the 1970s saw the spawn of that soup sustaining themselves. Finally, heavy metal was not just a description of a type of rock music. It was a lifestyle, a community. Heavy metal broke off from the mainstream and began to operate in its own world, its own ecosystem. Secondly, the NWOBHM was the catalyst for heavy metal dividing up within itself to form new sub-genres. In the wake of NWOBHM came black metal, thrash metal, speed metal, death metal, doom metal and the millions of sub-sub-categories that followed.

One band in particular were the prism that split the beam. Venom.

1. See Chapter 16, 'Retro'.

5

The First Wave of Black Metal

You can trace any event back through the cluster of factors that made it happen and dissect its causes to the point of absurdity. If Hitler had been a more successful painter, the Second World War may never have happened. If John Lennon and Paul McCartney had never met, guitar music wouldn't have made its sixties resurgence and Black Sabbath and thus heavy metal wouldn't exist. And if it weren't for a holiday camp in Benidorm, and a British government youth training scheme, black metal might never have been a thing.

Between 1979 and 1981 a teenager called Conrad Lant worked for Impulse Studio as part of the Conservative government's Youth Opportunities Programme – a scheme in which the government paid for youths between sixteen and eighteen to be employed and train on a job, instead of receiving benefits. YOP and its successor, YTS, were the butt of jokes throughout the eighties as the typical recipient was often said to be a gormless waste of space, imposed upon an unwilling employer. But the scheme did have positive outcomes, as people like the soon-to-be-named Cronos could work in jobs where there otherwise would not be a place for them.[1] Despite the very specific job

1 The comedy duo Reeves and Mortimer benefited from a similar scheme. Vic Reeves (real name Jim Moir) took advantage of Thatcher's Enterprise

title, Lant was basically there to make the tea, run errands and in one case throw a mic'd-up bin full of scrap metal down the stairs for the end of Tygers of Pan Tang's first single. It placed him at the heart of the New Wave of British Heavy Metal.

NWOBHM had been a shot in the arm for an ailing scene. It revitalised interest in heavy metal and provided a much-needed injection of youthful vitality. The band that Conrad Lant went on to front had more significant impact on the metal that followed than any other. Iron Maiden and Def Leppard conquered stadiums and charts worldwide, but stylistically what they were doing was nothing all that new. Venom were harder, faster, heavier and more Satanic than any band that preceded them.

The history of Venom is mired in misinformation, retractions, rewriting of history, bickering and general bullshit. The orthodox version is that Venom formed from three different bands – Guillotine, Oberon and Dwarf Star. The guitarist Jeffrey Dunn denies that any of these were real bands. Even the one he was supposed to have been in . . . 'All this about all these other bands, I've got no evidence to suggest that they ever existed,' he said in the wonderful *Neat & Tidy*.

The facts are that three Geordies[1] named Conrad Lant, Jeffrey Dunn and Anthony Bray changed their names to Cronos,[2] Mantas and Abaddon, dressed up in more leather and spikes than Judas Priest on a gay pride march, and invented extreme metal.

Allowance Scheme to fund the running of his weekly club in New Cross, 'Vic Reeves' Big Night Out', which was picked up by Channel 4 and made the two famous. The same scheme allowed Napalm Death/Cathedral vocalist Lee Dorrian to set up Rise Above records.

1. If you are unfamiliar with the word 'Geordies', it's what happens when Scottish people fuck Vikings.

2. Roman god of watches.

'We decided on using stage names very early on. I thought it would be lame to be singing about Satan and demons and all the dark forces, and to have basic normal names. I felt it wasn't right, we needed names to fit the personalities, something more formidable and demonic,' said Cronos, as quoted on their 'official' website.

Venom were a total aberration in NWOBHM. They just didn't sound like anyone else. While the approach of most bands echoed that of the old-guard stadium-fillers (albeit on a smaller scale – just look at the number of vocalists who modelled their stagecraft on Robert Plant), Venom were ground-breaking and uncompromising in their aesthetic. Everything was extreme. Their first single, 'In League with Satan'[1]/'Live Like an Angel (Die Like a Devil)', was a Molotov cocktail thrown into a party. They were explicitly satanic. Black Sabbath's apologetic, scared-Christian approach to the infernal was replaced by a celebration of Satan as an ally. Venom considered Ozzy a disappointment because every time he talked about Satan he'd go 'OH NOOOOOOOOOO!'

> That was always my problem with Ozzy. He'd sing about dark figures then spoilt it all by going, 'Oh God, help me!' Duh, wrong! That was stopping one step short of where I wanted to take this band. We were prepared to go beyond the Hammer Horror of Black Sabbath. – Cronos, www.venomslegions.com

For the first time a metal band presented themselves as the bad guys; as evil. This may have something to do with their love of wrestling, taking their cues from wrestling heels, the bad guys.

---

1. Which was brilliantly misprinted on the original pressing as 'In League with Satin', which sounds like a euphemism.

They weren't scared of Satan, they were *in league with Satan*! Ozzy warned you against what he saw; Venom warned you against *themselves*! 'LOOK OUT! BEWARE! When the moon is high and bright!' The extremity of their lyrics was like nothing that had gone before. They celebrated rape, masturbation, venereal disease, prostitution . . . The satanism is explicitly blasphemous. Not only that, they use *actual reversed satanic messages*![1]

Neat released Venom's first album, *Welcome to Hell*, in December 1981. Made up of tracks that originally were only intended for release as a demo, it had a raw ferocity that divided critics, though Geoff Barton gave it a full five stars in *Sounds* and described it as 'possibly the heaviest record ever allowed in the shops for public consumption'.

Sonically, they were more extreme than anything before them. Raw, loud, overblown . . . HEAVY. Their music was underpinned by a 'bulldozer' bass sound which came about by accident when Cronos was forced to take over on bass at short notice and played through his guitar rig. The guitars are harshly distorted, and vocally Cronos sounds like a pissed-off Lemmy, adding more aggression to his delivery than any metal vocalist before him – more akin to the furious growl of Cal from Discharge. Whereas other Neat bands found the studio a limitation, for Venom it totally worked. From their first single they drip with atmosphere. Black metal bands have ever since sought to find a lo-fi sound. It suits black metal: atmosphere trumps sonic perfection.

The follow-up album, *Black Metal*, spawned metal's first sub-genre. Most of metal's micro-niches get their names from

---

1. The backwards incantation on 'In League With Satan' when played forwards says, 'Satan! Priest in hell! I'm gonna burn your soul, crush your bones! I'm gonna make you bleed! You're gonna bleed for me!'

music journalists and are named some time after their conception. Black metal is much more clean-cut. On 1 November 1982 the album named *Black Metal* started the genre of black metal. Job done. Venom coined the term to distinguish themselves from the rest of heavy metal, which they saw as weak pop music.

In a total reverse of the normal approach, Venom built a reputation by *not* gigging. Stating that the normal club venues were too small for their stage show, they turned most offers down. Nonetheless they toured America and Europe, claiming to be the biggest independent metal band in the world, which is a bit like claiming to be the biggest writer of comedic books on the history of heavy metal in the world . . . However, they also toured with such credible support bands as Metallica and Slayer.[1]

At the time, Venom were never taken seriously. But, much more importantly, Venom did not take themselves seriously. They had a hedonistic attitude – encouraging the listener to sign pacts with the devil so we can join their party. The song 'Teacher's Pet' ends with a raucous chorus of 'Get your tits out for the lads', a traditional folk tune beloved of vicars and maiden aunts. Not everyone picked up on their self-consciousness. Hardcore punk

---

1. Tom Araya from Slayer once pissed on Cronos's head. *Decibel* magazine reports the incident thus: Dave Lombardo: 'I remember Tom getting punched by Cronos [VENOM]. We were in the back of the bus drinking, and we were just totally hammered . . . Tom came in, hammered out of his mind, going, "I gotta take a piss! Where's the bathroom in this thing?" And Cronos goes, "Right here – right here in my mouth!" And Tom took him literally. He pulled down his pants, whipped it out, and went to the bathroom on Cronos' hair. Cronos got up, grabbed Tom, and punched him in the face. They spent the rest of the night blaming each other, and Tom did the rest of the tour with a black eye.' Kerry King: 'I still can't believe Tom pissed on his head.'

Or you can read about it on the best URL of all time: www.blabbermouth. net/news/slayer-recount-venom-pissing-incident/

band Black Flag supported Venom in New Jersey. Flag's frontman, Henry Rollins, ripped them apart in his tour diary, *Get in the
Van*:

> Venom is weak. Everything about them is weak. They
> can't even play. They had a bunch of roadies to do
> everything. Weak, weak, weak. I would love to play with
> fucking 'heavy metal' bands more often. It was fun
> crushing them. It's all lights and makeup. What bullshit.
> Venom suck. They are so full of shit. What a bad joke.
> They don't sweat and they probably don't even fuck.

He invoked *Spinal Tap*, saying, 'I expected them to go into "Sex
Farm Woman" at any second.' Alas, with this comparison the
young Hank does himself a disservice, because he has massively
missed the point – Venom were so tongue in cheek they nearly
permanently damaged their cheeks. Although it suits Venom, this
self-awareness didn't translate into the black metal that they
inspired. Which is largely a good thing, because the *lack* of sense
of humour of the second wave of black metal is what makes it
uniquely appealing.[1]

Venom are significant in several different ways. Their sonic
extremity led to the splitting up of metal into sub-genres. In their
wake came speed metal, thrash metal, death metal and, most directly, the sub-genre they named themselves, black metal.

Black metal's first wave is very much a retroactive classification. Venom coined the term to stand out from the rest of
metal – as a unique selling point, but much like 'heavy metal' the
term wasn't taken up with enthusiasm by the originators of the
sound. These categories didn't really get fixed until much later.

1. See the second-wave black metal chapter for the best and dryest
Scandinavian response to a question about Venom . . .

Venom can be traced as a direct, explicit influence on everyone making dark, extreme metal in the early eighties – Metallica,
Slayer, Possessed, Voivod . . . and they passed the black metal
torch on to a band who would develop the black metal sound
beyond recognition: Bathory.

Venom were the first, but far more influential on the style and
overall presentation of today's black metal were from next door
to its spiritual home of Norway. Sweden's Bathory were predominantly the project of one man – vocalist and guitarist Quorthon
(known to his gran as Tomas Forsberg). They first appeared on a
compilation album, *Scandinavian Metal Attack*, in 1984 and the
extremity of their two tracks had a massive impact, generating a
flood of fan mail. Re-recorded for their self-titled debut album,
the tracks are heavier and faster and the album as a whole is an
early blueprint for the modern black metal sound. Over the next
two albums, 1985's *The Return* . . . and 1987's *Under the Sign of the
Black Mark*, they developed that sound further, to the degree that
Under the Sign of the Black Mark is the single greatest black metal
album of all time.[1]

Quorthon's image is incredible – photos depict him breathing
fire, wearing ragged clothes and a necklace made of chicken
bones. It would be copied endlessly.

Bathory gave legitimacy to the concept of one-man bands
within black metal.[2] Although he did use other musicians

---

1. OPINION ALARM!

2. As in solo, studio-only recordings. Not a dude with a bass drum strapped
to his back and a guitar and a harmonica on one of those harmonica-holder
things. Although I'd love to see 'Woman of Dark Desires' played by one of
those guys.

(notably Jonas Åkerlund, who played drums on the *Scandinavian Metal Attack* recordings before leaving to pursue a successful career as a film director[1]), the liner notes for the first Bathory records only name Quorthon, and the notion that it was just him stuck.

> It was people who didn't like us who spread those kinds of rumours. Those who liked us spread rumours too, but they were a bit different. The reason those kinds of rumours started circulating was because my pictures and my name came up all the time when talking about BATHORY . . . The first line-up was together for a year, mainly because we were fairly good friends and because they always had access to a free rehearsal place. When things stared getting serious, after we had recorded two songs for the compilation album 'Scandinavian Metal Attack' in January '84, I simply couldn't keep those guys any more. Because with a bassplayer who can only play on the E-string and a drummer who doesn't know what to play there's no fun. To get hold of two guys in the Swedish 'climate' who looks good, understands what it's all about and can write music is more or less impossible. Everybody in Sweden has a good education so there is nothing to fight for within Rock. They [would] rather cut their hair to keep their job or stay home with their sick girlfriend than rehearse. There's no use keeping them in the band, so members have been kicked out all the time. There have been new names, new people all the time. We didn't want to confuse the fans, make them think that this will not last. That's why we never released any pictures.

1. In a fitting full-circle, Åkerlund is currently directing a film about the Norwegian black metal scene.

Maybe people thought it was mysterious and became
more interested in the band because of that so we played
along with it.

This disingenuity is a hallmark of Bathory's image:

'I can't believe everyone says we're a solo project! It's
because they hate us!'
'No, I think it's cos it's just you credited on the records!'
'NO. THEY MUST HATE US.'

In reality it was not until his sixth album, *Twilight of the Gods*,
that Quorthon would dispense with other musicians. However, it
is undeniable that he was the creative force behind the band. The
brains of the operation. The head honcho. The Big Cheese.[1]
While happily going along with the notion that he did everything himself, Quorthon also denied the (very fucking obvious)
influence of bands such as Venom, Slayer and, later, Manowar.[2]
Although Jonas Åkerlund entirely contradicts this and says they
were 'almost entirely' influenced by Venom.

'I can't believe everyone says we're influenced by Venom.'
'Well, you kind of sound like them. And have the same
song titles. And some of the same lyrics. And they're the
only other band that plays the same style as you.'
'NO. IT'S BECAUSE EVERYONE HATES US.'

Presumably wanting to fend off any notions of special treatment, Quorthon also denied the link between himself and the
owner of Typhon Records, who gave Bathory their first break on

1. The Guv'nor. Mr Big. Barry Big Balls.
2. Such denials of the obvious truth remain common in modern black metal,
like a lot of the bands who say that they are not racist.

the *Scandinavian Metal Attack* record and then created a dedicated sub-label, Black Mark Productions.[1] The link being that the owner of the label – Börje Forsberg – was his dad.

> 'I can't believe everyone says there's some link between me and the record label.'
> 'What, the one owned by your dad?'
> 'SHUT UP EVERYONE HATES ME I'M GOING TO THE GARDEN TO EAT WORMS.'

Though the Venom influence is clear, Quorthon developed Bathory's sound and over the first three records it drew considerably closer to modern black metal. The sound is raw, but much less rock and roll than Venom and with a great deal more atmosphere. And then there's the vocals . . . Instead of Cronos's throaty, guttural shouting, Quorthon's vocals are pained, screaming sounds. In 1984 they were easily the most extreme vocal sound in any metal band. It's an approach that was taken up by almost every black metal band that followed.

By the third album, Bathory had developed beyond their influences into something considerably more doom-laden and even frightening. With *Under the Sign of the Black Mark* Bathory were possibly the first band to truly achieve what Black Sabbath had set out to do – to make a record that is scary in the way a horror film can be.

As with every real pioneer in heavy metal, Quorthon was artistically restless and moved away from this primitive black metal sound into something quite different. He was dissatisfied with the black metal label, and labels in general. In an interview with *Metal Forces* in 1987 he said:

1. History doesn't tell us who 'Black Mark' was, or what his role was in the operation.

> I think it's totally wrong to put labels on a band's music
> because you should let the music speak for itself and it
> doesn't matter if you wear chicken bones, studded leather,
> spikes and upside-down crosses – the way you dress has
> nothing to do with the music at all. I mean you don't play
> any better because you wear studded leather or not, do
> you?

His fourth album, *Blood Fire Death*, is more melodic, epic and heroic, and lyrically begins to deal with topics such as paganism and Vikings. Then on *Hammerheart* Viking metal is truly invented. We'll come to that later in the book.

Quorthon died of heart failure in 2004. He left behind a legacy that few individuals within extreme metal can rival.[1]

One who can was Tom Gabriel Fischer, a unique and fascinating man. Known to metalheads as Tom G. Warrior, Fischer had an upbringing that was harrowing. His father absent, he was raised by just his mother, and at the age of seven was left alone for extended periods while she smuggled diamonds and watches into 'third world countries'. He was left to look after her collection of cats – up to ninety at one point – whose excretions made his house utterly uninhabitable. Filthy and stinking, he was bullied, abused and tormented by neighbours, school colleagues and even teachers.

The effect of this upbringing was a deep misanthropy and an outsider status he has never shaken. Many in heavy metal adopt this sort of attitude for effect, but for Fischer it is utterly real. Drawn to the darkest music he could find as both an outlet and as an escape, he felt utterly driven to make his own heavy metal – the darkest and heaviest he could produce. His childhood has

---

1. Also, he looked a bit like Bob Mortimer.

also given him a single-mindedness that would not only help him overcome the incredible limitations that geography and poverty imposed upon him, but also produce music with an incredible vision.

Fischer lived in a small village outside Zurich, and the earliest bands he managed to assemble in this rarefied music scene failed to satisfy his needs. He was so radically ahead of his time that there was only one person who shared his vision of being the darkest, heaviest band possible – Urs Sprenger. They changed their names to Tom G. Warrior and Steve Warrior, pretending to be brothers, and began to make music influenced by Venom, Motörhead, Discharge and NWOBHM.

Eventually the first incarnation of Hellhammer was formed from the other metal maniacs he found. If Fischer's brutal upbringing wasn't metal enough for you, they rehearsed in a fucking *nuclear bunker*! Called *Grave Hill*! Which was underneath a *kindergarten*! (Two out of three isn't bad . . .)

After struggling to find the right drummer they recorded a demo – in fact, *two* demos. The first, *Death Fiend*, showcased their earlier compositions, and the second, *Triumph of Death*, the later stuff. They shelved the first and released the second.

The sound of these recordings is extraordinary. They were captured on a portable eight-track in their bunker/rehearsal room. Undoubtedly crude and at times amateurish, the style is primitive, predominantly measured in pace, with the adolescent energy of a band desperate to smash through any boundaries. Despite these limitations the tracks are nonetheless pregnant with feeling.

The engineer, a friend of Fischer's dad, ridiculed them during the session and, apparently, afterwards for ever more. Much more significantly, and echoing what happened with Black Sabbath only thirteen years before, Hellhammer were torn apart by the music press. The reviews of the tape were appalling. Even Bernard Doe's *Metal Forces*, the magazine that vehemently supported such early extreme metal acts as Exciter and Slayer, vilified their recording.

> I like my metal heavy, and make no mistake, Hellhammer are h-e-a-v-y, indeed they make Venom sound like the Bee Gees! ... but surely you've got to draw the line somewhere?

Have you, Bernard? Have you?[1] This literary kicking wound the band up so much they vowed never to play in the UK – happily they relented on that in later years.

More line-up changes took place – Steve Warrior was fired for being simply not good enough at his instrument. Eventually he was replaced by Martin Eric Ain.

Meanwhile, word was getting out ... The negative reviews still managed to attract the attention of like-minded maniacs and soon Hellhammer were deluged with correspondence. The tape-trading network spread the word even further. Not long after, the impact they made was enough to gain the interest of a new record label – Noise. They were offered a deal, dependent on the production of a better demo. *Satanic Rites* was a step forward from the previous recordings but nonetheless still stands out as distinctly raw. But it got them a deal, and an EP was recorded – *Apocalyptic Raids*.

---

1. It seems every advocate of pioneering extremity felt the need to draw this sort of line in the sand. According to Pete Dee of Kremated/Acid Reign, even Neal Kaye of The Bandwagon Heavy Metal Soundhouse – pioneering supporter of NWOBHM (and massive advocate of Judy Garland and Al Jolson) – refused to play Metallica in the week of Cliff Burton's death, dismissing them as 'that noisy shit'. And that is PROPER gossip.

The press still hated them. Unhappy with the response they were getting, they killed Hellhammer . . .

But Hellhammer wouldn't die. Because Hellhammer has two histories. The first is bleak. Plagued by personnel difficulties, limited by family objections and work, and finally torn apart in the music press they had depended on so much, the band seemed a total failure . . . but Hellhammer never stopped growing in influence and reputation. By the time of the explosion of the second wave of black metal, they were a revered part of the history of extreme metal.

The thing that made Hellhammer such a cult band wasn't just the music – it was their wholehearted commitment. They were fanatics, producing newsletters before they'd recorded a note, delivering Venom their demo tape by throwing it at them at a press conference! They did photoshoots, endeavouring to produce a complete package. They lived it, wearing their leather and spikes in rehearsal, spraying their guitars and amplifiers to make them look more evil. They got a devoted local following. It's not hard to see why the second-wave bands loved them as much as they did, in their rejection of hi-fidelity death metal. The rawness of Hellhammer's recordings was a huge inspiration. And the lack of musical training at the outset meant that they forged their own style – thinking hard about what type of music they wanted to produce and going for innovation over imitation. The sparse, off-beat style is totally their own.

But Fischer and Ain wanted more. After killing off the Hellhammer project they spent a frantic night planning out an entirely new band – and THREE albums' worth of ideas down to the smallest detail: artwork, lyrical themes, musical tone . . . That band was to become Celtic Frost.

A press release was sent out announcing the death of Hellhammer, then another setting out the ambitious beginning of the new project, including titles of songs they had yet to write. Luckily their record label took them up on the idea and granted them a continuation of the deal Hellhammer were on.

Celtic Frost picked up where the previous project left off, despite their efforts to distance themselves from Hellhammer.[1] *Morbid Tales* is basically Hellhammer with higher standards. Fischer states: 'The main aim was to evade the restrictive characterization of "black metal". The contents of our lyrics had transcended this topic by far.'

Over the course of three albums Celtic Frost developed radically. Each record offered something fresh. They experimented, totally unwilling to rest on their laurels. *To Mega Therion* shows a leap in musicianship and production values, and their third album, *Into the Pandemonium*, is a brilliant, difficult, expansive avant-garde masterpiece.

Though the legacy of Hellhammer followed them and it took years to shake off the reputation, Celtic Frost would go on to have a terrific influence on extreme metal. Even though what they did next was really, properly awful.

There is something about the Nordic countries and metal. Finland has the highest number of metal bands per capita in the world. Sweden punches well above its weight, and produced by far the best death metal. Norway is synonymous with black metal. The odd country out is Denmark. Weirdly, Denmark has produced almost fuck-all in the way of successful or notable metal bands. There's quarter of Metallica, and then there's Mercyful Fate.

Something of an honorary member of the black metal 'Big

---

1. Not helped by their record label's insistence that a sticker be placed on the first Celtic Frost record proclaiming, 'ex-members of Hellhammer' . . . Cheers, lads. Thanks for that.

Four', Mercyful Fate are considerably more hi-fidelity and melodic than Venom, Bathory or Hellhammer. What set them apart from any other metal band in the first half of the 1980s was their unapologetic and serious commitment to satanism. While Venom talked the talk on record, Mercyful Fate's frontman, King Diamond, was a fully paid-up member of Anton LaVey's Church Of Satan and a friend of LaVey's too. Their satanism was sincere, compared to the more light-hearted approach of Venom or the satanism-as-metaphor approach of Bathory and Hellhammer. They conveyed an occult authenticity.

Musically, Mercyful Fate owed a great debt to Judas Priest, in their use both of dual guitars and of falsetto vocals, though whereas Rob Halford uses both ends of his considerable range, King Diamond stays in that upper register the whole time – making for a distinctive and divisive style. (Controversy alarm – I don't really like it. I know, right? I'm totally letting the side down.)

A big influence nonetheless on the Norwegian scene, Mercyful Fate continue to prove relevant and massively popular.

The Big Four of the first wave of black metal are no longer the force they once were. Venom are split into two competing units, the Cronos-fronted Venom, and Venom Inc., who featured the rest of the classic line-up and are fronted by Tony 'Demolition Man' Dolan (who had recorded four albums with a Mantas-less, Cronos-less incarnation of Venom between 1989 and 1992 and also fronts the superb Atomkraft). As such Venom have never really gone away, but they are a divided force.

Bathory went Viking metal and then Quorthon selfishly died. Hellhammer became Celtic Frost and moved away from the raw black metal sound into something vastly more experimental, then they went glam, then they split up, with Tom forming the industrial metal band Apollyon Sun. In 2001 they reformed and made a wicked album, then they split up again and Warrior formed Triptykon, who are fucking amazing and you should listen to them. Mercyful Fate split up and King Diamond went solo, continuing in much the same vein.

But this clutch of bands were by no means the only black metal that happened before the Norwegians got involved. The black flame was very much kept burning across the world.

In May 1984 the German band Sodom released a bestial slab of noise called *In the Sign of Evil*. With extreme vocals, buzzsaw guitars and a frenetic pace, it's heavier than Venom and tighter than most black metal. The follow-up album, *Obsessed by Cruelty*, continues in much the same vein. They then switched direction and in their later years they were a leading light in the 'Teutonic' thrash metal movement, but their early work remains influential! Their blackened reputation was helped no end by the iconic early frontman of Mayhem, Per 'Dead' Ohlin, wearing a Sodom shirt in most of his photographs. The Norwegian black metal kingpin Euronymous named his record label after the Sodom song 'Deathlike Silence'.

Job-wise Sodom were even more metal than Black Sabbath. They formed a band so they wouldn't have to continue WORKING DOWN A COAL MINE. A clear win in the game of Industrial-Revolution-harsh-job Top Trumps!

Often the most inventive and original bands in heavy metal come from scenes that are geographically isolated. Unable to homogenise in the way bigger scenes often do, with no touring bands coming through and influencing everyone in the same way, musicians in more remote scenes have to make their own fun, as during the war. Brazil is an excellent example. In 1985 Belo Horizonte had a very fertile black/thrash metal scene, producing Sepultura, Sarcófago, Vulcano and Mutilator. In a similar fashion to Sodom, Sepultura's early recordings are raw, blackened thrash. *Bestial Devastation* is brilliant, primitive and heavy. The album that followed, *Morbid Visions* (the title owing a debt to Hellhammer's *Morbid Tales*) has a lighter production but still totally kills. The original frontman of Sepultura, Wagner 'Antichrist' Lamounier, left/was kicked out[1] before they recorded but went on to form the massively influential Sarcófago. Crudely translated blasphemy is the order of the day with these guys, coupled with primitively played, crudely recorded dark as the toilets-in-hell thrashing metal. The cover of their debut album, *I.N.R.I.*, was a major influence on the aesthetic of the Norwegian black metal scene, particularly in their use of evil-looking make-up, which evolved into the black-and-white 'corpse-paint' that would come to define the genre. The broken English in the lyrics adds to their raw charm, spawning the eternal catchphrase of cult black metal: 'IF YOU ARE A FALSE DON'T ENTRY!'

What was created by the pioneers of black metal in the first years of the 1980s was a series of sparks . . . Sparks that would become a blaze.

A blaze . . .

. . . in the Northern . . .

. . . sky.

---

1. Delete as appropriate.

6

Thrash Metal Ascends: 1981–9

Adrenaline starts to flow! You're thrashing all around!
Acting like a maniac! WHIPLASH! – Metallica, 'Whiplash'

Thrash metal is heavy metal's teenage younger brother. In the throes of puberty, acne-scarred and riddled with ADHD, it's eaten all the sweets, guzzled its weight in fizzy drinks, watched a film about nuclear war and is grilling its older brother's girlfriend: 'Have you ever seen a dead body? Have you seen what happens to dead bodies in a nuclear war? I once farted and burped and sneezed all at the same time and Colin Beverley from school says if you do that you can die. Are you two gonna do kissing?'

Around 1981, metal's never-ending quest for extremity took a fertile side road. In the wake of Venom's satanic racket a clutch of bands emerged from the shadow of the New Wave of British Heavy Metal who were intoxicated by its speed and extremity and wanted to push it as far as they could. Push it to the next level.[1] These enthusiastic, creative teenagers were spread through-out the globe. Addicted to extremity, they had record collections that swelled with every metal release they could get their hands

---

1. Crank up the power. Set the engines to warp drive. Stand for the French national anthem. Go ballistic. Rip it up like a motherfucker.

on – Motörhead, Judas Priest, Iron Maiden, Diamond Head, Tank, Tygers of Pan Tang – and accompanied it with aggressive British punk and American hardcore: Black Flag, Dead Kennedys, GBH, D.R.I., The Exploited and – more influential than any other – Discharge. Out of this sum of influences came thrash metal. A snotty, blitzkrieg-fast, aggressive and distinctly teenage metal movement. Dominated by a so-called 'Big Four' – Metallica, Slayer, Megadeth and Anthrax (but in reality populated by hundreds of bands equally worthy of acclaim) – it would go on to become the most prolific and successful of the metal sub-genres, dominating the scene for the best part of a decade and producing the single biggest band in heavy metal. And for the first time in heavy metal's history the centre of this new movement was not the UK but the United States, marking a permanent shift away from metal's birthplace.

The influence of NWOBHM on American metal came through indirect channels. Before the explosion of Iron Maiden in 1982, NWOBHM had made a relatively small impact upon the American music scene. While Maiden and Venom were big in Europe (Venom being 'the biggest independent band in the world', according to Mantas), there was no real distribution for them in the States. It was up to rabid record geeks like Metallica's Lars Ulrich[1] and Anthrax's Scott Ian to scour record shops for imports and buy through mail order (much like John Lennon and Keith Richards sourcing obscure American blues records from sailors in their local docks twenty years before). Having to struggle to find music seems to be the making of many musical pioneers.[2]

1. SIT DOWN, LARS.

2. I put my own lack of musical pioneering down to the existence of Hot Rocks in Sutton. More on that shop and its proprietor, 'Fat Matt', later. It's a good story.

The origins of thrash can be heard in some of the earliest heavy metal. Black Sabbath's 'Children of the Grave' is a decent prototype, and 'Symptom of the Universe' has a palm-muted riff that is a direct ancestor of the defining thrash sound:

DUH-DUH-DUH-DUH DUH-DUH-DUH-BRAAAAAAM!
DUH-DUH-DUH-DUH
DUH-DUH-DUH-BRAP-BRAAAAAAAM!

Judas Priest were the first metal band to be truly fast, dialling up the speed with songs like 'Exciter', 'Hell Bent for Leather' and 'Rapid Fire'. They introduce palm-muting on 'Victim of Changes' – a guitar technique that is the cornerstone of thrash metal. The subsequent influence of thrash upon later Judas Priest can be heard loud and clear on their 1990 track 'Painkiller'.[1] But it was Motörhead's 1979 album *Overkill*, and more particularly the opening title track with its double-bass drum intro that forged the first template for thrash metal. Double-bass drumming was used as far back as the early sixties among jazz drummers, but it was Motörhead's drummer 'Philthy Animal' Taylor who introduced it to heavy metal and turned heavy metal drumming into something utterly distinct.[2]

1. A great song to headbang to, but be warned – it's longer than you think and just when you think it's going to end and you can stop, they stick in another solo . . . I have seen many comrades fall this way. It is a loss that haunts us all.

2. If you are unfamiliar with the sound of Philthy's double-bass drumming, allow me to demonstrate using the name of a high-street noodle restaurant. Say these examples out loud. Single-bass drumming sounds like: BANG-THE-BASS-DRUM, BANG-THE-BASS-DRUM. And double-bass drumming sounds like: WAGAMAMA-WAGAMAMA-WAGAMAMA-WAGAMAMA. See? Easy.

Motörhead directly influenced every early thrash band – but they also seeded two intermediary bands who in turn had a big hand in shaping thrash.

The first was Discharge. After Venom and Motörhead, Discharge are the band that comes up most often when the pioneers of extreme metal describe their influences.[1] Formed in 1977 in Stoke-on-Trent, Discharge stuck out like a sore thumb among their punk contemporaries. Their debut album, 1982's *Hear Nothing See Nothing Say Nothing*, is an excoriating wall of noise – far more aggressive than anything recorded by the like of The Clash or the Sex Pistols. A scene coalesced around them, along with two other main bands, The Exploited and Charged GBH. Called 'UK82', to distinguish it from the more commercial-sounding ''77 punk', this scene along with more experimental bands like Amebix had a seismic effect on the approach of what would become thrash metal.

Discharge's socially and politically aware lyrical approach would also be lifted by their thrash offspring. The focus on nuclear war, in particular (with an iconic sample from the harrowing BBC documentary *The War Game*), was a big influence. Nuclear paranoia is possibly the biggest lyrical preoccupation within thrash metal.

Discharge even spawned their own genre – d-beat, named after their distinctive Motörhead-ish drumbeat.[2] Tons of bands began to emulate Discharge's sound and they nearly all managed

1. Just as for surreal and experimental comedians like myself it's Bobby Davro, Joe Pasquale and Jimmy Tarbuck.

2. I have tried to come up with a high-street-noodle-restaurant-based example to demonstrate d-beat but I've got nothing. I wouldn't blame you if you put the book down right now. Basically it goes: DO-GAT DOO DO-GAT or DO-GAT DO-DO-GAT. Got it?

to name themselves dis-something. The large d-beat scene in Sweden was a big part of what became Swedish death metal, with bands such as Anti Cimex and Mob 47. While '77 punk influenced the NWOBHM to write more simply and to put out their own records, the influence of the second wave of British punk on metal was a massive increase of speed, aggression and political awareness.

The second Motörhead-influenced precursor to thrash was Venom. Some have claimed that Venom were the first thrash metal band. For the purposes of clarity, let's keep Venom in their own self-made genre box and call them black metal. Clearer candidates for the first thrash metal band come from Canada. They originally formed as Hell Razor in 1978. Changing their name to the Judas Priest song of the same name, they became Exciter. They recorded a demo in 1980 and their debut album, *Heavy Metal Maniac*, was recorded in August 1982 and released in January 1983. So, a clear winner . . . But wait – the waters get muddied by another genre term, because a bunch of people reckon Exciter aren't thrash at all, but are instead . . . SPEED METAL.

So what gives?

Some people – awful, terrible people – say that speed metal and thrash metal are the same thing. I mean, how stupid can you GET?! Speed metal and thrash metal are COMPLETELY different. The difference is obvious. Speed metal is really fast and slightly more aggressive than NWOBHM. It has a focus on velocity. Thrash metal, in stark contrast, is really fast and slightly more aggressive than speed metal. It has a focus on *velocity*.

Nearly everyone who attempts to make a case for 'speed metal' as a separate category names bands I consider to be definitive thrash bands. Some say that speed metal is more melodic. But then thrash uses melody too, but maybe not quite as much.

Perhaps it's just something to do with bands that come from Canada. In truth, no one really knows and anyone who says they do is a liar. And possibly a racist.

So, with Exciter very definitely the first thrash band, at least in terms of album releases, who was next? Exodus formed in 1979, but line-up changes and issues with artwork (!) meant that they didn't release a full album until 1985. Sorry, lads, you're out of the running. Next came a small band who formed out of an LA outfit with the esoteric name of Leather Charm, later to become the corporate behemoth known to your nan as Metallica.

Metallica's history is well-documented. Lars Ulrich was a rich kid from Denmark with a bright future following his father's career as a professional tennis player. After moving to America, Lars became obsessed with the New Wave of British Heavy metal and began to learn the drums. He met Lemmy and became pals with Motörhead after following them on tour round California. He travelled to the UK and followed Diamond Head on tour, even going as far as sleeping on Sean Harris's floor, and then returned to LA determined to form his own band.

Metallica pretty much owe their existence to a friend of Lars's – Brian Slagel. Slagel was a fanzine maker and huge metal enthusiast. As an outgrowth of his zine-making he decided to put together a compilation album representing the underground Californian metal scene. Lars asked if he could have a track on the album. The only sticking point was that Lars didn't actually have a band . . .

Vocalist and rhythm guitarist James Hetfield had been playing in several bands by this point: in Obsession, who played covers of Sabbath, Led Zeppelin and Deep Purple, and in Syrinx, who covered Rush. Next came Phantom Lord (brilliant name), which morphed into Leather Charm (terrible name), and he wrote a few original tunes, including 'Hit The Lights', which would be the seed from which Metallica would grow. In 1981, Lars had auditioned for Leather Charm, but was rejected for being too shit. However, after his return from his NWOBHM gap year and having secured the spot on Slagel's forthcoming compilation, Lars called Hetfield up again, now with the incentive of the record. Leather Charm were in a hiatus, having lost their drummer. James and Lars jammed again, changed the name to Metallica, and recorded a primitive version of 'Hit the Lights' for the compilation on a Tascam four-track – Lars on drums, James providing vocals, bass and rhythm guitar. A guitarist called Lloyd Grant provided a solo and they got the tape to Brian Slagel just in time to be included on the record.

Metal Massacre #1 was released in June 1982. It sold in unprecedented numbers and helped establish Metallica (or 'Mettallica', as it's written on the first pressing) as the fastest band anyone had ever heard. The track was re-recorded for the second pressing and featured a new lead guitarist, Dave Mustaine, and Ron McGovney playing bass. This version is faster than the first, and has a punchier sound.

Live shows followed, initially with Hetfield just doing vocals. Their second show, secured due to Ron McGovney's connection with Mötley Crüe, was at the Whiskey A Go-Go supporting NWOBHM heavyweights Saxon. Several demo tapes were recorded, and one – *No Life 'Til Leather* – found favour with the international tape-traders, and Metallica began to play to larger audiences around LA and especially in San Francisco.

If the geographical heart of heavy metal is the West Midlands, the geographical heart of thrash metal is undoubtedly the Bay Area – the clutch of towns and cities that form the urban sprawl surrounding the San Francisco Bay.

Metallica's nineteenth show was at the Stone in San Francisco.

They were hugely impressed by the size and enthusiasm of the crowd. It was the first time that an audience knew all their lyrics; a stark contrast to the crowds in LA who preferred the glammed-up pop bullshit of bands like Mötley Crüe to Metallica's unalloyed extremity. The Bay Area was already home to a bunch of like-minded misfits who formed part of a growing extreme metal scene.

When their bassist, Ron McGovney, left (or was kicked out, depending on whose version you believe), their favoured replacement, Cliff Burton (from Bay Area band Trauma), agreed to join on the condition that the band move up to San Francisco. It was a no-brainer. Cliff was the best bassist they had ever seen and the Bay Area scene was clearly their natural home. So they shoved all their stuff in a van and moved north.

The Bay Area thrash scene was by the kids, for the kids, and possibly the first of its kind within metal. Taking its lead from the hardcore punk scene there was no distinction between the bands and the audience. Everyone knew each other and everyone was a raving metal maniac. The most prominent thrash-friendly band in the Bay Area in 1982 was Exodus. Exodus had started in 1979, formed by subsequent Metallica guitarist, Kirk Hammett, but didn't manage to get an album out until 1985 and so missed out on some of the 'influential' status afforded those with official releases in '83 and '84 (although their influence through demos and live performances on the bigger thrash bands is undeniable, they never achieved the popularity of the Big Four).

Guitar-based music in California in the early 1980s was a diverse scene. The radio was dominated by over-produced adult-oriented rock like Boston and REO Speedwagon.

The biggest band to come out of California in the late seventies were The Eagles. A perfectly decent band, but not a fit soundtrack for youthful rebellion. In stark contrast to this was the West Coast underground hardcore punk movement, dominated by the incomparable Black Flag and the politicised anger of Dead Kennedys, which infused youth with energy, speed, aggression and, most importantly, an underground DIY ethic that entirely bypassed the normal record label, booking agent route to musical success. Black Flag would spend whole weeks wheat-pasting flyers for their self-promoted shows in gruelling ten-hour shifts, fuelled by help-yourself buffet food piled onto the tray, not the plate. They had a total commitment to playing music, doing things their way and being as good as they could be. Famously they even rehearsed on Christmas day. It was music for its own sake – with no hint of the reward of fame or fortune. They were anti-authority, genuinely subversive and, most importantly, down to earth. Plus their guitarist, Greg Ginn, played using all downstrokes and he played fucking *fast*.

All this would have an immense effect on thrash, with its street-level aesthetic, socially conscious lyrics, relatively small-scale ambitions (at least early on) and commitment to right-hand speed.

Equally influential for thrash was a strong notion of what it was rejecting – namely the entire glam metal/Sunset Strip narcissism-fest that was happening in LA.

In 1980, LA was witnessing the birth of a scene that took the excesses of seventies hard rock and dialled up the sleaze. Glam metal, hair metal, poseur metal . . . It was over the top, and it wasn't good. An emphasis on image over musicality, a focus on success rather than integrity, an obsession with sex and drugs massively outweighing any love of rock'n'roll – glam metal was everything thrash metal hated. Its influence was negative. Metallica rejected it. Slayer kind of adopted some elements of it but then changed their minds. Exodus reacted to it like Damian going into Guildford Cathedral in *The Omen*.

In December 1982, Metallica added a dude who couldn't be

further away from glam bullshit. Cliff Burton wore flares . . . He added a new dynamic to the band's sound, playing bass like a lead instrument and headbanging in a weird half-time and generally being a hypnotic stage presence. Metallica recorded another demo, which secured them a record deal with an emerging underground label, Megaforce. Originally intending to call their debut album 'Metal Up Your Ass', the band were persuaded that such an inflammatory title might harm distribution. They headed to New York to record it, but one thing was left to fix.

Shortly before heading into the studio, the guitarist Dave Mustaine was kicked out of the band for drinking too much (which, considering the band soon picked up the nickname 'Alcoholica', is quite an achievement).[1] Mustaine has kept pretty quiet about the whole thing and doesn't seem to harbour any bitterness.[2] James and Lars drafted in the Exodus guitarist Kirk Hammett, a softly spoken, almost meek character who was the total opposite of the chaotic, aggressive Dave. Their first album, *Kill 'em All*, came out on 25 July 1983 and it was a defining moment in extreme music. It made a huge impact on the underground, spawning imitators and encouraging bands in other genres to push themselves faster and heavier. And it was ground zero for thrash metal.[3] *Metal Forces* said in their breathless review:

> It's certainly one of the most awesome, fastest and heaviest pieces of vinyl I've ever heard. I'd urge every heavy metal

1. It's a bit like getting kicked out of the Tory party for being a sexual pervert.
2. Lol.
3. *Kill 'em All* isn't an album for all occasions. An ex-girlfriend of mine was once having sex with a guy while listening to *Kill 'em All*. When track two – 'The Four Horsemen' – came on, he began fucking her in time to its galloping rhythm. She reckons she laughed so hard she probably psychologically scarred him for life . . .

fan to grab a copy of this album, and if when you've heard it you dislike *Kill 'em All* then you can no longer call yourself a heavy metal fan. You just don't understand what heavy metal is all about.

Kill 'em All is considerably heavier than their demos. Hetfield's vocals are no longer a cheap imitation of Diamond Head's Sean Harris. Influenced by the punkish aggression of Venom, he shouts, screams and snarls his delivery. The whole record is much tighter and faster, and the production, considering the limitations of budget and time, is crisp and punishing.[1] The Cliff Burton showcase instrumental 'Anaesthesia – Pulling Teeth' is a unique and experimental piece that elevates the entire record above any accusations of boneheadedness. (Not that boneheadedness is necessarily a problem. Venom have made a career out of it, though not quite the career Metallica have had . . .)

A tour followed, supporting Neat Records' favourite sons, Raven, who were promoting their album *All for One*. They called it the *Kill 'em All for One* tour.

Meanwhile, back down in LA, a satanic rumble was heard in the underground . . .

Not quite as 'street' as Metallica or Exodus and fond of leather, spikes and stage make-up, Slayer were from LA and early on had something of a whiff of the glam scene. Nonetheless their music had a ferocity and an evil atmosphere that made them out-heavy anyone in the Bay Area.[2] Slayer formed out of

1. For its time, which is a caveat you should always have in your head from now on – all extremity is eventually superseded, every band is eventually outdone.

2. Although it is reported that they only ever did one gig in the Bay Area wearing make-up and dropped it overnight due to the reaction it got. This ain't LA, boys . . .

neighbourhood covers bands and started off copying Judas Priest and Iron Maiden. Jeff Hanneman's love of hardcore pushed them to write harder, faster riffs. Slayer's stage show set them apart from the LA glam scene that was erupting around them. Adopting the leather and spikes of Judas Priest,[1] they did a photoshoot dripping in gore. Taking their nod from Venom, they adopted pentagrams and inverted crosses – iconography which is passé and overdone today, but in 1982, in what is still to this day pretty much a fundamentalist religious country, it was bold.

Like Metallica, Slayer got their first break on the third of Brian Slagel's *Metal Massacre* compilations, having been influenced by songs on the previous two to push themselves even harder and heavier. The song 'Aggressive Perfector' was recorded for that compilation, and it raised the bar for metal extremity once again. Off the back of that one track, Slagel offered them a record deal, though without an advance, which led to Slayer self-funding the recording of their debut record from Tom Araya's savings and the Bank of Kerry King's dad. The album was recorded in a distinctly unorthodox fashion, with the engineer telling the drummer, Dave Lombardo, that the cymbals had to be recorded separately from the rest of the drums.

While they were definitely pushing boundaries,[2] Slayer's debut album, *Show No Mercy*, is very much still the sum of its influences – Iron Maiden, Judas Priest, a touch of Venom. Tom Araya's vocals are a mix of aggressive growls and distinctly old-school

1. . . . but without realising the homo-erotic overtones. Kerry King has displayed a pretty pathetic homophobia in interviews over the years for someone who began his career dressing up in Rob Halford-inspired leather and spikes. He once stated in an interview that the last thing he'd want to be stuck in a lift with is 'a faggot'. Methinks he doth protest too much . . .

2. And, don't forget, Evil has no boundaries . . .

metal singing, with high-pitched, Rob Halford-esque wails. The riffs are incredibly catchy. But there is a darkness about the record, too. It is considerably more atmospheric than Metallica's debut. In common with many successful and long-established bands, Slayer are pretty dismissive of the production values of their early records, yet there is a resurgence of interest in albums like *Show No Mercy* which exist on the cusp of what became bands' more familiar sounds. Sepultura's *Morbid Visions* and *Bestial Devastation* and Sodom's *In the Sign of Evil* and *Obsessed by Cruelty* have all been reappraised by fans of raw production. *Show No Mercy* was a massive success in underground metal terms, and the following year Slayer recorded a 'live' album,[1] *Live Undead*, and an EP, *Haunting the Chapel*. The song which marks Slayer's turning point from a turbo-charged NWOBHM band to the titans of thrash metal that they became is that record's incendiary 'Chemical Warfare'. It is a watershed in speed and aggression.

The first thrash album of 1984 was Anthrax's *Fistful of Metal*. Three years earlier, and 5,000 miles away from the Bay Area scene, New Yorkers Anthrax had formed. Inspired as much by the vibrant New York hardcore punk scene as any heavy metal, Anthrax were the East Coast's sole major thrash band. (Two of Anthrax's founder members – Dan Lilker and John Connelly – would go on to form Nuclear Assault, a heavier and more hardcore-influenced outfit.) It was Anthrax who were partly responsible for the term thrash . . .

What's in a name? Well, arguably thrash wasn't born with Venom or Exciter or Metallica or Exodus or Slayer. In the beginning was

---

1. To what degree it's a genuine live album as opposed to an album recorded as live in front of a handful of other people is a matter of some debate.

the word. The word was thrash. And the man who first coined the term 'thrash metal' was a long way from California. Malcolm Dome is not what you think of when you project heavy metal into human form. He looks more like a pair of glasses grew a human to carry them round. The word 'thrash' was floating around before Dome plucked it from the air and pinned it to this particular sub-genre. *Thrasher* magazine was first published in 1981 and a hardcore punk compilation called *New York Thrash* was released in 1982. It's very likely that hardcore-mad lyricist Scott Ian owned that album, because in January 1984 Anthrax released the album *Fistful of Metal*, which included the song 'Metal Thrashing Mad'. And in his review of that album in the 23 February issue of *Kerrang!*[1] Dome coined the phrase 'thrash metal'. It was with this classification that thrash metal was formed. Not born, so much as swept into a neat pile. Classified. Just as with Alan Lewis's coining of the term New Wave of British Heavy Metal, the phrase became a lightning rod for other bands. Suddenly we had a name for what was different between Metallica and Iron Maiden. Metallica *THRASHED*! And thus began a pattern that would be replicated endlessly within heavy metal. The genre term forms the idea of what that genre should subsequently sound like. Every time a kid puts 'thrash' in an advert for people to join a new band, they know what that band will sound like. No doubt, like Vim from the comedy film *Bad News*, they will later argue about breaking out of that category,[2] but sub-genre labels are the boundaries that tell us which field to plough. We now had a benchmark. Before this classification it's Schrödinger's genre. Metallica's original bassist, Ron McGovney, called them power metal. *Show No Mercy* was described as 'heavy

1. Which has Phil Collins on the front. I shit you not.
2. 'I'm not getting in the van until Alan says we're blackened thrash.'

metal punk' – in *Rock Hard* magazine and 'speed metal' and 'hardcore metal' in *Metal Forces*.

I would argue that thrash is something of an umbrella term, and that through its wider usage can be seen as encompassing many other sub-genres such as death metal, black metal, etc. In terms of the modern taxonomy of metal, its use is something like the term 'heavy metal' being used to describe both the wide genre as a whole and the classic heavy metal sound as produced by the original early seventies bands, as well as those who emulate that sound. See?

By the time of this 'official' classification you couldn't move in the Bay Area for thrash metal bands. Arriving on the scene a little later, Testament occupy a similar place in the thrash pantheon – outside the Big Four but only just. (The dudes from those bands are quite fucked off about the whole Big Four thing . . . Eric Peterson told *Hard Rock Magazine*, 'We can keep adding numbers to it – the Big 10, the Big 5, the Big 4, whatever. It was the Big 5 for the last four years to everybody, that kinda makes sense, 'cause it's a pentagram.') Also from the Bay Area were Possessed – we'll return to them later in the story – Death Angel, Forbidden, Hexx, Lääz Rockit and Vio-lence. Many of these bands shared members. Testament have had no fewer than fourteen drummers.

Meanwhile the pioneers were moving things forward. In 1984, Metallica followed *Kill 'em All* with the impeccable *Ride the Lightning*. Despite the fact that the production is tighter, the riffs are faster and Hetfield's vocals are considerably more aggressive, they had begun to develop more depth alongside the raging thrash, adding melodic flourishes and even a ballad. Well, what sounds like a ballad to those who were expecting another full-thrash attack. 'Fade to Black' is actually a pained cry of depression.[1] But it's not exactly Chris de Burgh. Instead it uses the power of a full-on metal band to add weight to a dark lament. It led to cries of 'sell out'.[2] Elsewhere, they step up the speed and heaviness and lay down several songs that are total archetypes of thrash metal – 'Trapped Under Ice' being one of the most splendidly dumb but unashamedly enjoyable thrash metal songs of all time. It's literally about being trapped under ice. Awesome.

In April 1985, Exodus finally got around to releasing their debut album, *Bonded by Blood*. Held back by issues with the cover, it finally sported a sub-GCSE art painting of some conjoined twins. One of which is evil. Right. Well, that was worth waiting for . . . The title track is an anthem to the cheeky violence of Exodus shows in their hometown, specifically the time at the venue Ruthies Inn when a glass shattered in the front row and the stage ended up covered in blood. *Metal*.

Slayer's 1985 album shows them moving towards something new. After stopgaps in the form of an EP and a live album, *Hell Awaits* is a huge leap forward. The title track is blistering. A spooky intro implores '*join us*', and then it explodes like a rocket. Tom's vocals speed along at mach 3, and a vocal effect on *Hell Awaits* is reminiscent of something from *The Exorcist* or *Evil Dead*.

In 1985 thrash went truly international. Records from fast, thrashing bands began to crop up all over the place: in the UK with Onslaught's *Power From Hell*, in Brazil with Sepultura's *Bestial Devastation*, from Switzerland with Celtic Frost's *To Mega Therion*. Loads of bands formed – Xentrix and Carcass in the UK, Sarcófago

---

1. Apparently inspired by the time they had nearly all of their equipment stolen.

2. Seriously, guys – don't cry wolf! You'll have plenty of opportunity to call them sell-outs later . . . eventually they do a song for a Tom Cruise film, for fuck's sake.

and Mutilator in Brazil . . . Possessed released *Seven Churches*, which was so extreme it warranted a whole new genre category.

But 1986 was the peak year for thrash metal. Three of the Big Four released arguably their definitive albums: Metallica's *Master of Puppets*, Slayer's *Reign in Blood* and Megadeth's *Peace Sells . . . But Who's Buying?*. Joining them was a cavalcade of thrash awesomeness: Carnivore's *Carnivore*, Cryptic Slaughter's *Convicted*, Dark Angel's *Darkness Descends*, Destruction's *Eternal Devastation*, Kreator's *Pleasure to Kill*, Mortal Sin's *Mayhemic Destruction*, Nuclear Assault's *Game Over*, Onslaught's *The Force*, Possessed's *Beyond the Gates*, Razor's *Malicious Intent*, Sepultura's *Morbid Visions*, Sodom's *Obsessed by Cruelty* and Voivod's *Rrröööaaarrr*.

By the time of their third album, 1986's *Master of Puppets*, Metallica had exploded out of the metal underground and were playing arenas supporting Ozzy Osbourne.[1] And still the music was totally uncompromising. *Puppets* is even faster, even more brutal. From the blistering opener, 'Battery', to the blistering closer, *Damage Inc.*, via the sludgy doom of 'The Thing That Should Not Be', it continues to dial up the heaviness while still managing to be even more expansive and even more musical. Tracks such as 'Welcome Home (Sanitarium)' offer melody and atmosphere. The light and shade serve to add dynamic and make the heaviness even heavier. And the by-now traditional instrumental number, 'Orion', is nothing short of epic. *Master of Puppets* is Metallica's masterpiece. A shining example of what thrash metal can achieve in every aspect – musicianship, speed, power and scale.

By this point Metallica (Lars[2] in particular) were already

1. Ozzy now proving both that he could make it on his own as a solo artist, and that he couldn't pronounce the word 'moon'. But 'Bark at the Moan' is still a great song.

2. SIT DOWN, LARS!

uncomfortable with the limitations suggested by the term 'thrash metal'. This overlooks an important point. Rather than being limited by thrash, these four men were massively *expanding* what the term thrash metal could mean! Thrash was moving along and evolving with Metallica's innovations. All three albums were selling well, they were consistently blowing Ozzy off the stage night after night. Metallica were riding high, enjoying a level of success unprecedented for a band making such heavy music.

In the same year Slayer released their third album, *Reign in Blood*. In my opinion it is the single greatest record of all time. It's twenty-eight minutes long, and it is perfect. (It was over thirty-five minutes long in rehearsals, but Slayer are competitive.) Not only is it a sublime thrash album – it is possibly the heaviest thrash album of all time. It is dark. Seriously dark. Possessed had already made the first death metal album, and *Reign in Blood* categorically is NOT death metal. But it is brutal. Dark. Mean. Uncomfortable. It opens with a blisteringly fast tremolo-picked riff, an inhuman scream, and then the word 'AUSCHWITZ'. Way to go, lads. Open your ALBUM with the one word that encapsulates the single worst aspect of the worst atrocity of all time. At a point where most other thrash bands were throwing somewhat naive political observations into their songs – war is bad, politicians are corrupt, the justice system is rubbish – Slayer were diving into the very darkest corners of humanity. At a time when most thrash bands were exploring more melody, a lighter tone, a touch of humour, Slayer were pushing for the most brutal sound they could find.

It marks another significant milestone in the history of the *perception* of metal. From 1986 onwards, *Reign in Blood* in particular and Slayer in general would become the benchmark of 'metal'. They took the centre ground of metal even further away from the Led Zeppelin/Deep Purple end of things. Extreme metal had become the default setting for the definition of heavy metal.

More traditional forms of metal now had their own sub-category which defined them *against* the extreme metal norm.

There is still a whiff of controversy surrounding *Reign in Blood*. Dimwitted people seemed to think that their method of story-telling – in which they inhabit the point of view of someone doing the horrible things – is a bona-fide statement of support. Slayer treating their audience like adults, able to make up their own minds, is apparently a step too far for some. Looking at the lyrics for 'Angel of Death' the band's opinion is pretty clear. The atrocities carried out by Joseph Mengele are *very obviously a really bad thing*. The song is a piece of horror. Horror films do not feel the need to flag up that people being killed is a bad thing. As an audience we are expected to have some sense and make that decision ourselves. The question is, rather, whose side does the listener take? Well, as a fourteen-year-old listening to 'Angel of Death' while doing my paper round I was pretty fucking obviously horrified by the descriptions of Mengele's crimes. I associated with the victims. Slayer work on the assumption that their audience are not genocide-supporting psychopaths . . .

Nevertheless they received accusations of being Nazis. This wasn't really helped by their adoption of sub-Nazi iconography and calling their fan club *Slaytanic Wehrmacht* . . . However, in reality Tom Araya isn't white (he's from Chile) and Jeff Hanneman's Second World War obsession came not from neo-Nazi leanings but from reverence for his father who fought in that war.[1] Furthermore, on the same album is 'Altar of Sacrifice', a song about satanist ritual and human sacrifice. Tom Araya, the singer of that song, is a Catholic. He's singing the opposite to his own viewpoint.

(They shored up this perspective with the song 'Jihad' on

---

1. On the American side, in case you were wondering.

2006's *Christ Illusion*, telling the story of 9/11 from the point of view of one of the terrorists. The song was expected to cause the inevitable boring level of controversy, though all that seemed to happen was the album being recalled in India, and even that was mainly due to its anti-Christian themes. It's a lot harder to shock people these days.)

The first time I saw Slayer they permanently damaged my hearing. It was 7 July 1996 at the Brixton Academy and they were touring *Undisputed Attitude*, their controversial album of punk covers. At the time I had a stereo which made a barely audible high-pitched whine when it was set to 'standby'. After spending the whole gig in the front row, I never heard that noise again. They were the loudest thing I had ever heard.[1]

Slayer occupy a unique place in metal. For most of their career they have been the most extreme band at such a high level of popularity.[2] They are a crossover point between mainstream and underground metal. As a result of this there is a legendary, mythical aura around them (despite them being accessible, personable and

1. Since then I have heard louder things. Sometimes I fart so loudly in my sleep I wake up the cat.

2. In recent years it is arguable that Slipknot have overtaken them. They're certainly a bigger band, but whether they are as heavy as Slayer is a point of contention. I'd argue they're not, but then I'm biased, and old, and I don't know what all this new-fangled music the young people listen to is, and you can't tell which ones of them are boys and which ones of them are girls and you used to be able to leave your doors unlocked and your windows open and the Krays only killed their own and you might have had Jack the Ripper and rickets and rationing but we were happy they come over here and they get a house right off the plane and they're taking our jobs and they're all on benefits and it's like living in bloody Afghanistan round here they want to ban Christmas and Brussels are trying to make us all have human rights it's political correctness gone mad.

down to earth[1]). The excellent metalhead comedian Brian Posehn sums up their magical power with the joke: 'If you're getting a blowjob off another guy, it's not gay if you shout "Slayer".' Slayer are the go-to band for communicating fundamental metal-ness.

Slayer, Metallica and Anthrax form three-quarters of what has been termed the Big Four of thrash metal. The term is controversial, as it is based on the first four bands to get major-label record deals, not the actual influence they had. Exodus are an unforgivable omission and Testament, Kreator, Destruction and Sodom are all worthy of inclusion.[2]

The last of the Big Four thrash metal bands formed like a cutting from a rosebush.

After being kicked out of Metallica for having too much of an ego,[3] Dave Mustaine formed Megadeth. Initially they were musically very similar to Metallica, which makes sense given Dave was a major songwriter on Metallica's early stuff. They had enormous success with their debut album, *Killing is My Business . . . And Business is Good!*, and the follow-up, *Peace Sells . . . But Who's Buying?*, is considered one of the most important thrash albums of all time.

1. Both times I've met Slayer I've been impressed by how incredibly friendly and gracious they are. Tom seems excited to hear that you like his band. The second time I met them was an after-show signing at Nottingham Rock City. Most of the crowd had gone home so there was lots of time to chat. I asked Kerry King who played the opening riff on 'Sex, Murder, Art' because I was trying to learn it. He air-guitared the part in order to remember whether is was all downstrokes or alternate picking. It's alternate picking. The first time I met Slayer I completely lost my mind and essentially bellowed 'YOU ARE ALL VERY GOOD AT BEING SLAYER' at their faces. I have not always been the cool-headed dude you see before you.

2. Fuck it, let's be like millennials are supposed to be like and agree that EVERYBODY WINS . . .

3. Which is like getting kicked out of The Stone Roses for being a cunt.

Alas they have been plagued with line-up problems, partly due to Mustaine's substance abuse.[1]

While thrash metal is a subset of the wider genre of 'heavy metal', it still represents a fairly wide and varied range of styles. So what defines thrash metal? What are its qualities?

Where Black Sabbath's power had come from the slow build-up of a feeling of impending doom, like being crushed under a ten-tonne weight, thrash was the aural equivalent of being hit by a speeding train. It had a youthful energy. Sabbath were Quaaludes and wine, Thrash was amphetamines and cheap lager. An often overlooked element of thrash is its professionalism. In a radical shift away from Venom (and from the path taken by the early black metal bands in general – Hellhammer, I'm looking at you) thrash metal musicians were incredibly musically ambitious. Thrash is fast and aggressive, but it is also precise. The addition of classical elements and proper, actual trained musicians expanded the palette of thrash metal. Cliff Burton's musical background played a large part in Metallica's (then) uniquely expansive, rich sound: as James Hetfield said, 'Cliff brought certain melodies into our music, which he had learned at school through his classical training. He knew how certain harmonies function.'

The addition of the Joe Satriani-trained Kirk Hammett to Metallica gave them a European classical flavour in the form of his solos. (Later, Sepultura would be radically shifted away from their primitive black-thrash sound to something much cleaner by the addition of the classically trained Andreas Kisser – who also idolised Metallica . . .)

1. They were also cursed with his singing voice, which sounds like someone who isn't very good at voices pretending to be annoyed.

   The foundation of the thrash sound is palm muting. By muting the strings with the heel of their hand, the guitarist produces a
tighter, more percussive sound. With distortion, this makes a satisfying 'CHUG' sound. Tremolo picking – literally just fast
picking – with palm muting makes the signature
'CHUGGA-CHUGGA-CHUGGA' guitar sound that typifies
this genre. The use of downstrokes rather than alternate picking
creates a heavier sound still, which really tests the right-hand
speed of the guitarist.[1] Lyrically thrash covers a lot of different
subjects, including – much like NWOBHM – the experience of
heavy metal itself. Metallica sang of 'Hotel rooms and motor-
ways' and state they'll never stop and they'll never quit, 'Cos
we're Metallica!' Had a metal band mentioned themselves in their
lyrics before? Sabbath certainly never did that.
   One of the most interesting elements of thrash metal is its
experimentation with vocal styles. Until Venom tore up the rule-
book, nearly every metal band had clean singing, usually with a
suggestion of some sort of vocal training. Black Sabbath set the
template, with Ozzy's frosty, high-register voice soaring above
the bassy, down-tuned guitars. But after Venom's Cronos used a
gravelly, aggressive, rough delivery, heavy metal vocalists tried
all sorts of approaches to communicate a more aggressive atmosphere. As a result, thrash is a really mixed bag and there are
plenty of thrash bands that I personally cannot stand purely
because of the vocals.
   In my naive youth I used to consider myself a big fan of thrash
metal. As I was researching the comedy show that became this
book I listened to a huge number of thrash bands I'd never given
a great deal of time to. It turns out that despite the fact that my

1. 'Fnar fnar. Pwick pwick. Snub snub,' as Finbar Saunders would say.

top-ten list of metal bands[1] includes Metallica, Slayer and Sepultura, I realised that I like very few of the thrash bands that
are considered essential. I make no apologies – that wouldn't
be very metal – but I don't like Anthrax, Megadeth, Exodus
or Testament[2] . . . It turns out I am really picky when it comes
to thrash vocals. 'Bad' thrash vocals sound staged. I find it
absolutely baffling how anyone can listen to Megadeth and
not just hear the sound of a petulant teenager. He sounds
like when kids repeat what their parents have said but go
'NER-NER-NER-NER-NER-NER'. The riffage is so good that
it makes up for it, but to me that can be the only way in which
someone could really enjoy them – despite and not because of the
vocals. But, hey – each to their own, right?

Beyond the United States, thrash metal took hold in a way
that the NWOBHM never had. Scenes sprang up all over
the world. Germany provided three of the best – Sodom and
Kreator both started with a sound more akin to black metal,
as we saw in the black metal chapter; they are joined by fellow
Germans Destruction to form the 'Teutonic Big Three' thrash
bands.

In Canada, Exciter were joined by the avant-garde Voivod, the
sublime Slaughter and the relatively successful Razor and Annihi-
lator. The effect of the thrash explosion on British metal was
pretty harsh. NWOBHM seemed out of date and local bands

1. Metallica, Slayer, Black Sabbath, Sepultura, Darkthrone, Cannibal Corpse,
Dismember, Watain, Death, Emperor.

2. Thrash bands I really like: Kreator, Sodom, Onslaught, Cryptic Slaughter,
DRI, Nuclear Assault, Exciter, Toxic Holocaust, Municipal Waste, Kremated,
Witchmaster, Aura Noir, Dungeon, Coroner, Destroyer 666.

seemed parochial and uncool. A few bands followed the American lead. Onslaught's second album, *Metal Forces*, is fucking awesome. The British take on thrash was notable for its piss-taking sense of humour. British bands often seem limited by their inability to be po-faced. Take, for example, the band Lawnmower Deth (note the spelling of 'deth' is the same as Megadeth) and their seminal release, *Ooh Crikey It's . . . Lawnmower Deth*. There is a distancing taking place, as though to commit to the intense seriousness of, say, Slayer would be to open them up to potential ridicule. Yeah, we don't really mean it. A divide began to emerge, which exists to this day, between the 'fun-core', in-it-for-the-laughs attitude of Lawnmower Deth and 'apple-core' band Acid Reign,[1] and their ilk, and the more serious approach of the satanic end of thrash. Venom can be seen as a Rorschach test in this – whether you listen to them ironically or not shows where you place yourself.[2] This crack in thrash later became a fissure. The beachwear and sense of humour of a lot of death metal bands eventually led to the back-lash which was the second wave of black metal.

The late eighties saw the emergence of crossover thrash – hardcore punk bands who took influence back from thrash metal and combined the two. Pretty much the fastest thing going, DRI were from Texas but were pulled in by the Bay Area's tractor beam. Releasing their *Dirty Rotten EP* in 1983 they inspired Slayer's drummer, Dave Lombardo, to faster speeds, and in turn moved towards a more thrash metal sound during the late eighties. Cryptic Slaughter from Santa Monica shared DRI's anti-authority lyrical approach as well as their speed and indeed their record label. Metal Blade also signed Corrosion of

1. 'Apple-core' being a pun on the -core suffix, as in hardcore, grindcore.

2. Personally, I fucking hate ironic consumption of any artform. Life's too short and good bands too numerous to waste time with anything that is so-bad-it's-good.

Conformity, who would later change their sound to a bluesy, Southern-rock-influenced type of metal but began as a crossover band. Other bands such as Suicidal Tendencies and Cro-Mags introduced a testosterone-fuelled tough-guy feel due to them both being products of actual poverty and street gangs, which is somewhat at odds with the skinny suburban teenage feel that typifies most thrash.

Meanwhile at the top of the tree . . . on 27 September 1986 there came a sickening plot twist. On tour in Europe, Metallica were being driven through Sweden. At around 7 a.m. their bus skidded and overturned. The bassist, Cliff Burton, was thrown through a window and the overturning bus crushed him to death.

In common with many Metallica fans, even though I hadn't even heard of Metallica at the time of Cliff's death (I was seven), I still somehow miss him. Cliff was a crucial part of what had made Metallica so amazing; being at the heart of their melodic innovations. It was James who pushed them faster, but it was Cliff who added the depth and the atmosphere that made *Master of Puppets* in particular such a singularly brilliant record. The surviving members of Metallica credit his musical education with pushing them in more interesting and complex musical directions. His replacement, Jason Newsted, told *Guitar World* magazine, 'Lars is Metallica's logistic leader, but Cliff was the musical and spiritual leader.' After his death they became a significantly simpler band – notwithstanding the over-complex arrangements on . . . *And Justice for All*.

Cliff's death would prove to mark a turning point in Metallica's artistic and commercial fortunes. The band barely missed a beat, burying their grief and employing Jason Newsted from

Flotsam and Jetsam. They hazed him viciously, leaving him with restaurant bills, telling him that wasabi was mint ice cream, there to cool his mouth and thus he should eat loads of it . . . but carried on touring, recording an EP of covers and then a new album.

The $5.98 EP: Garage Days Re-Revisited is a gem, and stands as one of Metallica's best recordings, with arguably a better sound than the album that followed it. Covering NWOBHM and hardcore bands and very much showing the influences that shaped them, Metallica showcase themselves at their tightest and fastest. Lars has never been better than on this record. (Jason is credited as Master J. Newkid.)

And yet somehow after these dizzying heights their fourth studio album, . . . *And Justice for All*, is imperfect. The songs are overlong, the arrangements self-indulgent. It was an attempt to prove themselves musically to justify their enormous success, but audiences were visibly bored by the album's ten-minute epics. The production is strange, with the bass entirely absent in the mix. Though Jason claims it was all a frequency-clash issue, James admits he basically just turned the bass down when mixing. It seems their mourning of Cliff was coming out in peculiar ways.[1] The album is not bad by any means – a solid 8/10, a brilliant album by any normal measure, but this is the follow-up to three perfect records. It lacks the coherence and elegance of *Master of Puppets* and the immediacy of *Kill* and *Ride*. One song stands out. The song 'One'. Based on the novel *Johnny Got His Gun* by Dalton Trumbo, 'One' tells the brutal story of a man destroyed by a landmine in the trenches of the First World War and condemned to live without arms, legs, speech, sight or hearing. The opening is deceptively mellow, though minor key, as it describes his

1. An alternate mix called . . . *And Justice for Jason* can be found online.

situation. It ends full-thrash, with Hetfield's scream blending with a shrieking solo.

'One' was another turning point in Metallica's fortunes, as it inspired their decision to make their first promo video. Up until this point, Metallica had refused to make videos for any of their first three albums. In the context of the mid-eighties music industry this was completely extraordinary. To achieve such enormous success purely through radio, live shows and word of mouth was utterly remarkable, considering every other band was pouring thousands of dollars into clips for MTV.

When they eventually did make a clip, it was totally on their own terms. Black-and-white, stark and massively depressing, it illustrated the song's narrative through footage from the film version of the novel. The video ends with the protagonist's desperate internal monologue, fruitlessly pleading to be killed. Considering MTV at that point was giving heavy rotation to the Mötley Crüe abomination 'Girls, Girls, Girls . . .', it's a bold move. They even struck a deal whereby if they weren't happy with the result the tapes would be scrapped.

The reaction to the video was mixed. It was a brilliant clip and it caused a surge in Metallica's popularity. Alas, some felt – once again – that it marked the point at which Metallica sold out. Well, those fans were in for something of a shock . . . The boost in fortunes caused by the regular play of the 'One' clip inspired a leap in Metallica's ambitions, in their notion of just how big they could get. The next album was to be unabashedly commercial. As thrash entered the nineties, big changes were about to take place.

Thrash was evolving. It was no longer the main focus of the underground – death metal had taken over and something considerably *blacker* was brewing in Norway. It's arguable that while death and black metal developed alongside thrash metal, they can be seen as sub-categories of thrash. Malcolm Dome's book on thrash metal, published in 1990, has Cronos from Venom on the cover and features Napalm Death, Carcass and Morbid Angel alongside the usual Big Four suspects. Death metal did to thrash what thrash had done to NWOBHM – it made it look outdated and replaced it in the extreme metal top spot. But unlike the collapse of the vast majority of NWOBHM bands in the mid-eighties, most thrash bands kept going, keeping the pilot light on – a pilot light which would later ignite a whole new thrash movement, as we will see in the later chapter on metal revival movements.

As the London neo-thrash/crossover band Kremated eloquently put it:

> *THRASH AIN'T DEAD!*
> *THRASH AIN'T DEAD!*
> *THRASH AIN'T DEAD!*
> *BANG YOUR HEAD!*

7

Fucking Glam Fucking Metal[1]

It's all Marc Bolan's fault.

In the strange years following the decline of sixties idealism Britain became a depressing and grey place once more. It was almost as if the colourful, psychedelic late sixties had been an illusion, and the grim reality of the depressed black-and-white post-war era was suddenly visible again, slamming back into people's faces. This downer feel was of course best typified by the emergence of heavy metal – bands like Black Sabbath who had reacted against sixties idealism by facing the negative head on. But not everyone wanted to be reminded of the truth. And in the UK of the 1970s the truth was bitter. Hendrix was dead. The violence at Altamont had soured the hippy dream. An energy crisis was causing nationwide blackouts and a breakdown in industrial relations was causing regular, disruptive strikes. Then

---

1. I will state for the record here that on the whole I fucking hate this style of music. It represents everything I despise musically, aesthetically, politically and morally. It is a corruption of a thing I love and I would happily kill it with knives. In the live-show version of this book I have only ninety minutes to cover everything and so I can arrogantly and blissfully dismiss it as shit and move on. Sadly for both of us, dear reader, this book needs to be a bit more comprehensive and so we just have to do our best to glean something positive out of our coverage of a musical movement that can only accurately be described as a stinking ditch full of rotten pus.

in 1971 Marc Bolan appeared on *Top of the Pops* wearing glitter on his face and the whole country went fucking nuts.

Mark Feld had been pursuing a musical career for some time before he made it, playing acoustic-guitar-led songs and having a couple of minor hits in a very different style to that for which he would become known. He went through a mod phase, and changed his name to Marc Bolan, thinking Mark Feld too prosaic. Friends talk of his desire to be famous. Legend has it that he knocked on the door of the manager Simon Napier-Bell and 'proclaimed that he was going to be a huge star and needed someone to make the arrangements'. Contrast this with the more pragmatic start-a-band-and-just-get-on-with-it attitude of Sabbath, his near contemporaries. The desire for fame eclipsing the desire for artistic merit or musical expression is a constant within glam. It's about stardom more than art, and that stardom weaves a powerfully deceptive spell. A great deal is made about Bolan's looks. In truth he was a fairly average-looking bloke. He lacked the alien weirdness of Bowie and the blue-eyed sparkle of someone like Kurt Cobain, who twenty years later managed to make lumberjack shirts look rock and roll. He spoke with the flat suburban accent of an administrative assistant at a branch of Currys. But he cast a spell on audiences. His 1971 appearances on *Top of the Pops* with a spur-of-the-moment addition of glitter on his cheekbones performing 'Hot Love' and later in glittery eyeshadow for 'Get It On' became the talk of the nation. Gender norms had been defied. Glam rock was born. And a tradition of dads asking incredulously whether that's a boy or a girl was started. Bolan offered glamour – in the magical sense of the word. His art was escapism – not even idealistic, just fantastic. 'You can't be real,' he said in an interview featured on one of his box-set collections, 'on that stage I'm in a realm of fantasy.' Nevertheless, Marc Bolan's was a stardom based on a solid foundation of great songwriting as much as glamour. He had worked hard on his musicianship and this solid work ethic was taken up by most of the glam rock bands that followed. Slade, Wizzard, The Sweet . . . they all knew how to write a proper tune (or buy one . . .). Bolan's look kick-started a movement in the UK. And people got used to seeing this doll-like man on their tellies.

Then, the following year, David Bowie appeared on *Top of the Pops* wearing a jumpsuit and the whole country went fucking nuts.

David Jones had been pursuing a musical career for some time before he made it, playing acoustic guitar-led songs and having a couple of minor hits in a very different style to that for which he would become known. He went through a mod phase and then changed his name to David Bowie, feeling David Jones too prosaic. 'Bowie' was chosen after the name of his favourite type of knife.[1]

The twin engines of Bolan and Bowie, with their androgyny and otherworldly glamour kick-started a movement that dominated the early 1970s pop scene. Every band seemed to throw on glitter and their girlfriends' clothes. The stomp of Bolan's 'Hot Love' was the musical blueprint and a dozen British bands immediately joined the movement, raiding their Christmas decoration boxes for television appearances. Wizzard . . . The Sweet, Mott the Hoople, Alvin Stardust. The music was fun and catchy and not-entirely-serious and had a broad appeal.

Glam rock bands had a weird knack for writing fucking excellent Christmas songs. Wizzard's 'I Wish It Could be Christmas

---

1. 'David Bowie' was only his fourth choice of pseudonym, after 'David Butter', 'David Hunting' and 'David Those Ones You Get On Cheeseboards With The Pointy Fork Bit At The End'.

Every Day'[1] and Slade's 'Merry Christmas Everybody' competed
in December 1973.[2] Both songs have endured to this day and
spawned a host of imitators. Mud channelled Elvis with their
'Lonely This Christmas' and made a singularly disturbing video
with a ventriloquist's doll and people up ladders depositing snow
on them.[3]

   Queen skirted round glam rock, and added a genuine bisexu-
ality to a scene crowded with hod carriers in drag. Black
Sabbath shared Wizzard's manager, Don Arden, and Sabbath
were not immune to the 'bold' fashion choices that glam rock
encouraged.

   Slade had a string of failed singles before making it, as well as
several image changes. In 1969 they were encouraged to dress as
skinheads. They quickly realised that doing so involved getting
into fights with actual skinheads and so sharply ditched that look
in favour of the glam thing that was happening.

   Slade are the most headbanger-friendly of all the glam rock
bands. They're from the metal heartland of the Black Country
and the combination of their straight-ahead rock and roll sound
and Noddy's raucous voice is just the ticket. In 1980 they
were a last-minute replacement for Ozzy Osbourne at Donington

1. Which, if you think about it, is the stuff of nightmares. Rubbish would pile
up, shops would be shut, there'd be no post.

2. I once heard Noddy Holder being interviewed on local radio in
Wolverhampton in the run-up to Christmas. He spoke at length about the
recording and enduring popularity of the song. They then asked him to give
them a belt of 'IT'S CHRIIIIIIISTMAAAAAS!' He replied that he was very
sorry, but he was under contract with an advert that year and as a result was
not legally allowed to shout 'IT'S CHRIIIIIIISTMAAAAAS!' on any other
medium for the duration of the advert.

3. Mud's other significant hit was a terrifying warning about the dangers of
genetic experimentation entitled 'Tiger Feet'.

Monsters of Rock. As a result they enjoyed a colossal surge in popularity among our lot and have been close to our hearts ever since.

At the other end of the glam rock spectrum were art school bands like Roxy Music. Despite Bryan Ferry's off-colour comments about the Nazis having 'amazing' imagery (which many metal bands clearly agree with), they're outside the remit of this book.

Glam rock's aesthetic is strangely inorganic. There is a cheapness to it. The seventies video stock on which most of its seminal performances were shot gives it a stark, brittle, plastic/nylon/aluminium quality. Furthermore, apart from Bowie and Bolan, the image looks fake – tacked on. Even Bowie's backing group, The Spiders from Mars, look a bit like they've had their costumes imposed on them. Nearly every glam group had at least one member who looked distinctly uncomfortable in his foil and stack-heeled boots – blokes you'd expect to see hanging out in betting shops rather than at a make-up counter.

The elephant in glam rock's room is of course the prolific paedophile Gary Glitter.[1] At the time the nation had no idea that when he sang 'Do you wanna be in my gang?' there was a sinister undertone. No, Gary, I do not want to be in your gang. 'Do you wanna touch me there?' Still no, Gary. Still a definite no.[2]

As the decade wore on, glam declined. Bowie moved on to

1. Glitter's backing group, The Glitter Band, make a very pointed statement about their distinction from him on their Wikipedia page.

2. Glitter's horrific sexuality is blatantly alluded to in several songs: 'Do You Wanna Touch Me', 'Alone in the Night', 'Remember Me This Way', as well as the lesser known 'Please Let Me Fiddle with Your Genitals', 'Special Secret Type of Cuddle', 'Crying Only Makes Me More Horny', and 'I Like to Have Sex (With Children)'.

other styles, Bolan's popularity declined, Slade were in the dol-
drums. Disco was taking over. And then, for a brief moment,
punk took over and changed the feel of every guitar-based band.
It seemed like glam was dead.[1]

But then something horrible happened over in LA.

At the same time that thrash was evolving out of the NWOBHM
influence and striving for authenticity and a street-level everyman
image, on LA's Sunset Strip a scene was emerging that was everything the thrash pioneers hated.

'Metal started on Sunset Boulevard,' says Vince Neil of Mötley
Crüe on the VH1 documentary I forced myself to watch to research
this chapter. Which just goes to show how full of shit he was.
It really, really didn't, Neil. Read the first three chapters of this book.

Nonetheless, LA's Sunset Strip had long been the centre of
the West Coast's music scene. In 1980 it was dominated by punk
and new-wave bands – the sound of anti-authority and rebellion.
Over the next few years the political pendulum swung to the
right. The UK already had Margaret Thatcher's Conservative
government and in the States Ronald Reagan enacted what
became known as Reaganomics – tax breaks for the rich which
he claimed would stimulate the economy and allow wealth to
'trickle down'. Which of course is total bollocks. While this political situation proved fruitfully inspiring for agitating punk rock,
in the wider culture these policies coincided with a culture of
conspicuous consumption and a focus on the pursuit of wealth,
typified by the film *Wall Street*'s slogan, 'Greed is Good', and the

---

1. The influence of this era of pop music would endure, and echoes could be
heard in later heavy metal. The stomping glam drum pattern turns up in Iron
Maiden's 'Running Free' and Marilyn Manson's 'The Beautiful People'.

'yuppie' phenomenon. This ugly culture was reflected in the ambition and hedonism of glam metal.

Glam metal celebrated sleazy sexuality, and the conspicuous consumption of everything from drugs to girls to hairspray. Misogyny ruled – the Strip was full of strip clubs and had a bizarre focus on mud wrestling. I guess all this would be okay if the music was actually good. Alas, it really, really isn't.

Glam metal is barely worthy of the name metal. It's certainly not what I personally think of as metal, but other people do and I am no longer in charge of language use[1] so I guess we're stuck with it being called metal.

The first band to make it in this scene were Mötley Crüe. Their antics have been documented in two compelling books, *The Dirt* and Nikki Sixx's *The Heroin Diaries*. Basically, they were really horrible and very unhygienic. There you go – saved you reading two books.

According to his published diary, Crüe were assembled according to bassist Nikki Sixx's vision of 'the ultimate rock and roll band', which he meant in terms of look, attitude and lifestyle. Whereas bands like The Who and Led Zeppelin used sex, drugs and vandalism to blow off steam in reaction to the weirdness and pressures of fame brought by being actual musical geniuses, Mötley Crüe existed in order to indulge in sex, drugs and vandalism and the musicianship was an afterthought. They took glam rock's image but ignored its genuinely great songwriting.

In the various slickly produced documentaries on the scene everyone in their circle talks about their look, their attitude, their antics, their pyrotechnics . . . not the music.

Their first album came out in 1981. *Too Fast for Love* starts promisingly enough with a decent riff opening the song 'Live

1. Ever since Brexit . . .

Wire' . . . And then the rest of it is fucking rubbish. Terrible vocals singing terrible lyrics compete in terms of pure suck with comedy drum breaks and hilariously bad guitar solos. Lending me Nikki Sixx's book for my research, the excellent music journalist Marc Burrows said, 'It will fool you into thinking you like Mötley Crüe until you remember to listen to them.' It's worth reminding yourself, though. Just find a way you can do it for free.

Against all the odds (unless like me you have a general disdain for the general public) the album sold incredibly well. But it was nothing compared to what was to come.

In September 1983 they played the 'US Festival' in San Bernadino, California. The 'heavy metal day' saw them share the stage with the likes of Ozzy Osbourne, Judas Priest and Van Halen . . . And they were totally shit.

'They stunk. They were an embarrassment. They played awful,' says one of their crew on the VH1 film. They were so bad that when their drummer, Tommy Lee, found out the show had been recorded he started crying.

It's hardly surprising they were bad. Singer Vince Neil had been recruited, according to a roadie, John Crouch, in the same documentary, because he 'had the look, but his voice was a little suspect, so we decided we'd go with the look and we'll have to work with voice as we go'. Let's examine that a little more closely:

HE WAS A SHIT SINGER BUT HE LOOKED GOOD SO THEY HIRED HIM.

Okay. Moving on. The producer for their second album complained that Nikki Sixx couldn't play bass. 'No shit,' says their manager, 'he never could. He's an entertainer.' It didn't matter. The crowd at the US Festival loved them. Because people are idiots. Their set was an immense success and led to regular radio play and massive record sales.

The most obvious reason for their success was the way they looked. Their image pushed the gender-bending instinct of seventies glam to its natural conclusion. They went full transvestite, wearing make-up and high heels, occasionally managing almost to pass as female. And their hair was MASSIVE. It caused a huge stir and in the conservative early eighties this could have been amazingly subversive. Alas they fucked that up by doing videos that could only be done if you were massive misogynists and strenuously disavowing any queer subtext.

This needs to be made clear. They *definitely* weren't gay. No siree. Not gay AT ALL. You can tell because of all the girls. So many girls. In case you were in any doubt at all, they even have a song called 'Girls, Girls, Girls'.[1] See? That's girls times three. That's maths. It's almost as if they are trying a little bit *too* hard to prove that they definitely like girls.

Being massively image-over-content, Crüe were *perfect* for MTV. Their second album, the hilariously titled *Shout at the Devil*,[2] spawned their first video, for 'Looks That Kill'. It's a confusing mess. Holding flaming torches, they herd some women into a cage. And then what looks like a really giant woman appears and sets them free and the pentagram from the drums whizzes off and sort of goes on her shield and there are some spikes and *what the fuck is going on they really shouldn't have all that fire around when they are using that much hairspray.*

If there is something positive to be said about Mötley Crüe, it's that they fucking went for it. They dreamed of being the

---

1. 'Girls, Girls, Girls' can be significantly improved upon by substituting a single 'GERLS' in the style of Father Jack off of *Father Ted* during the chorus.

2. Seriously, what the fuck does *Shout at the Devil* actually mean? Is it a shout out TO the devil? Or against him? They wore pentagrams and stuff. Are they in favour of the devil or not? This is very unclear, guys.

ultimate rock and roll band with the ultimate rock and roll lifestyle. 'I knew I'd be in Mötley Crüe,' says Nikki Sixx. 'I knew
how we would look, what we would sound like, how we would
behave (fucking badly, obviously).'

   They got fucked up on drugs, threw insane parties, crashed
cars (and killed people),[1] shot guns, married porn stars and strip-
pers, made millions, spent millions on drugs, flushed drugs down
the toilet. Tommy Lee had a dream that he was playing the drums
upside down so he arranged to have a drum kit that went upside
down with him still playing it. They totally and comprehensively
lived *sex, drugs and rock and roll* to its ultimate limit.

   It's just a shame they sounded like absolute dogshit.

In the wake of Mötley Crüe's success the worst-case scenario happened. A load of other bands like them got really big too.

> The bad news is all these bands are coming out that are B
> and C rate Crüe copies. In the end the record companies
> trying to cash in will be the death of us if this doesn't
> stop . . . – Nikki Sixx, *The Heroin Diaries*

They opened the gates for their Sunset Strip peers and spawned
imitators and *Jesus Christ why won't it go away*? The most I can
bring myself to do is give you a rough list of some bands and tell
you how shit they were. Okay? Let's go: Quiet Riot covered
Slade's 'Cum on Feel the Noize' and it was shit. Skid Row, Cin-
derella, Warrant? Shit. Twisted Sister? Right-wing shit. WASP
were shocking, gory shit. They copied Alice Cooper and turned

---

1. If you ever needed evidence that Vince Neil is a cunt, he describes the day
he killed his best friend by crashing his car while drunk as 'One of the worst
days of my life'. *One* of.

it up several notches. Their shows involved them throwing meat into the crowd, a gimmick that would later be repeated by death metal rednecks Deicide and satanic black metal cover stars Watain. Blackie Lawless contrived a device that made sparks fly off his crotch. Again, the music was shit.

Everything you need to know about Bon Jovi[1] can be summed up in the simple and revealing fact that Jon Bon Jovi has a Superman tattoo. Even Nikki Sixx thought Bon Jovi were lame. From *The Heroin Diaries*: 'I always dug Jon – I just hated his band's music. It was the opposite of everything I loved and believed in.'

Poison were even less metal than Crüe and they practically invented the glam ballad with their dire 'Every Rose Has a Thorn'.[2] How fucking DEEP, guys. That's, like, totally true. Total shit.

The worst thing about glam was its ubiquity. It even began to infect previously impeccable bands like Discharge and Celtic Frost, both of whom put out fucking terrible glam metal albums, complete with poodle hair and awful vocals. The glam power ballad ruined Scorpions. Which considering they had already used what has been described as basically child porn on an album cover is pretty devastating. Plus there's that time when Lars[3] started hanging out with Guns N' Roses and Sebastian Bach and started wearing a white biker jacket . . .

---

1. I once announced a Bon Jovi tribute band by saying, 'If unlike me you are a fan of Bon Jovi . . .' I was later approached by a guy in the toilet who remonstrated: 'That was a bit much, wasn't it? A bit out of order?' Dude. You really need to see what I used say about the Jonas Brothers.

2. Though Sebastian Bach of Skid Row reckons Crüe started that shit too: 'After "Home Sweet Home" came out it was de rigueur that you had a huge ballad.'

3. SIT DOWN, LARS.

In researching this scene, I tried to keep an open mind. I went in hating it and all it stood for, and I came out with something of a soft spot for some of the people involved but utterly despising their music, their image, and their gross misogyny and selfishness.

But one thing that really stood out in my reaction was the begrudging respect I ended up having for a band I previously hated – Guns N' Roses.[1]

It's little wonder GN'R got so huge – so many bands in their scene were famous for little more than a hedonistic rock and roll image. These guys had that *plus* they could actually write songs. Their debut album, *Appetite for Destruction*, is by far and away the best[2] music to come out of the Sunset Strip scene. With roots more in punk and metal than in glam, it has a much more aggressive edge than anything Crüe or Poison were putting out, plus real hooks and, I have to admit, some incredible riffs.

The glam was pretty low-key. They had a relatively street-level approach and best of all they could actually play. Alas, they were let down by the massive bell-endery of their frontman, Axl Rose.[3] Nikki Sixx's diary comments: 'Cool new band but the singer is an asshole.'

He grew increasingly difficult and frequently showed up late to shows. His lack of respect for his audiences is legendary, often delaying concert performances by hours. When GN'R toured

---

1. I used to *really* hate them but my position has softened over the years. This, younger readers, is something that will happen to you. A mate of mine who has otherwise really good taste in music just reviewed Take That and he really enjoyed it. Nostalgia is a powerful drug. Beware its toxic effects.

2. /least worst.

3. An anagram of 'Oral Sex'. Hold my sides. I think they've split. His real name is William Bruce Rose, which is an anagram of 'I, Crumblier Sea Owl'. Which is a MUCH better name for a frontman.

with Metallica it was a tremendous clash of personalities. A low-level feud erupted between the two bands (or, more specifically, between the two frontmen).

Guns N' Roses inevitably disappeared up their own arses. They outgrew their trailer-park relateability and spent millions on overblown music videos. Drugs took over and the music suffered. Eventually they imploded.

By the beginning of the nineties glam still looked unassailable. Glam was everywhere. Every label had over-subscribed to the genre and MTV was wall-to-wall back-combing and 'success jackets'. The term 'heavy metal' was now intractably associated with the most vacuous scene it had ever produced.

Happily, while all this shit was going on, a movement in complete opposition – death metal – was gaining strength. And a check-shirt-clad music scene up in rainy Washington State was just starting to snowball, and that snowball was to become an avalanche. And glam was at the bottom of the slope. Skiing. Or something. I dunno. This metaphor has gone on too long. Turn the page and read about death metal. Go.

8

Death Metal

Something inside me, it's — it's coming out
I feel like killing . . . YOU

It says a lot about the popular perception of my favourite type of music that heavy metal has been used as a form of torture in Guantánamo Bay.[1] To me this seems misguided. Metal is bracing like a cold shower. It can be endured and it is possible to acclimatise to. A far more powerful weapon is the novelty song. And indeed the song 'I Love You' by Barney the Purple Dinosaur is apparently used much more often. Personally, I'd go for 'The Birdy Song' or 'Agadoo' on a never-ending loop.[2] Now that is a true nightmare. Still, the use of heavy music for torture raises interesting questions: what makes something sound truly heavy? Is heavy just the same as unpleasant or annoying? Which are the heaviest bands? IS BARNEY THE PURPLE DINOSAUR HEAVY?![3] Metalheads are, of course, divided on the subject. For

1. The *Guardian* reported in 2008 that Metallica's 'Enter Sandman' was being used in Guantánamo and Deicide's 'Fuck Your God' on prisoners in Iraq.

2. Imagine Black Lace, stamping on a human face, for ever.

3. Not to be confused with Barney Greenway of Napalm Death, who disappointingly got his nickname not from the dinosaur but from Barney Rubble from *The Flintstones*.

some purists, heaviness is nothing other than FEEL, man. For them, the heaviest bands might range from the straightforward doominess of Sabbath and Trouble to the riff-power of Diamond Head or Judas Priest. These people believe that heaviness is not about sonic extremity but a deep emotional feeling of weight communicated by the music. Something more abstract, that you feel in your soul. For other people, heaviness is something you feel in your ears. According to that principle, death metal and grindcore are two of the ultimate expressions of heaviness. Over the years I have heard claims made for Obituary, Agoraphobic Nosebleed, Napalm Death, Deicide and Cattle Decapitation being the Heaviest Band of All Time. Fans of electronic noise bands would argue that Whitehouse or Merzbow are heavier than any metal band. Then there's Swans . . .[1] Heaviness is in the ear of the beholder.[2] Whatever your opinion on the subject of heaviness, death metal is a pinnacle; one of the peaks in heavy metal's topography. Here we find many of the extremes totally exemplified. Death metal is where heavy metal turns up to elev-enty. The pioneers of death metal and the current crop of musicians who follow in their footsteps share a massive craving for sonic extremity. Death metal is the answer to the question: 'How can we make this heavier?' Well, you take the heaviest stuff anyone has made so far and you start from there. Sabbath down-tune? You downtune even more. Sabbath play slow? You slow down. Anthrax play fast? You speed up. Or you do both IN ONE SONG!!! You find amps and pedals that distort the guitars to the point that it sounds so unlike the acoustic ancestor to that instru-ment that it might as well be entirely unrelated. How do we make

1. A quick poll on Twitter brought some hilarious results. 'Late-era Pantera'? Yeah, I like them but, seriously, you need to listen to Teitanblood.

2. Or, if you're listening to . . . *and Justice for All*, in the 'Eye of the Beholder'.

the lyrics more extreme? Well, instead of portraying a creeping sense of doom or a wail of isolation you describe in explicit, gory detail the most horrific torture and murder scenarios imaginable. And then you take those lyrics and vocalise them so that they sound like they are being narrated by an actual monster. Possibly a huge purple dinosaur . . .

When Black Sabbath decided in 1969 to replicate the feeling of horror films in music, they invented heavy metal. By the mid-eighties the influence of horror on heavy metal was of a very different stripe, because horror itself had significantly developed over the intervening years. The horror films that influenced Black Sabbath were rather polite: early Hammer horror is artful, elegant and restrained. At their best those films are masterpieces of atmosphere and the slow building of dread. A great deal of this is due to the film-makers working around classification and censorship considerations, and as the censors became more liberal so the films lost their subtlety and refinement and became more exploitative. (The older black-and-white Universal Studios horror films that they grew up on were even more buttoned-up.) Over the course of the 1970s, horror became gorier and more extreme, and after the watershed that was Roman Polanski's *Rosemary's Baby* a new occult 'realism' crept in. The pinnacle of this tendency was *The Exorcist*, whose malevolent influence is still felt in cinema today and in the declining fortunes of the pea soup industry.

The advent of home video machines revolutionised the film industry. Suddenly films were consumed in a different environment and low-budget features could make their money back while bypassing the need for cinema distribution and thus the normal channels of censorship. As a result, horror got even more exploitative, and even less tasteful. It was the era of the 'video nasty'. These extreme underground films were devoured by the very same young men (almost always) who were also consuming the extreme underground music produced by Hellhammer and Bathory, Discharge and GBH. While Sabbath endeavoured to make the musical equivalent of a Dennis Wheatley adaptation, these kids wanted to make the musical equivalent of *Zombie Flesh Eaters*. This was death metal.

It is worth stating again that in the early 1980s the extreme sub-genres were all mashed up together,[1] without distinction from each other and without the names we now rely upon for easy categorisation. What became thrash metal and black metal and death metal and grindcore were all lumped together under various ad-hoc terms such as 'hardcore metal' or 'speed metal' or 'total head-banging thrash rage-out music'. (I may have made one of those up in an attempt to channel Tommy Vance.) The five-year period from 1982 to 1987 is the most creatively fertile and productive period in heavy metal's entire history. Out of this half-decade we got black metal, thrash metal, death metal, grindcore, doom. An explosive diversification and stratification of metal genres.

In the predefined morass of sub-genres that existed in the early 1980s, death metal was indistinguishable from the dirtier end of thrash and of the first wave of black metal. It all went into the mix and the influences mixed and interacted all over the shop.

Most accounts of the development of death metal describe it as being the next step on from thrash metal. This is misleading. Death metal's roots are the same as those of thrash, and it developed pretty much *alongside* thrash metal and actually influenced thrash's development. Thrash was a step in a different

1. In ways which are once again being explored by the burgeoning retro-metal scenes.

direction from the inevitable and inexorable journey from Venom
to full-bore death metal.[1] In a way, thrash can be thought of as
'proto-death metal'.

Examine the timeline of development:

1982 – Venom release *Black Metal.*
1983 – Metallica release *Kill 'em All.*
　　　　　Slayer release *Show No Mercy.*
　　　　　Exciter release *Heavy Metal Maniac.*

Although landmarks in the development of thrash, they are still
bathed in NWOBHM's amniotic fluid. Thrash is still not a viable
genre. And, at the same time, other groups are forming and
attempting to beat a darker path . . .

　　　1984 – And death metal is already with us, albeit not yet
　　　on an official release, only demos. But in this year Mantas/
　　　Death, Repulsion/Genocide, Slaughter and Possessed all
　　　release proto-death-metal demos. All are considerably
　　　heavier than anything Exodus or Slayer would EVER
　　　release, but they're all considered part of the same
　　　'hardcore metal' style. No one is really using the term
　　　thrash metal and yet Possessed's effort is actually called
　　　'Death Metal'. Meanwhile the thrash bands are still tied
　　　by an umbilical cord to NWOBHM.
　　　1985 – Possessed release their debut album, *Seven Churches*,
　　　death metal's first official album release.

It wasn't until 1986 that thrash metal fully matured, with the
release of Slayer's *Reign in Blood* and Metallica's *Master of Puppets*.
So if the apex of thrash (particularly in terms of its extremity) is

---

1. Thrash was the equivalent of the weaker members of an expedition stopping
halfway up a mountain. It spun off from the main thrust.

'86, then it's significant that Possessed had given birth to death metal with their release the year BEFORE that . . .

It all began with tape-trading.

> One of the most important means of finding out about new bands was the elaborate, worldwide tape-trading scene that circulated underground metal demo tapes and fanzines. Trading was an often tedious process, utilizing home-copied cassettes, slow postal mail and international reply coupons. – Thomas Gabriel Fischer, *Only Death is Real*

The international tape-trading scene that had been so important in the development of thrash metal also spawned a significantly heavier underground-to-the-underground. Among the proto-thrash and post-NWOBHM stuff that was floating around, most bands were trying to copy the sounds on Metallica and Slayer's first albums, but a few outsiders with a desire for something significantly more extreme began to find each other in an attempt to reach a new level of intensity.

One direction this drive took was the European black metal rawness produced by Hellhammer and Bathory, as outlined in the previous chapter. In the States, a different, considerably gorier scene erupted.

> I think that because Possessed were the very first to intentionally create 'Death Metal' it was like an epiphany that true metalheads just couldn't ignore. Back then there was nothing close to what we did with Seven Churches and I think we opened a lot of eyes to the possibility of doing much, much heavier types of metal. – Jeff Becerra, Possessed's frontman, interview on MetalSucks.com

Possessed were born out of the fertile Bay Area thrash scene, but had the same hunger for extremity that had driven Venom and Hellhammer to greater heaviness. Their first album, *Seven Churches*, is commonly accepted as the first 'pure' death metal album, which is impressive for a record which appeared as early as 1985. Although massively influential on death metal, this record is the only one they made in the genre (the follow-up, *Beyond the Gates*, being more in the thrash vein). Previously discounted as mere Slayer clones, Possessed came up with a debut album that delivered the death metal goods and made Possessed stand clear of their influence. *Seven Churches* begins with the incidental music from *The Exorcist* before descending into a maelstrom of total death. The atmosphere is dark, dank and terrifying. Becerra's vocals are more extreme than ANYTHING previously put onto vinyl. Still recognisable as a type of thrash metal, the guitars are heavier, and the songs include extra details like demonic backwards vocals.

At each stage of metal's development there are bands who stand out for their commitment to furthering metal's extremity. It's a noble lineage from Sabbath to Priest and Motörhead, to Venom, to Slayer, to Hellhammer and then on to Possessed. The hunger for heavier is passed on like a torch.

Ultimately they were short-lived. After their second album Possessed split, in 1988. The guitarist Larry LaLonde went on to form the funk metal band Primus with Les Claypool and has played on several Tom Waits albums.

In 1989 Becerra was shot in a robbery, and paralysed from the chest down. The gunman aimed at his head, but his gun jammed, saving Jeff's life. Now confined to a wheelchair, he strikes an impressive and distinctive figure fronting a recently revived Possessed from his chair. Now THAT is extreme. Fucking hero.

Possessed may have coined the term 'death metal', but Death[1] were *called* 'death'. There's nothing subtle about that. Death metal, made by a band called Death, whose demo was called *Death by Metal* and whose career was cut short by the frontman's untimely death. I shit you not. Now THAT is commitment to a concept.

Possessed were seminal, but the body of work created by Death laid a much more significant foundation for the huge death metal movement that would follow in their wake. The band consisted of a revolving line-up of musicians centred around the creative genius of guitarist, vocalist and songwriter Chuck Shuldiner. As well as the initial influence he had on the expansion of popularity of what we now consider 'old school' death metal – i.e. the original movement – the musical experimentation and progress made over their seven studio albums opened the doors for the death metal sub-sub-genres of gore metal, technical death metal and melodic death metal.[2] Shuldiner was an originator of the whole genre, and then had a significant hand in developing it far beyond its roots. Starting off relatively primitive and with cartoonish, horror-film-inspired gore lyrics, Death developed over the years into a more technically accomplished act who dealt with real-world issues and a deeply thoughtful worldview. Shuldiner, in common with all the best pioneers, was never content to rest on his laurels. He drove relentlessly for invention and innovation, and he also treated Death as a very personal expression of self.

1. They are not to be confused with the Michigan punk band of the same name, who are very much worth listening to in their own right, but are not part of this narrative . . .

2. Yes. Melodic death metal. That is a thing. That actually exists. 'You know what's really missing in death metal?' 'Women?' 'Nope. Melody.'

Growing up, Shuldiner was a middle-class suburban kid. He was born in Long Island, New York, and grew up in Tampa, Florida. His parents were supportive, both morally and financially, funding his musical endeavours and allowing him to rehearse in their house, even supplying the banch with food and 'non-alcoholic drinks'. The fact that she specifies 'non-alcoholic' is pretty much my favourite quote in the whole death metal story. As his mother says in the book *Choosing Death*, 'When [Chuck] called after two weeks to tell us of his change in plans, we wired the money to him to fly home. His father and I respected his decisions and gave him financial freedom to go wherever his search led him for his career.' KVLT!

This type of parental support was also a part of the story of the Florida band Obituary, whose first entry in their thanks list on their debut album is 'our parents – for putting up with the shit and living with us long hairs'. And the opposite of what happened with Hellhammer . . .

In completely opposite circumstances to the poverty, isolation and neglect suffered by Tom G. Warrior in his Swiss village, Chuck had it made. He had no financial worries, incredibly supportive parents and an itch he needed to scratch. Inspired by the sounds of Venom, he decided he needed to make music that was more extreme than anything he could find, and in 1983 formed Mantas, releasing a demo entitled *Death by Metal*.

Nowadays it's easy to find personnel for a death metal band. But when the few people making death metal were drastically ahead of their time, it was extremely difficult. Shuldiner struggled to find the right line-up, playing first with Kam Lee and Rick Rozz (who would later rejoin and play on several Death releases), then Matt Olivo and Scott Carlson of Repulsion, who moved to Florida for a couple of weeks to try out with him, then went back home sharpish when that didn't work out . . .

Repulsion had begun life as a thrash metal covers band called Tempter, based in Michigan. Matt Olivo and Scott Carlson then added drummer Phil Hines,[1] who played with a hardcore punk style, and wrote original songs heavily influenced by Slayer. In heaviness they were years ahead of their time.

> Because we were fans of extreme music we wanted to come up with the most extreme music; something that we could be fans of. What we were trying to do was be extreme. – Scott Carlson

In style they crossed death metal with a hardcore sensibility and aesthetic, playing punk shows and destroying people's ears. Although their first incarnation lasted only a short while, they were prolific recorders of demos and these were a huge influence on what became grindcore, so much so that Carcass started up their own label in order to release the demos as the album *Horrified*.

After the comically brief dalliance with Repulsion, Chuck's next move was to thrash hotbed San Francisco to play with Eric Brecht, drummer in the crossover band DRI. With a horrible inevitability this collaboration was short-lived, and like a galactic yo-yo he returned home when that didn't work out. Then he moved to Canada to play with the incredible Slaughter. Then, when that didn't work out[2] . . . he moved back to Florida for a bit, then back to San Francisco to play with drummer Chris Reifert

1. Not to be confused with the Chaos Magic pioneer Phil Hine. Unless there's something he's not telling me.

2. I do sometimes get the impression that the problem might have been Chuck himself. Like you know when you have friends whose problems seem to really mount up, and it seems really obvious that the one consistent thing is . . . THEM?

(who would later form the very Death-like Autopsy). Finally, with this line-up, Death recorded their debut album, *Scream Bloody Gore*. Released in 1987, it is considerably heavier than Possessed's *Seven Churches*, with production lending it considerably more weight and the vocals being more extreme – more aggressive. In that sense, it vies with *Seven Churches* as the first death metal album.

What was it about Florida that bred such an influential death metal scene? Possibly the influence of Chuck Shuldiner, possibly the effect on the brain of that level of sticky heat. Maybe it's the right-wing, gun-toting, racist, Cuba-invading culture? Maybe it's the fault of the Golden Girls. Possibly it's the malign occult influence caused by the presence in the state of the Walt Disney Corporation and NASA.

The Florida-based band Obituary claimed many times to be the heaviest in the world. Their debut album, *Slowly We Rot*, is certainly a perfect template for the traditional approach to death metal. Their tempos are slower, and then there are those vocals . . .

Two things are notable about Obituary's vocalist, John Tardy. One is that he has long curly blond hair which makes him look like a nineties Sarah Jessica Parker off *Sex and the City*.[1] The other is that his vocals were the most extreme thing heard on record at that time. Not so much screaming or shouting as VOMITING out the words, they are so indecipherable that on their debut he didn't even bother writing lyrics for a bunch of the songs! He just went '*BE-BLEEEERRRRRG!*'[2]

---

1. Seriously – you never see them in the same room . . .
2. 'What you singing about in this one, John?'
   'Oh you know, death and that.'
   'Cool.'
   '*BU-BLERRRRRRRRRG!*'

This was a distinct change from the high-register screams of *Scream Bloody Gore.*

That guttural vocal style is the single defining feature of death metal.[1] It's variously called death grunts, dethvox, vokills and 'Cookie Monster' vocals . . .

> I didn't like the first wave of what everyone called death metal. The Cookie Monster vocals turned me away. If I can't get into a singer, it's hard for me to get into the music. You've got fifty bands out there right now who sound exactly the same. – Kerry King, Slayer

It's hilarious that the king of extremity himself sees this vocal style as beyond the pale. Though, to be fair to him, it's this vocal style that is most off-putting to outsiders. I guess everyone has their limit.

There then began something of an arms race, with vocalists endeavouring to sound less and less human, and to go deeper and deeper. Whether directly or indirectly influenced by the vocals of zombies or possessed beings in horror films – Regan in *The Exorcist*, for example – they went well beyond what anyone had done in music before. Chris Barnes, vocalist on Cannibal Corpse's first few records, pushed his vocals so low that on their fourth album, *The Bleeding,* his voice is virtually unrecognisable as human.

Extreme vocals are in evidence as far back as recorded music if you know where to look. In popular music, the Beatles' recording of 'Twist and Shout' is a great early example of a throat being shredded. Screamin' Jay Hawkins, Little Richard and Howlin' Wolf all did it too. Then of course there's Tom Waits, whose vocal cords must now resemble beef jerky.

There's a relatively clear lineage in the development of

---

1. Which, as with any genre-defining trope, not all DM bands use . . .

extreme vocals in metal, starting with Lemmy's gravelly roar, which then led in turn to Venom's Cronos, Slayer's Tom Araya, Hellhammer/Celtic Frost's Tom G. Warrior and Possessed's Jeff Becerra.

Although the technique was initially extremely male-dominated, death metal vocalists today are just as likely to be women. Angela Gossow, the former vocalist with Arch Enemy, was the first high-profile woman doing death growls and took a load of patronising-to-outright-sexist-flak for it. In her wake hundreds, maybe thousands, of woman have proved that there's no advantage in having a cock if you want to sound like a monster. (A couple that come to mind are Landmine Marathon's Grace Perry and Makiko from the frankly rubbishly named but actually very good Flagitious Idiosyncrasy in the Dilapidation, from Japan. Maybe it's a translation thing. Or maybe they just really like Carcass.)

Not every death/grind vocalist can produce an inhuman sound on their own, as the does-what-it-says-on-the-tin grindcore band Anal Cunt suggest in their song 'Benchpressing Effects on Kevin Sharp's Vocals'. Morbid Angel use ring modulators and phasers for a truly monstrous sound on 'Where The Slime Live'.

While most early death metal bands focused on zombies and murder, Florida's Deicide chose a more aggressive path, peddling a distinctly Christian-flavoured type of ad-hoc satanism.

Deicide began life as Amon. They recorded an album, *Feasting the Beast* which never saw the light of day. Changing their name to Deicide, which means 'the killing of God', they struck out in a confrontational and aggressively blasphemous vein, baiting the religious extremism that was (and still is) so prevalent in Florida.

Deicide's intimidating sound was created by the Hoffman brothers on guitar and Steve Asheim on drums, but their notoriety was almost entirely down to their 'colourful' frontman, Glen Benton.

Benton branded his forehead with an inverted crucifix, presumably to make airport security more of a fun pursuit. (Asheim has stated in an interview that this was most likely an act of competitiveness following the media interest Brian Hoffman generated by branding a cross in his arm with a cigarette.) Benton claimed it didn't hurt all that much, because 'there aren't many nerves in that part of your head'. He created a satanic media persona, making shocking statements which over the years he has slowly reneged on, showing the persona to be more of a construction, especially in the light of the genuinely extreme lifestyle and behaviour of the subsequent Norwegian black metal scene. It's unclear how Benton's behaviour affected that scene, though it makes a lot of sense that a high-profile death metal figure making extreme boasts to the press would encourage the Norwegians to compete and to outdo their Florida rivals.

Benton's antics were in danger of obscuring the music. An ex-girlfriend of mine once said they were 'the sort of band that sells more T-shirts than records'. (This was back in the nineties when people actually did sell records, of course. Nowadays shirt sales are the only thing keeping bands on the road ... so put your hand in your pocket at the merch table, kids.)

Deicide were the first satanic band I listened to. While their commitment to blasphemy is undeniable, the theology of their avowed satanism is a bit woolly, to say the least. Theirs is the Satan of the televangelist. The Satan of the Bible Belt. The Satan that would be your Christian grandmother's worst nightmare. A suburban rebellion – useful in itself (it certainly encouraged me to question my own Christian upbringing) but theologically hollow.

A more interesting and considered theology is that of yet another Florida band, Morbid Angel. Less aggressive than

Deicide, but with an occult darkness that is considerably more atmospheric, they explored the world of H. P. Lovecraft's Cthulhu stories and their spin-off text the *Necronomicon* for a more eso-teric, authentic-sounding occult mythology. (And apparently his racism, too – rumours abounded in the early nineties that their frontman, David Vincent, was a big old racist, losing them a lot of fans. He claims 'people misconstrue' and that he was trying 'to illustrate points of breaking the patterns in thinking'.) They're definitely one of the more creative and interesting bands among the top tier of death metal, and really pissed everyone off with their last record, which included a load of industrial dance crap.

The Florida bands had a rare advantage – a producer who really understood the extreme sounds they were after. Scott Burns at Morrisound Studios was a death metal fan. He provided a wel-come change from producers who expressed bafflement and annoyance at the extremity of the sounds death metal bands were seeking. Burns was a key part of the development of the death metal sound from the early raw demos to something with clarity, dynamic range and polished production values. He seems to have produced practically every major death metal record between 1988 and 1996, recording Death, Obituary, Cannibal Corpse, Master, Pestilence, Sepultura, Deicide, Suffocation ... When Napalm Death decided they wanted more of a death metal sound, they went to Scott Burns.

So death metal found a natural home in Florida. Hot, swampy and rabidly right wing. Weirdly, it also thrived somewhere com-pletely the opposite: cold, liberal Sweden.

Extreme metal in Sweden started with Bathory, but extreme music in Sweden started with crust punk. The d-beat sound of Discharge found a massive fanbase in Sweden and d-beat as a genre is pretty much propped up entirely by the relatively small population of that country. But the d-beat scene is nothing compared to the insane bands-per-capita output of Swedish death metal, much of which grew out of that fertile punk scene.

They found their stars in Entombed, a band whose debut, *Left Hand Path*, is so perfect the only reasonable thing to do was to go off in a different direction, and by album number three, *Wolverine Blues*, Entombed had intertwined their HM-2 sludge with a rock and roll swing that was still incredibly heavy. Line-up problems have massively hampered their career, and much like Venom they now have two versions playing live – Entombed and Entombed AD.

The cornerstone of Entombed's sound (and that of nearly every other Swedish DM band) is the Boss HM-2 guitar distortion pedal. Made in Japan in the mid-eighties, the HM-2 sounds crap when used normally, but with everything turned up to 10 and a guitar downtuned to C, you immediately sound like Swedish death metal.

A band so closely related to Entombed they can be thought of as brothers are Dismember, creators of the single greatest death metal song of all time, 'Dreaming in Red'.

Not content with one style of death metal, Sweden hit upon another with the success of At the Gates and In Flames – a distinctly more tuneful approach which was dubbed the 'Gothenburg sound', also known as 'melodic death metal'.

While death metal was finding its core sound in Florida and Sweden, in the UK a related but different beast was being conceived: GRINDCORE! To the uninitiated, grindcore and death metal sound very similar. To us who are in the know they sound . . . very similar. They are very similar.

Punk had begun in Detroit in the late sixties with MC5 and the Stooges. Then it got picked up in New York in the early seventies by the Ramones, Television, Suicide and the New York Dolls. Then began a game of transatlantic punk tennis. We had the Sex Pistols, The Clash, The Adverts, The Damned etc. Then America struck back with hardcore punk – Bad Brains, Black Flag, Dead Kennedys, Minor Threat, Deep Wound. Then we had anarcho-punk: Crass, Discharge, Conflict, Amebix. Then it went back over to the States and nothing much happened. And then we got our ball back but it said 'Green Day' so we threw it in the bin.

The next step on from anarcho-punk in the UK was ... GRINDCORE!

Founders of the genre are Birmingham's Napalm Death. If brevity is the soul of wit, then Napalm Death are funny as fuck. Beginning as a political punk band, they gradually got heavier and faster, recording demos and swapping members along the way. The speed notably increased with the addition of their hyperactive drummer Mick Harris. Harris invented the term 'blast beat' for his insanely fast method of drumming that has since become ubiquitous in extreme metal. Napalm Death invented the micro-song, culminating in the epic one-second-long 'You Suffer'.

The fast turnaround of personnel in their early career is exemplified perfectly by the fact that their debut record, 1987's *Scum*, has two different line-ups. Side one has Nick Bullen on vocals and bass and Justin Broadrick on guitar, while side two has Lee Dorrian on vocals, Jim Whiteley on bass and as guitarist Bill Steer. Both have the eaten-all-the-red-Smarties energy of Mick Harris on drums. Played extensively by BBC Radio 1's John Peel, the album was a massive and unexpected success, and Napalm Death very swiftly became a benchmark for brutality.

Bill Steer's departure in 1989 was due to his commitment to a similarly fast and brutal band – Carcass. Beginning with a noisy grindcore style, Carcass focused on extreme gore in their lyrics and collage artwork, both gleaned from medical textbooks for a more authentic grossness.[1] They released their debut album in 1988. *Reek of Putrefaction* is even less coherent to the untrained ear than *Scum*. Over several albums Carcass refined their sound and became more melodic and less gore-obsessed, influencing both the gore-grind sub-genre and the melodic death metal movement that later flourished in Sweden. With their album *Necrotism: Descanting the Insalubrious* they also influenced every band who use ludicrously long titles.

Another band to evolve from punk into metal are the majestic Bolt Thrower from Coventry. Writing songs almost exclusively about war, they are named after a weapon from the ultimate geekness that is Warhammer. They even use Warhammer's artists for their albums – so uncool it's all the way back round to cool again.

Back in the United States, the biggest death metal band of all time was forming. For me, Cannibal Corpse remain the archetype of death metal – being a great example and also the first death metal band I ever heard. They are famous for obscene and horrific album cover artwork and such extreme song titles as 'Entrails Ripped from a Virgin's Cunt', 'I Cum Blood' and 'Necropedophile'. But as notable as they are for their extremity, Cannibal Corpse are also incredibly proficient musicians. Their compositions are complex and technical and they're incredibly fast. It's a misguided effort to defend extreme music through arguments of musicianship, but it's also worth stating that while these bands

---

1. Their original vocalist – an elusive guy by the name of Sanjeev – apparently used to alternate writing 'Siege' and 'Deep Wound' on his hand. What a dude. Not for him the commitment of patch denim. A marker pen and the back of his hand was all it took to praise his favourite hardcore legends.

were pushing the boundaries of heaviness and shocking horror, they were also breaking new ground as musicians.

Death metal spread like the contagion it talked about. Australia spawned Slaughter Lord, Sadistik Exekution (who when classed by their record label as the more trendy black metal replied, 'WE ARE DEATH . . . FUKK YOU!' . . . and the label mistakenly took that as the title of the album). Scenes cropped up in every imaginable country (except Norway).

Then something weird happened. Death metal got massive. It was never supposed to happen, but for a brief while, alongside its sister genre grindcore, death metal was all over mainstream TV and radio.

It began with John Peel. His BBC Radio 1 show was a uniquely eclectic mix of styles. Among the dub reggae, German techno and obscure bluegrass 78s, Peel's enthusiasm for finding new music led him to embrace the UK's burgeoning death metal scene, and bands such as Extreme Noise Terror, Carcass and Napalm Death got heavy rotation and were invited to perform live sessions on the show. Such was the influence of Peel's programme that this coverage soon bled into television, turning into the sort of media circus usually reserved for the launch of the biggest pop bands. There seemed to be genuine media interest in, and appreciation of, death metal.

In 1989 Napalm Death were on the children's BBC show *What's That Noise?*, featuring Craig Charles. The clip is easily found online, and it's incredibly charming. Lee Dorian and the rest of the lads are clearly slightly fazed by their harsh noise not only being taken seriously, but being used as something of a teaching aid to get kids to open their minds about different types of musical expression. The same year Napalm's Bill Steer appeared alongside Craig Charles in a different televisual context, this time with his Carcass bandmate Jeff Walker. In the *Red Dwarf* episode 'Timeslides' they can be seen portraying Dave Lister's band, Smeg and the Heads. An experimental, almost ambient band very far from Carcass's gore-grind noise![1] The BBC was a bit heavy metal mad in 1989. The documentary series *Arena* produced a slightly odd film about heavy metal in general, which featured Bill Steer once again, this time in a bedroom with the bassist Shane Embury, talking in a delightfully teenage know-it-all fashion about the fastest bands.

This mass-media portrayal of death metal and grindcore was not only unprecedented: it has never happened since. Death metal went mainstream, with major label deals and blanket coverage. To top it all off, in 1994 Cannibal Corpse appeared in the Jim Carrey film *Ace Ventura, Pet Detective*. Carrey was a big death metal fan and their appearance was at his personal request. Death metal had jumped the shark.

Today, death metal is over-familiar. It seems that everyone thinks they know something about the heaviest of metal sub-genres;[2] the music with the indecipherable guttural vocals and extreme horror film imagery. The one with the illegible logos and brutal blast-beat drumming. It's part of the collective

---

1. This episode contains my favourite line in the whole of *Red Dwarf*. After Lister gets hold of Adolf Hitler's briefcase, he examines the filling of the sandwiches included in his packed lunch, and exclaims, as only Craig Charles can, 'Banana and crisps?' This has nothing to do with death metal, by the way. I just think it's funny.

2. One of my favourite online pastimes is to search for people using the phrase 'Norwegian death metal'. They catch themselves out. They're trying to sound clever and worldy-wise by name-dropping Norway while referring to death metal, but fall foul of the fact that despite Norway's extreme metal scene being easily the world's most notorious, it is BLACK METAL and not death metal. Norway has fewer DM bands than pretty much anywhere. Sweden, of course, has shit-loads. The fucking IDIOTS. Try it. It's fun.

consciousness of popular culture. As a term, death metal is now so familiar it is widely used without context and referring to the wrong sub-genre. Its neat, self-contained linguistic extremity has turned it into a meme, a catch-all label for heavy music. When I want to talk about extreme music on stage as a comedian I reach not for *grindcore* or *black metal*, but for a term I know my predominantly 'civilian' audience will recognise. When I want to reference my old band SunStarvedDay to a comedy crowd I don't say 'chaotic metalcore in the vein of Kiss It Goodbye, early Cave In or Botch' . . . I say 'death metal'. Death metal is practically a brand. A linguistic shorthand. There's even a band called Eagles of Death Metal who are *not* a death metal band. Fucking unbelievable. Post-modernism has stripped our culture of meaning. The snake is eating its tail.[1]

Death metal began as an attempt to make the most extreme music possible. It promised to be the unacceptable outer edge of heavy metal. The pinnacle of HEAVY. Now it has an almost cosy ubiquity. It has largely lost its power to shock, as post-modern appreciation of everything-as-art and hipster assimilation of all outsider music into the Borg-like cool-ship have rendered it safe; a known quantity. It is neutered, defanged, defused.

In much the same way millennials have a shallow but broad understanding of the political arguments my nineties generation

---

1. The name apparently comes from a conversation in which Josh Homme from that band said that the brutal Polish death metal kings Vader were the Eagles of death metal. Somewhat ironically this largely inoffensive band, whose lyrics deal with girls and stripping and pretending to be some sort of sleazy Southern rock-type person, were witness to easily the most horrific scenes ever played out at a rock and roll show when ISIS-affiliated terrorists committed a mass shooting at one of their gigs in Paris. They now suffer post-traumatic stress disorder. If only they played a style of music within which they could express such an extreme experience . . .

had about the fur trade and sweatshops and corporations and can regurgitate prefabricated counter-arguments, so death metal is such a part of our cultural fabric that it will never again be seen as new or alien or genuinely extreme.

There's a cynical, jaded notion that there's nothing new under the sun, that everything has been done. The excellent website TV Tropes calls this the 'Seinfeld is Unfunny' trope:

> *'I don't know what the big deal with* Hamlet *is, it's just one famous saying after another, strung together by a moldy old plot.'*
> — Old Joke

There are certain shows that you can safely assume most people have seen. These shows were considered fantastic when they first aired. Now, however, these shows have a Hype Backlash curse on them. Whenever we watch them, we'll cry, 'That is *so* old' or 'That is *so* overdone'. The sad irony? It *wasn't* old or overdone when they did it. But the things it created were so brilliant and popular, they became woven into the fabric of that show's genre. They ended up being taken for granted, copied and endlessly repeated. Although they often began by saying something new, they in turn became the status quo.

This ubiquity, the feeling of familiarity (even if not borne out in ACTUAL familiarity — most people do not own any death metal records and fewer still have actually been to shows) is due to the sub-genre's incredible and unlikely mainstream media coverage in the late eighties and early nineties. When talking to middle-aged music fans in particular, there is a sense almost that because death metal has 'been done' there is no need for death metal to be a thing. As though death metal's extremity is a means to an end (rebellion? shock?) rather than an end in itself. This 'bindun' sentiment dogs all outsider art. 'How can it be relevant/shocking/ whatever if even *I've* heard of it?'

But this attitude, this weird acceptance of death metal, had an effect on extreme metal: over-exposed, no longer underground, and performed and consumed by people who don't even look metal. This was not good enough. A backlash was inevitable, and that backlash came from an unexpected place and took the form of the second wave of black metal.

But, meanwhile, death metal itself was evolving . . .

The history of death metal is the history of a genre constantly splintering, cross-pollinating and creating new strains of itself.

One of the defining characteristics of the originators of heavy metal sub-genres is a thirst for experimentation and an unwillingness to ossify into easily definable categories. Early members of Napalm Death quickly became bored with the limitations of grindcore once they'd played with it for a bit, and variously went off to play doom metal (Lee Dorrian with Cathedral) and industrial metal (Justin Broadrick with Godflesh). The early pioneers of a sound are often restless, seeking new things. Often they horrify the diehard fans of certain parts of their career by taking wildly divergent paths. Darkthrone, for example, have had at least four distinct phases: a short-lived death metal phase, the atmospheric minimalist lo-fi black metal of their next three records, a crossover crust punk element that began to creep in, and now it's all NWOBHM and thrash. Bathory went mental. Him off Emperor is rubbish now, but creating, still. Chuck Shuldiner went from primal, brutal death-thrash to pristine technical stuff.

And death metal continued to develop beyond the basic blueprint laid down in the late eighties. With the emergence of more melodic death metal came the splintering off of a new subgenre – brutal death metal (or BDM). As a result we now have a flourishing ecosystem of death metal sub-genres: melodic DM, brutal DM, technical DM (like normal DM only harder to play), blackened DM (death metal crossed with black metal), death-thrash (thrashy death metal), death-core (death metal made much, much worse with the addition of bad hardcore and neck tattoos when you haven't even got your arms done yet), deathgrind (two things that sound quite similar crossed with each other), death/doom (death metal where they're quite sad about all the deaths).

Death metal may never again hit the heights of popularity it enjoyed in the early nineties, but the scene is healthier than ever before, with new bands constantly adding new, experimental sounds to the mix. Which mainly sound fucking awful. But that is as it should be. As I careen towards middle age it would be a sorry state of affairs if young people weren't producing music I hate.

Cos I don't care how many neck and hand tattoos they've got, deathcore bands just aren't as heavy as Obituary.

BE-BLEEEERRRRRG!

'More ragga, more boggle, more death metal and Belgian house.

You hear me. Less get TV banging, mud der-far cuss.'[1]

1. Member of the public, reading off a card, oblivious to the meaning of the words he's been made to say. 'Speak Your Brains' – *The Day Today*, episode six.

9

The Second Wave of
Black Metal

Isolated groups can seriously fuck themselves up. Just look at the Conservative Party. Or the Spice Girls.[1] The psychological theory of 'Group Polarisation Phenomenon' suggests that groups often form more extreme ideas and plans than the individuals within them would form on their own.[2] Individuals exaggerate their opinions and suggestions in order to seek acceptance within the group. They state more extreme opinions than they actually hold, partly to test the limits of the group, partly in hope of finding favour with the more extreme members of the group. This distorts the perceived consensus, as other group members then shift their own ideals towards more extreme ends. Groups often take more risks as a result of this phenomenon. The theory has been used to explain acts of terrorism, gang violence and even the Holocaust.

The group of teenagers who comprised Norway's black metal 'inner circle' cut themselves off from mainstream society and competed for status. They endeavoured to outdo each other in terms of their evil, grim, serious behaviour. Their notion of black metal was

1. Or Bon Jovi. Or improv comedy troupes.
2. Just look at the bedroom tax, or the song 'Two Become One'.

a far cry from Venom's fun hedonism. This attitude found its most direct expression in the motto of Euronymous's record label, Death-like Silence – 'No mosh, no fun, no core'. The blackened thrash[1] band Nifelheim once sacked a guitarist for having a girlfriend.[2]

In the first few years of the nineties, group polarisation within the black metal scene led to arson and murder. It started as a rejection of the aesthetic and attitude of death metal,[3] a scene which they perceived as having lost its appeal due to its popularity with jocks and its lack of real grimness. Death metal bands used their subject matter almost as a costume that they could take off, whereas the ultra-grim Norwegians had a true obsession with death. 'I don't understand why death metal bands don't want to kill people,' said Varg Vikernes, a man who certainly put his money where his mouth was. It became an almost comical competition to out-do each other in acting out a notion of evil.

Ironically, all this happened after entirely more innocuous and innocent metal had attracted a pathetic amount of backlash and ire. The petrol-station-Halloween-display imagery of Ozzy Osbourne and the fantasy themes of Judas Priest had been investigated, probed, banned, railed against, and taken to court. It's possible that the tabloid exaggeration of the evils of heavy metal made people more determined than ever to make that a reality.

Death metal had plumbed the depths of horrific imagery. But the bands themselves were more often than not clean-cut suburban guys. There was a gap between the imagery of the music and the

1. Cross between thrash and black metal, like early Sodom or Sepultura.

2. Which led to me coining the insult 'in no danger of getting kicked out of Nifelheim'.

3. According to Alistair Riddell off Age of Taurus, Mayhem's 'rejection' of death metal and adoption of black metal was basically down to Mayhem not being very successful and looking for a unique selling point.

way the musicians themselves lived their lives. Norwegian black metal was the answer to that. It asked for total commitment.

   Norway's descent into darkness started with a band called Mayhem. Mayhem were the passion project of guitarist Øystein Aarseth, later known as 'Euronymous'. They started life as a primitive extreme metal band, covering Venom and Celtic Frost. Through the use of newsletters and fanzines, they soon gained a reputation as boundary-pushing and extreme even before recording anything. Their first demo *Pure Fucking Armageddon* – released in the same year as Slayer's *Reign in Blood* but on a different planet – is virtually unlistenable, even by black metal standards. The follow-up, *Deathcrush*, is a much more bold and distinctive recording. The cover depicts the severed hands of an Ivory Coast thief, a strikingly stark image for the time, more akin to a crust punk release. After a bizarre electronic drum track (made by a separate musician called Conrad Schnitzler[1]) the songs are heavy; catchy as well as crushing. Free of the sub-Hellhammer lack of production that diminished the first demo, the tracks sound more like the blueprint for the second wave of black metal, while still retaining more eclectic influences from punk, thrash and proto-death metal.

   The addition of Per Yngve Ohlin, or 'Dead', on vocals was the turning point for Mayhem and for the whole Norwegian black metal underground. He recorded two studio tracks and is commemorated on the incredible *Live in Leipzig* – in many ways black metal's *The Who Live at Leeds*. Obsessed with death, and prone to such bizarre behaviour as collecting dead animals and sniffing their rotting corpses between vocal takes,[2] Dead fulfilled his dark

1. Who sounds like a spicy German meat dish.

2. This story was stolen and appropriated by the cartoon metal band Slipknot to further their image; image being of huge importance to a band with masks and numbers and such.

potential by committing suicide. He blew his brains out with a shotgun, having first slit his wrists and throat – to make sure. He left a suicide note:

> Excuse the blood, but I have slit my wrists and neck. It was the intention that I would die in the woods so that it would take a few days before I was possibly found. I belong in the woods and have always done so. No one will understand the reason for this anyway. To give some semblance of an explanation I'm not a human, this is just a dream and soon I will awake. It was too cold and the blood was coagulating all the time, plus my new knife is too dull. If I don't succeed dying to the knife I will blow all the shit out of my skull. Yet I do not know. I left all my lyrics by 'Let the good times roll' – plus the rest of the money. Whoever finds it gets the fucking thing. As a last salutation may I present 'Life Eternal'. Do whatever you want with the fucking thing. / Pelle.

Euronymous found the corpse. Ohlin's blood was everywhere and the brain had come out of the skull. Before calling the police Euronymous went to a nearby chemist and bought a disposable camera, rearranged the scene to make it more photogenic and took several photographs. One of these ended up on the cover of a semi-official live Mayhem record – *Dawn of the Black Hearts*. He collected parts of Dead's shattered skull and made several neck-laces, which he distributed among his inner circle.

Euronymous had an incredible capacity for self-promotion and myth-building. He took advantage of Dead's death and issued a statement declaring Dead had killed himself because death metal had become 'trendy' and commercialised. Far from going along with this behaviour, his bandmates were shocked at his coldness. Necrobutcher told the *Guardian*: 'Øystein called me up the next day . . . and says, "Dead has done something really cool! He killed himself." I thought, have you lost it? What do you mean cool? He says, "Relax, I have photos of everything." I was in shock and grief. He was just thinking how to exploit it. So I told him, "OK. Don't even fucking call me before you destroy those pictures." '

Euronymous used Dead's suicide to foster Mayhem's 'evil' image. But by the time this paid off and Mayhem finally had a successful record, Euronymous himself was dead. He had set in motion a series of events that would end in his own murder.

Metalheads can be contradictory. On one hand heavy metal is absolutely a democratic, open, mainstream form of music, which at times has operated entirely on the level of pop music. Iron Maiden, Motörhead and Diamond Head used to feature in the teen pop magazine *Smash Hits*. Go to any big metal show and you will see a mix of the diehard long-haired, patch denim types (like me) and also the short-haired, boring-trousered metal-at-weekend normal types (like you, you loser). You don't have to look particularly metal to be a metalhead. You just have to like the music and you are in. Compare this to goth, in which the uniform is the only thing that really matters.

The flipside of metal's democratic, open-door policy is our staunch opposition to what is now commonly called cultural appropriation. Basically – if you don't like metal, please don't dress like you like metal. It seems obvious when you write it in plain English. I don't like reggae. So, for me, wearing a T-shirt with Bob Marley on it would be a pretty weird thing to do. I think Coldplay suck so I wouldn't get a Coldplay patch and sew it onto my denim cut-off. I don't like the TV show *The Great*

British Bake-Off so it would seem like a strange decision to write GBBO in studs on the back of a jacket.[1]

And yet time and time again we see examples of people wearing heavy metal band T-shirts for bands they clearly know nothing about and do not listen to. We see the signifiers of heavy metal – our clothes, our artwork – appropriated by fashion. They sell Slayer shirts in Top Shop and it is not just metalheads who are buying them.

Now, not everyone is annoyed by this. Rob Halford of Judas Priest says it makes him happy to see non-Priest fans wearing Judas Priest T-shirts because it shows how universally awesome the iconography of heavy metal is. He is wrong. It's bullshit. And here's why.

Number one – quite a lot of metalheads identify with the culture exactly because it is not mainstream and they have always felt alienated from mainstream society. To them metal is a refuge from the bullshit wider world.

Number two – being a metalhead is sometimes in itself alienating. I have been started on, shouted at, ripped the piss out of and heckled and mocked for being a metalhead. I don't give a shit and I'm not complaining. I am confident enough that metal is best so I am immune. However. When mainstream dickheads appropriate our thing in order to somehow be 'cool' it is fucking annoying.

The contrast to this is another aspect I find incredibly annoying – people who have adopted the traits of an outsider culture like unnaturally coloured dyed hair, piercings and tattoos then moan about how they are treated differently because of it. 'Oh boo hoo I have a tattoo of a skull on my neck and I can't get

1. Brilliantly, when in his punk phase the comedian Vic Reeves had 'Debussy' in studs on his jacket. What a fucking genius.

an office job.' GOOD! You shouldn't want an office job if you also want the outsider cool of a neck tattoo! You can't adopt signifiers which *literally come from prisons* and then expect to be a normal part of mainstream society.

Metal has a cultural capital exactly because it rejects the mainstream. Which is why the mainstream wants to appropriate it. I have never thought metal was particularly 'cool'. I just felt it spoke to me. It drew me in. I am a metalhead not because I want to be an outsider. I am a metalhead because I want to belong, and I don't particularly feel like I belong in normal society.

Number three – people who don't like metal have all of the rest of culture. Metalheads mainly just have metal. It's like someone owning a massive hotel asking if they can sleep in your bed. *That's my bit! You have all of the rest of it.*

This feeling was very much what was expressed by the Norwegian black metal scene. Death metal was supposed to be outsider art – a counter-culture, not just a sub-culture. But it got appropriated by the mainstream and it became the property of any keg-drinking bonehead who wanted it. It was no longer 'ours'. It was 'theirs'.

Black metal's second wave was a reaction. This reaction led to some of the best music ever made.

Hailing from Oslo, Darkthrone produced their first album in 1991. *Soulside Journey* is an accomplished technical death metal record in the vein of the Swedish DM sound. The follow-up represented one of the most radical departures in style ever witnessed from one album to the next.[1] *A Blaze in the Northern Sky* is the first

1. An intermediary album, *Goatlord*, was demoed but not released until 1997. It demonstrates a more gradual shift. But that's less interesting, right?

full release of a Norwegian black metal album.[1] It is an astonishing record. The cover is a stark black-and-white image of their guitarist Zephyrous, his face obscured by corpse-paint, practically flying witch-like in the night. It's the total opposite of the gaudy full-colour covers death metal bands were using. Sonically, it's so stripped down it's in danger of disappearing.

The opening track, 'Kathaarian Life Code', has an alienating, atmospheric intro. A low buzzing, a solo monk-like chant drenched in reverb and a second rasping, vomiting voice, the words indiscernible until '*we are . . . a blaze . . . in the Northern . . . sky*'. And the song rears up and kicks off – relentless blast-beat drumming, harsh, low-fi guitars that sound like a strimmer going through barbed wire, a demonic laugh . . . then a recognisable riff grounds the whole thing before a demented, Slayer-like solo.

And then it slows down and fucking POUNDS . . . The influence of Hellhammer and Bathory is obvious. The dynamics are amazing. Fuck, I love that song.

Nocturno Culto's vocals are generally deep, but not the guttural growls of death metal. There's a top note of shrieking. It's abrasive. The whole effect is undeniably raw, and cold-sounding. Almost hostile to the listener. Sonically it is the opposite of the trendy death metal that was being put out on major labels. Whereas death metal bands spent weeks perfecting a high-fidelity, full, bassy and rich sound in studios, *A Blaze in the Northern Sky* is thin and trebly – to such a degree that the band's label initially refused to put it out, saying it sounded 'weak'. In fact, it's anything but – the record was the beginning of a redefining of heavy. The language of extreme metal was being rewritten.

---

1. At this point Immortal had released a self-titled EP and Sweden's Marduk had released their *Fuck Me Jesus* EP. I had a T-shirt with that on. I'm fairly sure my mum threw it away.

This was the first of three stone-cold classic black metal records from Darkthrone. The follow-up, *Under a Funeral Moon*, is arguably better, more efficiently atmospheric, even more black and less death metal. And then *Transylvanian Hunger* just blows the fucking doors off. The guitars and drums for this third masterpiece were recorded entirely by the drummer, Fenriz, who sent the tapes to their usual guitarist and vocalist, Nocturno Culto, to record vocals. The approach is a droning, almost ambient sound with sparse riffs.

Although not caught up in the violence of 1992 they are not without controversy. The press release for *Transylvanian Hunger* was accompanied by the bone-headed comment, 'We would like to state that *Transylvanian Hunger* stands beyond any criticism. If any man should attempt to criticise this LP, he should be patronised for his obviously Jewish behaviour.' An unconvincing non-apology attempted to distance the quote from any anti-Semitic sentiment, stating that 'Jewish' was Norwegian slang for 'idiotic'. Hmm. Well, maybe, but the phrase 'NORWEGIAN ARYAN BLACK METAL' on the back cover was like petrol on a smouldering church. The following album was accompanied with a statement that Darkthrone were NOT a Nazi band.

As with all the greatest musical pioneers, Darkthone were keen to explore beyond the raw black metal template they had set, and later records adopt other influences such as crust punk, NWOBHM and epic power metal. With the possible exception of their demo album *Goatlord*, it's my humble opinion that musically Darkthrone have never put a foot wrong and that they are the greatest black metal band of all time.

The year 1992 saw the release of a self-titled album by the controversial band Burzum. If you thought being a fan of Metallica was difficult, allow me to introduce you to the moral quagmire that is 'enjoying the music of an actual murderer'. The solo project of Count Grishnakh, aka Varg Vikernes is a clusterfuck of contradictions.

After recording four impeccable, raw, atmospheric black metal albums in the early nineties, Varg let himself down and he let the school down by being a big old racist and murdering Euronymous. And it really is a shame, because his music was so, SO good.

The competition within the Norwegian black metal scene that led to his increasingly extreme activity also led to an incredible burst of creativity. Obsessed with live acting role play (or LARPing) and the writings of J. R. R. Tolkien, Vikernes was desperate to be accepted, though he attempted this through the most unacceptable behaviour. His pre-prison output is essential listening for any black metal fan: incredibly atmospheric, genuinely inventive and original. He produced an astonishing amount of high-quality material in an incredibly short space of time. Taking advantage of being a solo artist he recorded four albums in a period of fifteen months. Ranging between furious thrashing black metal and atmospheric, ambient stuff, it evokes a frozen landscape and a mythical medieval world. Like *Game of Thrones* without all the sexism.

In 1992, a series of churches were torched in Norway. It didn't take long for the Norwegian black metal circle to reveal its involvement. The attacks were part of the competition for status and for outdoing each other, so naturally credit had to be claimed.

The main stated reason for the burnings was that the churches were built on old pagan sites. This is a common phenomenon – St Paul's Cathedral in London is believed by some to be built on the site of a Roman temple to Diana, St Paul being the symbol of opposition to the Diana cult due to his remonstrations against it in the Bible.[1] Christianity's growth in Europe was facilitated by

1. This is disputed, naturally, but fuck it. It's not like I'm an actual historian. I did film studies. At a university that doesn't even exist any more.

its absorbing local religions, Borg-like. The violent overthrow of indigenous beliefs and practices was much less effective than basically going, 'Right, we can accommodate your winter feast as long as you pretend it's Jesus' birthday party. Okay?'

The second important factor in the Norwegian church arsons is that the churches in Norway are made out of wood.[1] Which is just asking for trouble. What is this, a fucking fairy tale?[2]

The effect of the church arsons was that all the Christians in Norway realised they had been wrong all along and abandoned their beliefs under the weight of the opinions of some lonely teenagers. They packed up the churches and Bibles and put them away for ever. And nobody was Christian ever again.

I joke, of course; every church grew stronger. Funds were raised to rebuild, attendance sky-rocketed and Christianity flourished. But so did black metal. The church burnings became deeply symbolic: a lightning rod for worldwide anti-Christian sentiment. Erik Danielsson of Watain, the theist-satanic[3] Swedish black metal band, has a more darkly spiritual impression of the church burnings: 'the only Christianity they defeated was the last piece of Christianity within themselves'. Even more than the murders, church burning is the iconic symbol of Norwegian black metal and the second wave.

---

1. Attempted copycat church burnings in the UK were distinctly less successful, what with our churches being made out of stone. They mostly just led to slightly singed stonework and a prayer book looking a bit like a kid's pirate map.

2. 'And the big bad wolf did try to burn the church down. Which was an absolute breeze because in a breathtaking act of naivety, the church had been made from wood. Which is one of the easiest things to burn. Although less easy than the previous church, which had been made out of dry tinder and firelighters, and not forgetting the church before that, which was made out of matchheads and the strips that you get on the side of matchboxes to light the matches on.'

3. Satanists who believe in God. But they think he is a baddie.

Varg boasted of his involvement, even going to the extent of releasing an (excellent) EP called *Aske* (Norwegian for 'ashes'), which depicted a burnt church and came with a promotional lighter.

On 10 August 1993 Varg murdered Euronymous, stabbing him twenty-seven times and then disposing of his bloodstained clothes in a nearby lake. He was arrested shortly afterwards and served thirteen years of a twenty-one-year prison sentence. He has never expressed remorse for the killing of a man he considered his enemy. Prison seems to have removed his musical ability. He's not made a decent record since.

As if being an actual murderer wasn't bad enough, Varg also espouses radically right-wing, explicitly racist views. Happily, this ideology does not infect his music. A parallel can perhaps be drawn with the science fiction writer H. P. Lovecraft or comedian Jim Davidson. Except for the fact that Jim Davidson is shit.

If Vikernes were an intelligent, charismatic leader he might possibly pose a threat. Laughably he is anything but. Constantly being arrested by the French police under terrorism legislation, he is a laughing stock with a burnt-out musical talent and pathetic, paranoid conspiracy theories. He's written a book about his 'knowledge' of Norse mythology and it's fucking hilarious. Like a Ladybird book or some shit.

As a racist, Varg is not alone within black metal. The far right has always sought musical affiliations, previously targeting the skinhead, punk and folk subcultures. Black metal seems an obvious choice. It is elitist and misanthropic. It is belligerent and offensive and has no truck with diplomacy or undue kindness.

This fundamental misanthropy has allowed ultra right-wing and racist ideologies to proliferate. It's a stratum that cuts right through, starting with Emperor's early flirtation with Nazi iconography. Their use of it – in crude early photo collages – seems to be in the vein of early punks who did it as a simple act of rebellion to wind people up. Siouxsie Sioux of Siouxsie and the Banshees wore swastika armbands and Johnny Rotten of the Sex Pistols wore a T-shirt with a swastika alongside an upside-down cross and the word 'DESTROY'. It was an act of rebellion against the establishment, particularly the Second World War generation who still made up the majority of people holding real power at that point. Black metal sought to explore the darkness in humanity, and Nazism is an obvious place to find such darkness. As a band Emperor quickly moved beyond such basic shock tactics, though the guitarist Samoth later formed the death metal band Zyklon, named after the gas used in Nazi death camps.

Plenty of black metal bands have espoused far-right politics, from the outspoken anti-feminist and homophobic comments made by Cobalt's Phil McSorley about some bands with more openly leftist/progressive views (he got kicked out of the band over it) to the organisation of explicitly fascist meetings by bands like France's Peste Noire. And I'm really fucked off about Peste Noire cos I really fucking loved their music and now the borderline weirdness I dug about them has spilled over into being part of everything I hate.

Then there is a much more hardcore far-right element, dubbed National Socialist Black Metal or NSBM. Reassuringly most of it is laughably bad. There often seems to be a connection between far-right views and crap artistic output.

Much of the NSBM seems to come from Eastern Europe – indeed 'Eastern European' is a dog-whistle term used for NSBM bands. While some such as Poland's Drukh have a whiff of rumour about their politics, others such as Graveland are explicitly white supremacist. Even at shows in London people turn up with white power patches.

An unfortunate reaction to this tendency in black metal is an over-zealous and often plain stupid campaign by anti-fascist groups to shut down shows by bands they deem to have fascist leanings, often without really doing actual research into whether that's true or not. This has led to some cartoonish errors like the recent cancelling of a Marduk show in the US, Marduk often using the Nazis as subject material but in ideology being about as fascist as my nan. (Actually, that's probably a bad example.) They're not fascists anyway, any more than the guys who made the documentary *The Nazis: A Warning from History*.

Happily there is a glorious flipside to this bullshit – bands like Iskra and Panopticon who take an explicitly anarchist agenda and a crust punk influence and make music that is way better than the vast majority of NSBM. Panopticon in particular take themes like coal-mining unions and environmentalism and make fucking brilliant music.

Nazi ideology aside, the very worst thing about Varg is something that I have never seen in print. Sure, he's a murderer. Sure, he's a massive white supremacist. But there is something even worse. He wears T-shirts of bands he doesn't listen to.

Now, while I am happy to accuse someone of racism without necessarily backing it up, the accusation of wearing T-shirts of bands you don't listen to must not be made lightly. It is the very worst thing a metalhead can do.

Varg was pictured many, many times wearing a T-shirt with Venom's *Black Metal* album cover on it. Google it. They're easy to find. And yet he states on his website:

> Well, just like I have never listened to Venom I have never read 'The Satanic Bible' or any other books by La Vey.

. . . and:

> I mentioned Venom and the fact that I never listened to their music. In fact the only person in the whole Black

Metal scene in Norway who *had* listened to Venom was Aarseth [Euronymous]. Everybody else in the scene either hated Venom or didn't even know who they were [. . .] The fact that I wore a Venom T-shirt in court does not change this fact. I wore it because it had the text 'Black Metal', and for no other reasons. – from Varg's own website

What a twat.

So the big question, Andrew, is how can you justify listening to the music of a white supremacist murderer? The short answer is, 'With a growing unease.' I don't place much value on the politics of the musicians I enjoy. My personal political views are represented by almost no good bands. If I only listened to bands whose politics I agreed with I'd be stuck with only Panopticon, Catharsis and all the anarcho-crust bands. Which is limiting. A lot of metal musicians have conservative politics. Bruce Dickinson is a Tory. James Hetfield is a gun nut. Slayer seem to think that More Must be Done by a Stronger Government, if the song 'Dittohead' is anything to go by. If Burzum were political musically it'd be a different matter. Happily, the music made by Burzum is apolitical. My advice is, find a way of listening to it without giving him any money. I am obviously not advocating anything illegal. (Although that would be the simplest way.)

Norway continued to produce amazing bands. Gorgoroth, Satyricon, Enslaved, Thorns and the memetastic Immortal.

Immortal have become the most iconic Norwegian black metal band. They used corpse-paint that made them look like badgers and did a weird crab-walking thing. Their video for 'The Call of the Wintermoon' is unintentionally hilarious – shot in broad daylight it shows the band poncing about in a forest wearing capes and pointy wizards' hats and pulling strange faces.

Although it is genuinely impossible to take seriously, it typifies the approach of the Norwegians. It is deeply uncool. And thus totally removed from death metal's board-shorts and riffs, MTV-baiting style. Immortal have produced eight fantastic albums of mythical winter-blasted black metal and an offshoot in the solo project Abbath.

February 1994 saw debut albums by two of the most successful acts to emerge from black metal. Cradle of Filth's *The Principle of Evil Made Flesh* and Emperor's *In the Nightside Eclipse* both have considerably higher production values than the raw black metal produced by Darkthrone, Burzum and Immortal. Both records utilise keyboards and samples. Later to be described as 'symphonic black metal', the style is considerably less alienating and more reminiscent of goth.

There's something distinctly different about the approach to black metal made by the UK's own Cradle of Filth. Eschewing cult violence in favour of a more romantic, gothic style and very much steeped in the sort of sense of their own ridiculousness that underpinned Venom, Cradle went their own way. Ultimately they became something of a pantomime dame in the black metal scene, but they nevertheless sold a shit-load of records and drew a lot of people into extreme music.

They're derided now, as they have somewhat lost their way musically, but *The Principle of Evil Made Flesh* is totally mint. As well as the keyboards and samples there are female vocals among the punishing and raw and riff-tastic guitars, and it pushes the boundary of what black metal can be without breaking it. Cradle are possibly best known for their *Vestal Masturbation* T-shirt, which depicts a wanking nun on the front and the legendary slogan 'JESUS IS A CUNT' on the back. Several people have been arrested for wearing it. It's a design classic.

By the time of these releases the second wave of black metal was no longer a secretive, underground movement. The popular heavy metal magazine *Kerrang!* had run a feature on Burzum in March 1993 and the church burnings, murders, and subsequent arrests and convictions made the scene world-famous. The cat was out of the bag, much to the annoyance of the Norwegians. Very quickly the word spread and second-wave black metal bands sprang up all over the world.

Disparate bands from other countries began to coalesce into a worldwide scene. Marduk and Dissection from Sweden, Beherit from Finland, Rotting Christ from Greece, Sigh from Japan, and Samael from Switzerland were all competing with the Norwegians for brutality, atmosphere and originality. They were joined by a tidal wave of new bands who used the Norwegian template and built on it. Some with originality and some with none. Soon black metal overtook death metal as the biggest extreme metal scene in the world. This was never meant to happen. As Gaahl of Gorgoroth/Trelldom/Wardruna said:

'Black Metal was never meant to reach an audience.
    It was purely for our own satisfaction.'

10

Genre Inflation (Too Many Cooks, Too Many Cooks)

From the grass roots to MTV, heavy metal broadened out in the eighties and nineties. More bands fed into the system from the underground and more and heavier metal bands were featured in mainstream media. The DIY revolution that began with punk had an explosive effect on the number of bands playing heavy music. Without the need for label support for a band to get off the ground, the underground metal scene flourished, supported by the tape-trading network and DIY touring. This then became a feeding stream into the specialist heavy metal labels such as Earache, Roadrunner, Relapse, Nuclear Blast and Metal Blade, as well as the tiny independent labels who themselves specialised in more niche, heavy genres.

Meanwhile, social and economic changes were taking place that increased people's ability to form more bands. After the economic depression of the seventies, which continued to affect people in the first half of the eighties (the first UK Metallica tour with Exciter in 1984 was cancelled due to lack of sales; this was put down to people simply not having enough money) many households experienced an increase in disposable income. That trend continued until the banking crisis of 2008, which fucked everyone over except the bankers who did it in the first place and actually made money from it. Hence independent music venues

are shutting down while skyscrapers and corporate chains take
over. There is money, but metalheads aren't seeing it.

This combination of factors led to an absolute shit-ton of
bands and a sprawling diversification which makes for a very
messy narrative. The genre inflation that began in the mid-eighties,
spawning subsets of metal including thrash, death, black and
grindcore, has never stopped. The internet has added to this in
recent years with entire servers dedicated to hosting facile debates
about whether bands are or aren't a particular style, arguments
akin to medieval theologians debating the number of angels that
could fit on the head of a pin. Nonetheless, the distinct styles of
heavy metal that exist in the current era are diverse enough for
these categories to actually be useful.

A few genres don't fit neatly into a timeline the way black–
thrash–death–second-wave black metal all loosely progress from
one to the other. So here is a chapter where I will dig into a few of
the other areas of metal and stop you getting all uptight cos I didn't
mention them. Oh and cos they're important too. Yeah. That too.

Just as there is more than one way to skin a cat, there are many, many,
many ways to be heavy within heavy metal. Thrash and grindcore go
for speed. Death and black metal go for extreme, aggressive vocals.
Doom is heavy in its SOUL. (NB Doom the genre is not to be confused with the crust punk band Doom, the video game *Doom* or 'The
Doom Song' from the cartoon *Invader Zim*[1])

1. 'Doom doom doo doom doom, / doom doom do DOOM, / DOOOM
doom do-doom, / DOOM do-doom doom doooom, / doom doom dooom,
do-do-DOOOM! / (Three months later:) Doom doom doo doom doom, /
DOOMY-DOOMY-DOOM, / doom do do DOOM, / Do do DOOM, doomy-
doomy-doomy, / Doom doom doom THE END.'

Doom is like Black Sabbath on ketamine. (Which I'm sure Black Sabbath would have been if ketamine had been more of a thing in the seventies.) It followed directly on from Sabbath's influence, taking Tony Iommi's mainly slow, deliberate riffing and Ozzy's high, plaintive singing and then building from there. The British band Witchfinder General are arguably the first band to pick up Sabbath's sound and add more doom to it, releasing *Death Penalty* in 1982. American bands followed suit. Trouble from Aurora, Illinois,[1] built on Geezer Butler's Catholic influence and at one point were labelled 'white metal', which is fucking stupid. Their first album. *Psalm 9*, came out in 1984 and it is a thing of beauty. The Sabbath influence is obvious, but Trouble are prettier and more soulful than Sabbath. Saint Vitus released their self-titled debut the same year and Pentagram followed with *Relentless* soon after, forming an American doom holy trinity.

Later on in the US a mix of doom with hardcore punk led to 'sludge', particularly in Louisiana: Eyehategod, Crowbar and the supergroup Down all enjoyed success in the nineties with a doomy, bluesy guitar sound and harsh vocals. There was also a less-metal string of bands who emerged under the banner of 'desert rock', such as Kyuss.

Skipping back to the eighties, but moving our attention to Sweden, the enormously successful Candlemass were an influence not only on bands who directly followed their doom style, but also on the Swedish death metal explosion. Talking of their debut on the influential Swedish radio show *Rockbox*, Daniel Ekeroth says in his magnificent book *Swedish Death Metal*,

> At that precise moment a lot of us decided to start bands ourselves. I know I did. The legacy of extreme metal had

---

1. Excellent!

to be conserved. We all picked up our guitars and started
to mix the speed and energy of Metallica with the
heaviness of Candlemass.

That heaviness is of a very particular kind. That debut album,
1986's *Epicus Doomicus Metallicus*, has possibly the most Ronseal title
in all metal. It is epic, doomy and metallic and also it sounds like they
know Latin. Latin makes everything more doomy, right? Candlemass went on to great success and are still going, despite a couple of
breaks and a lot of line-up changes. Their second frontman, Messiah
Marcolin, joins a holy trinity of extreme hair frizz along with
Melvins' Buzz Osbourne and Napalm Death's Shane Embury.

A doom revival was sparked from an unlikely source. The
relentless speed and single-minded approach of grindcore seemed
to make its founders restless. After Carcass, Bill Steer turned his
back on metal and formed the blues-rock band Firebird. After
essentially writing the first half of Napalm Death's first album,
Scum, Justin Broadrick left and went esoteric and electronic with
Godflesh. More pertinent to this part of the narrative and a major
figure in the widespread increase in interest in doom was Napalm's
first long-term vocalist Lee Dorrian. He left in 1989 after disa-
greements about Napalm's direction and formed the doom metal
band Cathedral, releasing *The Forest of Equilibrium* to critical success (and no doubt some bafflement from Napalm Death fans).
Cathedral played the major-label game for a while, and have
since had a varied twenty-four-year career. Dorrian is also responsible for the record label Rise Above Records, which in 1991
released a doom metal compilation album, *Dark Passages*, which
further boosted interest in the style, particularly in the UK.[1]

1. He has also been extremely patient with me when I have talked at him at
length while drunk about bands he has no interest in.

Cathedral split up in 2013 and the members briefly formed the fucking amazing Celtic Frost-influenced Septic Tank.

For my money, Warning, from Essex, are the best doom band of the bunch. Their 2006 release *Watching from a Distance* contains possibly the most emotionally affecting song in all of heavy metal – the incomparable 'Bridges'.

The north of England produced three influential bands who crossed over from death metal to doom, and all later experimented with gothic influences.

The Peaceville Three, (so named because they were all on the label Peaceville and there were three of them), Paradise Lost (from Halifax), My Dying Bride (from Bradford) and Anathema (from Liverpool) all began really heavy and then went a bit flouncy. Anathema consist of three brothers, another two brothers and another dude. FRATERNAL! These bands clearly pine for their death metal roots, as Nick Holmes from Paradise Lost now fronts the death metal supergroup Bloodbath and the guitarist Gregor Mackintosh fronts the death metal supergroup Vallenfyre alongside Hamish Glencross from My Dying Bride.

If you were to, for comedy's sake, make out that the whole world fell into a strict binary of goth versus metal then you might, hypothetically,[1] find the whole genre of gothic metal a bit of a pain in the arse. Nonetheless, Cradle of Filth, Type O Negative, the Peaceville Three mentioned above, and a million different bands from Finland continue to be an inconvenient truth. Type O Negative began in 1989 after the break-up of Peter Steele's crossover thrash band Carnivore. Dripping with self-awareness and bone-dry irony, Type O managed to have their cake and eat it, ripping the piss out of goth culture while simultaneously becoming a key exponent of it. Their stand-out hit 'Black No. 1 (Little

---

1. For, say, a comedy show about the History of Heavy Metal, say.

Miss Scare All)' is a song about hair dye and has become a goth anthem.

Notable at this point are Marilyn Manson, whose break-through album, *Antichrist Superstar*, crossed over from goth into a form acceptable for a lot of metalheads, and Nine Inch Nails, whose extremely danceable industrial goth sound is ever-present in metal nightclubs. Even more on the borderline of the two are the most Teutonic band in the world: Rammstein, whose stage shows are the very best I have ever seen.

Gothic tendencies emerged elsewhere in metal. A trend appeared in the nineties of good-looking, classically trained women fronting gothic metal bands with dudes who look like music teachers and have very neat facial hair. Nicknamed 'beauty and the beast' metal and more often falling under the banner of 'symphonic metal', its greatest exponent are Nightwish from Finland, whose erstwhile[1] singer Tarja Turunen was a full-on actual opera singer. They fired her, though. By handing her a note at a gig. What a shower of dicks. The Dutch band Within Temptation are another in this mould, as are Italy's Lacuna Coil and Germany's Xandria, a group who get through vocalists like Spinal Tap got through drummers. This lot are essentially bands for people who like airbrushed pictures of angels and dragons. If you've ever wondered who buys those gothic candle holders you see in head shops, now you know.

Power metal began with the sounds of Judas Priest and Iron Maiden, combined with the lyrical approach of Ronnie James Dio, and then turned up the cheesiness to MAXIMUM. As a result it is really big in Germany, where they don't object to that sort of thing. German power metal bands include Helloween, the

1. I was fucking dying to get that word in this book somewhere. YESSSSS. (Fistbumps self.)

Queen-influenced Blind Guardian, and Edguy, who are not to be confused with Deadguy, the brutal American hardcore band. Sweden has produced HammerFall and Dragonland[1] who are not to be confused with DragonForce from Britain, who I once interviewed for TV not knowing the first thing about them. I've seen them three times since and I still don't really know anything about them. America has produced Iced Earth, the actually dead-good Manilla Road and Manowar, who maintain the rare accolade of being the single most po-faced band in all of metal. Signing their contract in blood and never knowingly covering their nipples, they are the most unwittingly homo-erotic thing I've ever seen. Their mantra 'Death to false metal' stands alongside Sarcófago's 'If you are a false, don't entry'. You get the impression Manowar maybe don't realise they're NOT living in *Conan the Barbarian*.

Talk of cheesiness leads me on to folk metal. The most unashamed of all the metal sub-genres. (Except maybe pirate metal. No explanation is needed for pirate metal.) A lot of my friends really like folk metal. But then a lot of my friends really like the *Hobbit* films. The two things are not unrelated. As you'd expect, folk metal combines traditional instruments with metal – often metal of the power variety – to varying degrees of success. Technically the peerless Panopticon, with his use of bluegrass, is a type of folk metal, but very far from what the genre name suggests to most people. To most people it's bands who wear fur and have violins and hurdy gurdies. It originated with Skyclad from the UK and was then taken up by a million bands from Finland. Amorphis, Finntroll, Korpiklaani, Moonsorrow, Ensiferum, Turisas. There are more metal bands per capita in Finland than in any other country. There is significant government funding of music

1. Who implore you to '*look to the sky / as the dragons fly by*'. I shit you not.

and possibly some sort of secret law where every household must produce at least one folk metal band or be thrown into the sea. It's all very jolly and upbeat, but not my bag. Which I must admit makes me feel the same way I do when I hang out with my hardcore gay friends: I'm almost annoyed I'm not into it because they seem to be having SO MUCH FUN.

11

Grunge and Groove: the Nineties

Tradition has it that punk was responsible for single-handedly killing off prog rock in the late seventies. It's a well rehearsed opinion. In reality, punk was too short-lived as an above-ground phenomenon to actually replace anything, and most prog bands of the seventies were in the process of fizzling out by the time punk really became a nationwide movement. A far bigger impact on rock music happened fifteen years later in the early nineties, and it was a much more positive change.

In 1990, as we entered the final decade of the twentieth century, hair metal seemed unassailable. It had dominated MTV ever since Mötley Crüe's *Shout at the Devil* and new bands such as Guns N' Roses continued to keep it at the top. Then a scene exploded in Seattle and overnight the make-up got put away and Warrant no longer had a market.

Grunge was a watershed. Practically instantaneously the atmosphere in popular music changed. The approach of the new movement seemed so natural, so down to earth it rendered glam ridiculous to the very audience who'd dug it. The scales had fallen from their eyes. The emperor was wearing no clothes. Glam was shit. *Now you've pointed it out, it seems obvious. We feel so stupid.*

Although its explosion and rise to ubiquity was swift, grunge didn't appear out of thin air. Far from being a reaction against the glam bullshit, it came about entirely of its own accord. During the period when the overground was dominated by the musical equivalent of Reaganite conspicuous consumption, with advert-like promo videos and shoulder pads and big hair and terrible songs about coke-fuelled nothing, a parallel universe existed where these values were turned on their head.

A direct line can be drawn from the explosion of grunge back to the underground hardcore punk scene of the early eighties. The likes of Nirvana, Soundgarden, Pearl Jam, and the Smashing Pumpkins all originated within a DIY music scene that had been previously set up by Black Flag and their peers. This was a healthy underground scene that employed the anti-commercial (or, if not anti-commercial, then it's-okay-to-not-be-particularly-commercially-successful) sense of the early-eighties punk scene, which by the middle of that decade had become violent and narrow-minded.

As with nearly all genres, most of American hardcore's pioneers and originators moved on from the seminal sounds they had made, to explore something new and different.[1] In their wake, derivative copyists policed a scene that had exactly the same kinds of rules it used to criticise. In addition to the potato-print bands indistinguishable from each other, audiences were increasingly made up of those attracted to punk's reputation for aggression.

As something of a reaction against this, bands began to reject certain aspects of punk's homogenised look and sound. Rites of Spring were an early example – growing up in the Washington DC hardcore scene they took hardcore's weight and fury and

1. Minor Threat's Ian McKaye formed Fugazi, one of the first bands to gain the post-hardcore label. They were a distinctly more arty, less aggressive band.

turned it in, making music that was introspective, sensitive and fragile, while still remaining heavy. Gradually this strain of hardcore developed into 'alternative rock' with the help of bands such as Hüsker Dü and the Minutemen, who were moving on from the restrictions of straight-ahead punk and experimenting with more melody, experimental sounds and influence from older music that had been rejected by punk. Grant Hart from Hüsker Dü summed up this attitude in the book *Our Band Could be Your Life*, saying, 'You know the whole deal with tearing down the old to make room for the new? Well, music isn't city planning.'

It was this growing alt-rock scene, still predominantly operating underneath the radar of the mainstream that branched off into the grunge movement with a coalescing of bands in Seattle, Washington State. (Not Washington DC. They're different places, 5,000 miles apart. But you're smart, you knew that, right?)

Two compilation albums provided coherence to a disparate set of bands. The first, 1985's *Deep Six*, featured Green River (members of whom would go on to form Pearl Jam), Melvins and Soundgarden. The following year saw the release of *Sub Pop 100*, by the label Sub Pop. Sub Pop was responsible for signing many of the bands central to grunge such as Mudhoney, Nirvana and Soundgarden and creating a localised scene. Much like Brian Slagel's Metal Blade, who'd given Metallica their first recording, the compilation grew out of a fanzine, and led to the forming of a full-blown label. Sub Pop's second compilation, 1988's *Sub Pop 200*, is the early grunge scene in microcosm, featuring Nirvana, Soundgarden, Mudhoney, Screaming Trees and Green River.

Geographically isolated from the usual touring routes, Seattle bands had a make-your-own-fun approach to music and developed a distinctive sound which mixed influences from punk and metal and classic seventies rock. In terms of look, grunge was distinctly anti-image,[1] stripped down and unadorned. After the artificiality of glam, grunge seemed *real*. Cheap thrift-store clothes and pawn-shop guitars replaced the make-up, success-jackets[2] and huge stage sets. While glam valued artifice and showboating, grunge valued authenticity above all else.[3]

The transformation of grunge from self-sufficient local scene with a few successful bands to landscape-altering phenomenon was sparked in 1991 by the release of Nirvana's breakthrough record, *Nevermind*, and its lead single, 'Smells Like Teen Spirit', which were impossible to escape in the year following their release. Combined with the constant airplay of Metallica's *Black Album* singles, heavy guitar-based music was mainstream in a way it had never been before.

Nirvana were the vanguard, and in their wake 'alternative rock' swept like a tidal wave over the musical landscape: Soundgarden, Smashing Pumpkins, Pearl Jam, Jane's Addiction, Red Hot Chili Peppers, Mudhoney.

The contrast between the lyrical approach that this new wave of alt-rock bands took and that of the glam pricks could not be more stark. Hubris and ego were replaced with introspection and vulnerability.

The ultimate extension of this overthrow of the machismo of glam metal was the Riot Grrrl movement. Closely associated with

1. Which can be seen from its distinctive image . . . In so many cases through this story, bands who claim to have no image often are more self-conscious about what they wear than those who DO have an image. At least images can be changed and shedded entirely.

2. The brilliant music journalist Simon Price coined the term 'success-jacket'. It refers to the long jackets guitarists in big bands wear just after they've made it. Now you've heard the phrase you'll see them everywhere.

3. And if you can fake that, you've got it made (to paraphrase Sam Goldwyn, as told by Bob Monkhouse).

grunge, but with both feet planted firmly in an explicitly punk context, Riot Grrrl was a feminist backlash against the male-dominated scene and a timely explosion of awareness of the role of women in the underground music scene. The movement started with a coalescing of fanzine writers, including Alison Wolf and Molly Neuman, who wrote *Girl Germs* and later formed the band Bratmobile, and Kathleen Hanna, Tobi Vail and Kathi Wilcox, who wrote *Bikini Kill* and formed a band of the same name. Together these women produced the fanzine *Riot Grrrl*, which was a lightning rod for a growing feminist current within underground American punk. Many other bands joined the movement and the influence was felt worldwide, leading to an increased visibility of women in punk and rock bands and an increased awareness among men around feminist issues.

Kurt Cobain punctuated the end of grunge by committing suicide with a shotgun, almost exactly three years after Dead from Mayhem had done the same. And much like Euronymous, Courtney Love is rumoured to have kept a bit of his skull. Rumours that Dave Grohl took pictures of Cobain's corpse are entirely made up.[1]

The alt-rock predominance found its most tangible expression in Lollapalooza, a festival originated by Perry Farrell of Jane's Addiction. The festival was such an avatar of alt-rock that Metallica's headlining it was taken as the final nail in their coffin – evidence they had sold out to the alt-rock trend.

I dug Nirvana for a while. They were an important catalyst in me getting into heavier music and ultimately into metal. But as an adult . . . personally, I always feel like I want to like grunge more than I do. These bands – Soundgarden, Stone Temple Pilots, Alice

1. By me.

in Chains, Pearl Jam, even Nirvana – make sounds that do some of the right things for me. But they fall short. In a similar way genre-definition-wise to proto-metal, they are NOT heavy metal.

All except one band. In the middle of this scene, like a pearl in an oyster, sit Melvins. More influential on the metal scene than any other Seattle band, and standing distinctly apart from grunge, Melvins combined punk with Black Sabbath and brought a heaviness to the American independent music scene like no other. Not only were they a key part of what fuelled Seattle's grunge explosion: they were a key influence on doom, hardcore, post-metal and stoner rock. Well done, lads.

Grunge totally destroyed glam metal, and a brief scene cropped up that made mainstream metal heavy once more. And this, dear reader, is where I got involved.

Looking back on it, the patterns were there. All paths lead to heavy metal. I grew up with two musical influences, the Beatles and BBC Radio 2. And sometimes the Beatles ON Radio 2. My dad is a big Beatles fan. I have heard *Sgt. Pepper's* a thousand times. An early memory of musical extremity was my dad borrowing a Beatles LP from Wallington Public Library and turning it up so loud he dislodged a load of ornaments from the shelf the speakers were on.

Radio 2 was always on in the background, so I got a comprehensive education in fifties rock and roll, sixties rock music, seventies glam, Motown, Stax . . . you name it, it went in my ears.

Then my older brother David brought a tape copy of Queen's *Greatest Hits* back from a scout camp and my life took a turn for the better. I have a distinct memory of us singing 'Bohemian Rhapsody' in the kitchen late at night – my part was the 'let him go!' bit. I recorded *Queen Live at Wembley* off the telly and watched it over and over and over again, copying Freddie's moves, air-guitaring to Brian May and dreaming of being in my own band. The heavier parts made me thrill. Guitar-based rock music was imprinted on my soul.

Then my older, older brother Steven got into Public Enemy and I followed suit. At the age of nine I was wearing the clothes my mum had picked from Marks & Spencer with a sideways Public Enemy baseball cap. I looked like a dick. Nothing has changed. The video for 'Bring the Noise' with Anthrax became my favourite thing.

Then *Wayne's World* came out and I discovered Jimi Hendrix. Still my favourite recording artist of all time. No one speaks to me the way Jimi does. The other effect of *Wayne's World* was more direct: I wanted to be a metalhead. I wanted to have long hair and go to the Gasworks and play electric guitar and headbang.

Then the descent began – Nirvana for a month or so, then Metallica. Then Slayer, then Deicide and Cannibal Corpse, Sepultura, Machine Head, Pantera. Then Fear Factory – my first gig, December 1995. I was now intractably a metalhead.

The early nineties were a good time to get into extreme metal. There were loads of on-ramps. In the underground, metal was moving into the post-thrash era. Death metal was coming to the end of its dominance and the black metal movement was on the rise. This period saw bands taking extreme metal influences and mashing them together to make what became a surprisingly marketable post-thrash sound. At the time, we simply called it 'extreme metal'. And this was the point at which I joined in the fun. And I've never been the same since. Partly because of all the injuries . . .

Mosh pits are fucking stupid. They are also fucking brilliant. Venues have attempted to stamp them out. Corporate festivals make bands sign contracts stating they will not instigate them (or anything at all that might cause injury . . .). But despite the bruises, broken teeth and busted phones, they remain a key part of the culture of heavy metal – the most direct way of reciprocating the energy a band is putting out on stage.

I distinctly remember the time my mate Charlie patiently explained to me what a mosh pit was. It was in my fourth-year art class at school. He had been to a few metal gigs, while I remained a virgin.[1] I was fascinated by the stories I'd heard about what happened at shows, and his lecture came complete with an illustrative diagram.

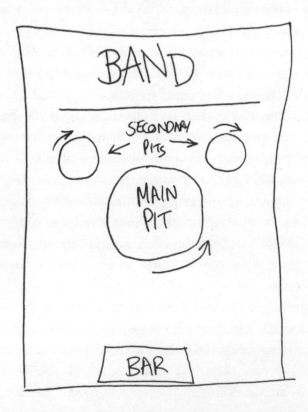

1. I mean, technically we were both virgins. And due to the fact that we went to an all-boys school, would remain so for some time. But we have both TOTALLY had sex with people since then. Not with each other though. Despite my best attempts.

'That's the stage, with the band on it,' he told me as he drew a rectangle, 'here's the crowd . . . and *here* and *here* you get the mosh pits.' He drew big circles.

'Mosh pits? What are mosh pits?'

'Basically . . .' He considered carefully. ' . . . basically, sort of fighting.'

Moshing isn't fighting, of course, although to the untrained eye it can look like it. Moshing is a controlled outlet for aggression and energy. All rock music is essentially dance music. Early rock and roll was good for actual dancing – the sort of swing dancing that is popular again among hipsters and women who do burlesque.

The screaming response of women watching the Beatles is a good example of a pure energy outlet. They didn't know how to react to the music, so they just screamed.[1]

By the late 1960s, once all the screaming at the Beatles had stopped, responses to live rock music seemed more introverted. Possibly due to the drugs. Audiences danced within their own space, in a sort of confined reverie.

With the arrival of extreme metal in the early 1980s, it was necessary to open up the physical response to the music to something new. The increased speed and violence of thrash and death metal meant that nothing short of full-contact slam-dancing would suffice.

As with a great deal of 1980s metal culture, we stole the mosh from punk. The hardcore punk scene had invented slam-dancing: Pete Dee from crossover thrash band Kremated tells me, 'Hardcore folklore says the word "mosh" was accidentally christened by HR from Bad Brains and was the result of someone mishearing him talking about either "crowd dem mash it up" in relation to

---

1. They also 'wet themselves' apparently.

the pits at BB shows, or alternatively "they look like they mashin' grapes" and the word "mosh" stuck.'

Moshing styles vary, from the circle pit, which is a mass circular motion, a bit like going down a plughole (they always seem to go anti-clockwise, although I hear they go round the other way in Australia . . .) to the more punk rock slam-dancing, in which bodies crash into each other like dodgems, to the fists and lost-teeth free-for-all you get when people don't know what the fuck they're doing.

Mosh pits can be simultaneously intimidating and totally hilarious displays of dumb machismo. There is an etiquette in which those who fall over are helped up, no one actually tries to hurt anybody and one massive topless gym-bunny must always be present. For some reason. These rules get ignored at times, of course. People sometimes fail to help others up, sometimes people go in too aggressive, but there is always a massive topless gym-bunny . . .

And then there's the kung-fu-style pits that happen at hardcore gigs, which are the single most ludicrous thing in all of heavy music.

The wall of death is a variant on the mosh pit. Many different bands claim to have invented it, though the most likely candidate is Sick of It All, the veteran New York hardcore punk band. More than any mosh variant, the wall of death involves significant direction from the band on stage. The audience is divided into two opposing teams, facing each other over a gap which runs down the middle of the room. On the band's signal, the teams run at each other and commence moshing. Imagine *Braveheart* with vest tops and crew-cuts.

I have made several physical sacrifices to mosh pits over the years. My two upper front teeth were snapped in two just after I left a pit that was getting too intense for me. I took a step back, then immediately took a blow to the face and screamed as half of one tooth was gone, and half of another was dangling from the nerves. (The show was Sub-Zero and I stayed to watch Rykers, the headline band.)

Stage-diving is launching oneself from the stage into the audience. Like a ball pool. I have landed on my head more than once, and there was that one time at a Fear Factory/Biohazard Donington warm-up show when my mate John dived off the stage, parted the audience like the Red Sea, landed on his back and, when he stood up, couldn't see. Brilliant!

One wreckless stage-diving incident has caused a significant step-up in venues' health-and-safety policies. In 2013 the 'slam poet' and 'rapper' George Watsky threw himself off a 35-feet-high lighting rig onto the fragile, snappable bodies of the audience below him, breaking one woman's arm and unfortunately not killing his dickhead self. Ever since this literal pratfall, bands (and comedians, believe it or not) have had to fill in forms before gigs stating that we won't be arseholes and cause harm to our audiences.

While we nicked moshing and stage-diving from our snotty younger brother, headbanging is purely ours. No other dance move quite expresses the beat of heavy metal like the headbang. It comes entirely naturally. It's the most organic, natural way to dance to music with such an insistent beat.

For beginners it causes headaches and disorientation. Inspired by the 'Bohemian Rhapsody' bit in *Wayne's World*, I made my first attempt in my bedroom – the laboratory in which I conducted most of my early experiments in being a metalhead. It was during my brief Nirvana phase *c*.1992.[1] I put on *Nevermind* and

1. Don't worry, I grew out of Nirvana as soon as I got into Slayer. I have yet to grow out of Slayer.

proceeded to throw my head about with a total lack of grace, skill
or concern for my own personal safety . . . What could POSSI-
BLY go wrong? Half an hour later I had a splitting headache, and
my neck was completely fucked. Much to the amusement of my
family I had to eat dinner with one hand, the other propping
my head up, doing the work of my now useless neck. And my
brother asked for his CD back. I didn't stop there, and the legacy of the subsequent twenty-plus years of headbanging is a
neck so disproportionately thick that I cannot buy formal shirts
that fit me.[1] I still practise at home, in order to show off on stage
while playing with my band. It's important to keep your hand
in – like an athlete. The consequences of being out of practice
will forever haunt me. When I was courting[2] my wife[3] I took her
to a metal club night at the Camden Underworld. 'Painkiller' by
Judas Priest came on and I proceeded to headbang to it. Anyone who's ever attempted this will know two things: number
one, it's a really good song to headbang to – it has exactly the
right tempo; two – it's really fucking long. It JUST. KEEPS.
GOING. Being out of practice, I began to struggle but really
didn't want to wimp out in front of this incredibly hot metalhead.
My brain had other ideas. Totally fucked from being sloshed
around inside my skull, it began to make the world spin about me
like I was on a fairground ride. To my perception I remained
standing entirely upright as the floor lurched up to meet me. I

1. Thick neck, skinny body. But, then, formal shirts aren't particularly metal.
Unless they're made out of metal. And then they'd be armour. And that's a
different shop.

2. Yes. Courting. I also say 'disco', 'O-Levels' and 'street-cred'.

3. Yes. Wife. I tricked a woman into finding me attractive and legalised the
situation before she could change her mind. We fuck other people though.
We're not idiots.

cracked my head and needed a sit down. Still. I married her. SO
I WIN!

The risk of a disorientated collapse into a concrete floor is one
of the less publicised side-effects of headbanging. Medical prac-
titioners and concerned mothers have for a long time strongly
advised against the whole thing. The long-term effects are just
starting to emerge. For the professional metal musician, headbanging night after night for years on end can cause severe spinal
problems. Tom Araya from Slayer used to headbang between
vocal lines for their entire set. He had a distinctive style, nodding
left, then right, then left, swinging his arse-length hair in a way
that looked really fucking cool. In 2010 he had surgery in order
to replace a spinal disc which he'd managed to grind down over
many years. It's a weird sight now to see him remain static
throughout their shows. For Philip Anselmo of Pantera, the spinal problems caused by headbanging ultimately led to the
break-up of his band. Around 1994 he began experiencing
excruciating back pain. He was told he'd need surgery which
would involve several months in recovery. Being something of a
macho dickhead he decided to forgo the surgery and self-medicate
with painkillers and a back brace. As normal prescription medi-
cation stopped covering the agony, he turned to heroin. In an
entirely unforeseen turn of events, he discovered that heroin is
rather moreish and became massively addicted, overdosing in
1996 and being pronounced clinically dead for five minutes.[1]
The personality change his addiction caused led to Pantera splitting up and then him derailing multiple times in one of the most
disappointing declines ever seen within heavy metal. And all
because of headbanging.

At their peak, Pantera were a perfect band. But they certainly

1. Whether these five minutes were spent alone, I cannot ascertain.

didn't start that way. Pantera managed to pull off an incredible trick. They used their major label debut to effectively make a fresh start, disassociating themselves from their back catalogue, essentially tricking everyone into thinking that was their first record. Most of us who loved them at their peak were unaware of their past. And this was a canny decision, because the major-label Pantera was a muscular, aggressive, testosterone-fuelled post-thrash behemoth. But, before then, they were a glam metal band. And they fucking sucked.

The band was formed by two brothers, Vinnie Paul and Darrell Abbott (Darrell was known originally as 'Diamond' Darrell and later as 'Dimebag'), and was filled out by the time of their first record by bassist Rex Brown ('Rex Rocker') and vocalist Terry Glaze (improbably – his real name!). Although head and shoulders above anything Mötley Crüe or Poison ever recorded, Pantera nonetheless released three albums that can be categorised as 'Fully Shit'. The first, *Metal Magic*, has possibly the most ludicrous cover I have ever seen in my life. A weird airbrushed man/ lion (or is it a panther?) holding a sword. Well, it's sort of a sword. It's hard to tell. I don't think the artist had ever seen a sword. The album was produced by their dad and released on their own Metal Magic label. The sound is okay for a self-recorded/self-released label, although the cymbals sound like they're from a kid's drum kit. Despite its limitations, the record is musically accomplished and ambitious. But it still sucks.

The next two albums see them moving slowly towards the sound that made them famous. They recorded a video for the track 'All Over Tonight', which showcases, among other things, their incredibly lovely hair. The cover for *Projects in the Jungle* manages to be even worse than the previous one. It looks like something I'd have drawn for my art GCSE.

By album four they had employed vocalist Philip Anselmo as part of a search for a heavier sound. His vocals are much more in the vein of Rob Halford, and the album marks a transition from glam into something I personally consider true metal.

Then they signed to a major label, overhauled their image and got huge. *Cowboys From Hell* still retains some of the Judas Priest influence but is way more muscular and has a simplistic, grooving riff style. This led to a genre title that never really caught on in the UK – groove metal. I find it an uncomfortable fit, possibly because of the embarrassing dad association with the word 'groovy'. It makes my teeth itch. (Worse, however, is the what-the-fuck term 'aggro metal', which I had literally never come across before researching this book, and the vomit-inducing 'sports metal', which can just go and suck on an exhaust pipe.)

Pantera then did something that almost no mainstream heavy metal band has ever done: they got significantly heavier with each record.

The cover of *A Vulgar Display of Power* depicts a man being punched in the face. It does what it says on the tin. *Far Beyond Driven* is a record of incredible focus. As Phil says in their home video, 'We want the next record to be . . . extreme. Not the band! We want people to say, "What . . . is wrong . . . with them."' By this time Phil was talking a great deal about listening to death metal and black metal and that fury was creeping into his vocals.

By the time of *The Great Southern Trendkill* internal problems were interfering with the operation of the band. Nonetheless, I believe it to be their best. Wildly ambitious, sprawling, furious and beautiful, it's Pantera at their most brilliant. Tragically by this point Phil was estranged from the rest of the band, self-medicating his back problem through heroin. He recorded his vocals in New Orleans, separately from the rest of the band, who recorded in Dallas, Texas. His heroin problem led him to bizarre onstage outbursts and aggressive behaviour. On 13 July 1996 he overdosed and had that whole 'dying for five minutes' affair after a show in Texas, before being resuscitated.

The next record sucked balls. *Reinventing the Steel* is a weird regression to their less ambitious roots and marks a decline that ended in an eventual split. Phil's side-projects were cited as evidence of his lack of commitment to the band. The members fought openly in the metal press. It was a dark time.

The Abbott brothers formed Damageplan, releasing their debut record in February 2004. In December that year Dimebag was shot dead while playing on stage with Damageplan. His twenty-five-year-old murderer, Nathan Gale, was reportedly suffering from schizophrenia. He also shot dead three others and injured two more before being killed by police.

Among the many heroes we have lost over the years (Cliff Burton, Ronnie James Dio, Jeff Hanneman), Dimebag felt the most like one of us. Almost like a friend. Dime was hilarious. It's funny how often descriptions of people who are dead include the phrase 'full of life', but it seems really appropriate here. Dime was larger than life. He seemed kind and generous with his time and I felt like had we met we might have got on. Part of Pantera's legacy is a series of home videos which I watched endlessly with my mates as a teenager. It formed a large part of our interaction with the band and a big reason for our affection.

Now, I am a big fan of Pantera and of various other things that Philip Anselmo has done. Growing up he was a musical hero and, more than that, something of a role model. It was to my enormous shock and lasting disappointment that this dude let himself down tragically on stage at a Dimebag memorial show in January 2016.

The video is stark. A very drunk, shaven-headed Phil sieg-heiling the audience and screaming 'White power'. Now, I am a comedian, and I have a very dark, fucked-up sense of humour. I love a sick joke, me. Anything that pricks my liberal-lefty sensibility with genuine cleverness really makes me laugh. But I can't see the context for this whatsoever. A video blog by Machine Head's Robb Flynn states the opinion that Phil has always been a racist and a bully. I hear from a close source whom I genuinely trust that Phil is 'absolutely, categorically not racist', and I want to believe it. I want to believe that he was dicking about being un-PC and was just so drunk that he didn't have the capacity to recognise the consequences of his actions – mainly on anyone who's not white, but also on his own career and on that of the musicians he plays with. I just don't know. The tricky part of negotiating this is that unlike, say, Burzum, Philip Anselmo's personality is a significant part of why I dug his bands. His lyrics are personal. I felt a personal connection to him. And so this makes it much harder to enjoy his music.

By far and away my favourite band of the mid-nineties were Sepultura.[1] This period saw them experimenting with non-metal influences to incredible effect. *Chaos AD* takes influence from industrial, crust punk and hardcore, as well as the more simplistic riffing of bands such as Pantera.

The result was complex, textured records that embraced thrash, death, doom, hardcore and industrial with a breathtaking virtuosity. Andreas Kisser's blazing discordant solos are even more fucked-up than Slayer. Their lyrical content and imagery moved them away from the fantasist territory of death metal into

---

1. My first tattoo is artwork from their 1993 release *Chaos AD*. Its dense, squiggly lines were a challenge for the tattooist, who on my next visit had started wearing glasses . . .

real-world problems: politics, rioting, the chaos of the modern third world. It was a statement of intent and a declaration of who Sepultura were, and where they came from. The album inlay plugs a charity working to stamp out 'illegal torture in Brasil'. Max Cavalera's vocals are furious, aggressive, totally crushing. The stand-out track is the acoustic-guitar- and drum-based instrumental 'Kaiowas'. Managing to be heavy without distortion, it's an astonishing song.

The next album was another left-field turn. *Roots* turned their focus from the urban blight of Brazil's slums to its rainforest. Taking some influences from the burgeoning nu-metal movement, including the use of Korn's producer, Ross Robinson, *Roots* is a considerably more organic-sounding record. They used analogue equipment and dramatic downtunings. It is slower and more inveigling.

Following on from *Chaos AD*'s instrumental 'Kaiowas' are 'Jasco', a simple classical guitar interlude, and the incredible 'Itsari', which is a field recording of Sepultura playing with an Amazonian tribe, building on their chants with drums and acoustic guitars. The song 'Rattamahatta' climbed to number seventeen in the UK singles chart, an incredible achievement given its experimental heaviness and the fact that the lyrics are all in Portuguese!

On 16 December 1996, Sepultura played London's Brixton Academy. I was there. It remains one of the greatest gigs I have ever seen. The set-list was impeccable. I wore no coat and all six of my Sepultura T-shirts, peeling them off one by one as the venue heated up.

There's something special about your first car, your first kiss, your first fuck. Americans in films seem to combine all three. I still can't drive, my first kiss ended up breaking my heart on my eighteenth birthday and my first fuck lives somewhere in east London.

My first gig, however, was Fear Factory. December 1995 at the London Astoria. Don't look for it, it's not there any more. I wore my Jimi Hendrix T-shirt because I didn't yet have any metal band shirts. I drank a beer and moshed and was sick.

Fear Factory combined death metal with an industrial edge and wrote songs about a dystopian future largely influenced by *Terminator 2*. Their breakthrough record, *Demanufacture*, is a slick, polished affair with an incredibly tight production. Almost as if TERMINATORS HAD MADE IT.

They couldn't be more nineties if they tried. Frontman Burton C. Bell even had tribal tattoos and arms covered in friendship bracelets. Bell was an early exponent of a bipolar vocal style, combining death metal growls with a hyper-clean singing which is highly effective on their records but came to dominate, some say plague, metal production styles later in that decade.

Subsequent albums saw them somewhat boxed in by their own concept and failing to build on the progressive element of *Demanufacture*. At one stage it looked like they would be huge, but they never quite broke through. In December 2015 they played *Demanufacture* in full to mark its twentieth anniversary and, I like to think, my twentieth anniversary of going to metal shows. Thanks, guys. Appreciate it.

Music journalists are always looking for the next big thing. In metal, that is known as the 'new Metallica'. At one stage it looked certain that Bay Area post-thrash band Machine 'Fucking' Head were going to go stratospheric and break out into the mainstream. Sadly they took an inadvisable change in direction and it never happened.

Stemming from a straightforward thrash metal background, Oakland, California's Machine Head had an enormous impact on the European metal scene with their debut album, *Burn My Eyes*. Machine seemed to signal a new era in heavy metal, *Guitarist* magazine commenting, 'gone is the patchouli and hair parted permanently dead centre. In its place are the most amazing braids and tattoos. Machine Head are truly cred.' Machine Head's ascent was dizzying. After an acclaimed tour with Slayer they played every European festival going, then followed up with their own headline tour. The timing was just right. MH cleaned up. It looked like they'd be the next arena-filling metal band.

The ascent of bands like Machine Head, Pantera and Sepultura heralded a brief period for the heavy metal mainstream, in the wake of the collapse of glam and before the torrent of effluent that was nu-metal. Bands with the bite of the extreme metal underground were conquering the world. But as the millennium drew near it all started going horribly wrong . . .

12

In the Late Nineties Every Band I Loved Went Shit

Anyone who had accused Metallica of selling out when they introduced actual dynamics in their songs on *Ride the Lightning* was getting massively ahead of themselves. In the 1990s Metallica changed beyond recognition. And that happened to be when I got on board.

Being a Metallica fan is like following a shit third-division football team.[1] After they've lost their star striker. And been relegated. And had a massive racism scandal.[2]

I am unashamed. I have loved Metallica since 1994; three years after they produced their last truly great record. I first saw them live in 1996 and have stuck with them through the ups and the many, many downs of the last two-thirds of their career. They are a hard band to justify to the unconverted. Partly this is a symptom of their success. Any artist with Metallica's level of fame will attract a large and very vocal horde of detractors. But there is something more to the antipathy that they draw, partly because

---

1. Without the feeling that you're championing an underdog. And without the affordable tickets to go and watch them. Actually, the more I think about it, the less this analogy works.

2. . . . and their ground burnt down and then you found out that it had been made out of children's bones. And asbestos. By slaves.

of the nature of heavy metal culture itself and partly because of the personalities involved. And their drummer.[1]

Metalheads like to feel a sense of ownership of the bands they follow. We often define ourselves against the mainstream and so when one of *our* bands crosses over into genuine commercial success it can feel like we have lost something that belonged to us.[2] Part of the enjoyment of metal is liking stuff that other people don't know about. Immature as it might be, there's real pleasure to be had in the mild feeling of superiority attained when listening to obscure bands. Elitism is fun, kids.

Metallica grew up in the extreme metal underground. Their early success, even before their first album was released, was due to the rabid tape-traders who made copies of their demo and sent them out to their network of metal enthusiasts. They made a style of music that was bold and new and seemingly totally lacking in commercial viability. It was popular exactly because of its extremity, the opposite of the polished pop that was being produced for mass consumption, and the opposite of the fakery and conspicuous wealth that hair metal aspired to. It was thrashing music for true headbangers.

After continuing along in this vein, developing thrash into something more complex and musically interesting throughout the eighties, they took a bold decision.

1. SIT DOWN, LARS!

2. A recent personal example is the Californian powerviolence band Nails. I got their first record pretty soon after it came out and was blown away by its power. It reminded me of a German band called Acme that I used to listen to back in the nineties. I managed to see their first London show and was one of only two people actively enjoying their set. It gave me a wonderful feeling of discovery. Like I knew a secret. Last week (as I write this) they were featured in the fucking *Guardian* promoting their third record. That ship has sailed.

They abandoned thrash, employed Mötley Crüe's producer and made an FM radio-friendly hard rock album. The self-titled *Metallica* came to be known as *The Black Album* due to its Spinal Tap-like all-black cover. It was a radical departure from the breakneck speed of their previous output. But although they were simplifying the songs, the recording process became way more involved. Recording *The Black Album* took eight months and cost one million dollars.

'They had broken through to one level, but they still weren't on mainstream radio,' says the producer Bob Rock, talking to *Music Radar*. 'When they came to me, they were ready to make that leap to the big, big leagues. A lot of people think that I changed the band. I didn't. In their heads, they were already changed when I met them.'

The video for 'One' had exposed Metallica to a much wider audience and their own arena tours followed. But touring . . . *And Justice for All*, the band noticed the live audience were disengaging at the complex arrangements and extra-long songs and they made the decision to make their next record stripped down and straightforward. They were going to simplify their approach to songwriting. Sort of.

'We really felt that there was something specific we wanted to do, which was to sit down and try and write . . . simple songs,' says Lars in the *Classic Albums* documentary on *Metallica*.

The opening track and lead single, 'Enter Sandman', is a straightforward rocker. Its clean intro and hooky riffs made it a huge international success. It's a heavy tune compared to what mainly gets played on the radio, but the edges are rounded off with a slick production. There are some hints of their former heaviness elsewhere on the album – 'Through the Never' is almost thrash (although it has the worst lyrics of any of their songs up until that point . . .'), 'Sad But True' is genuinely heavy,[2] but in a slow, powerful, grooving way . . .

But then there's 'Nothing Else Matters' – an actual ballad. A fucking LOVE SONG. Hetfield had written the tune with no intention of letting the other guys hear it. But once it was accepted as being a fitting diversion on the record, James committed to it being something of a departure from their usual influences. Any big fan of Led Zeppelin or even Judas Priest would admit that heavy metal certainly has space for ballads, but this quote from Bob Rock suggests their eyes were not on their metal forebears when they stuck it on the album:

> James was very enamored with Chris Isaak's song 'Wicked Game'.

Right. Chris Isaak. Not Venom, then.

The gamble paid off. Metallica sold 16 million copies of *The Black Album* in the USA alone.[3] It made them millionaires. It also lost them a large swathe of their original fanbase, who were disgusted at the change in direction. Many pointed to the lack of Cliff Burton's direction, some blamed Bob Rock (to the extent that Rock received death threats from people taking their love of old Metallica a little too far).

But the album also won them a legion of new fans. For every grumpy old-school Metallifan they lost, they gained a

---

1. 'Through the Never' is the lyrical equivalent of a stoned teenager's conversation. 'DUDE! Have you ever thought about, like, how big the universe is?' Sadly they were to top this later in their career . . . 'Frantic' is so, so bad.

2. 'You want heavy? 'Tallica gives you heavy, baby!' is the fucking baffling way Hetfield now introduces that song when they play it live. I really wish he wouldn't.

3. To put that in context, Motörhead have sold 15 million albums IN TOTAL.

thousand new ones.[1] Metallica might have sold out, but in doing so they helped millions of people make the reverse journey – from commercial music fans to loyal bastions of the underground.

Also, to be entirely fair, Metallica were massively ambitious from the beginning. In early interviews they talk business, about labels and deals. They talk about becoming huge while still making music their way.

But somehow they are still seen as having been champions of the underground. Despite never being anything other than hungry for commercial success, fans still project their own values onto the band. Lars's background in professional sport might well go some way to explaining his insatiable hunger for success, for recognition. Hence his disavowal first of thrash and then of heavy metal. He wants to be recognised among a wider group of peers – as artists, rather than as simply a metal band.

What they did next was even more controversial. They all cut their hair. This is simply not on. The Swedish blackened thrash band Nifelheim are led by twins Eric and Peter Gustavsson. Both Iron Maiden fanatics, they are going bald, but are staying true to metal's hair uniform. Comedian and metalhead Steve Hughes reports them as saying, 'Steve. Nifelheim are losing our hair. But if we have only one hair left . . . *it will be long.*' Metallica's visit to the barber was a sign for many people that they had finally turned their backs on heavy metal.

And the albums they released in 1996 and 1997 did little to overcome that feeling.

---

1. Including your author. I fucking love it. It was my gateway drug into heavy metal. It opened my ears to new sounds and began my descent into the abyss of extreme music. When I first got hold of it most of the tunes were too heavy for my unaccustomed ears. But I persisted.

Load and *Reload* are only heavy metal albums in the sense that, as previously explained, a lot of people misuse the terms heavy metal when they are actually describing hard rock. They are not particularly heavy, certainly not fast. They are influenced by country rock and blues; as well as bands like Corrosion of Conformity, who supported them on the tour for *Load*, and Down – a supergroup made up of members of Pantera, Crowbar and CoC. They fit quite well with the alternative rock movement of the mid-nineties.

My personal view is that *Load* is underrated and *Reload* is less bad than most people make out. They reward repeated listening. They are complex, textured and interesting – the mature sound of a band doing what they want to do and expanding their horizons. They are, however, significantly less good than anything the band had put out before. It was hard not to be disappointed. Even their unofficial but passionate biographer Joel McIver says, 'The one overriding fact is that these two albums simply aren't very good. They have their moments, but mostly they're boring, and in parts they're terrible.'

The controversy around *Load* and *Reload* belies the fact that Metallica fans carry about the sense of ownership. A contemporary comparison would be the hatred directed at the rebooted *Ghostbusters* film. It's one thing to think a piece of work is crap, quite another to take that personally and to get angry. But people feel invested in their favourite metal bands. By the time Metallica released albums I thought sucked I had expanded my listening to such a degree that no one band held all that much sway.

But then they went mental.

Lars[1] scored the biggest PR misfire in heavy metal's history by taking legal action against Napster and a load of Metallica

1. SIT DOWN, LARS.

fans for filesharing. While his fundamental argument is sound, his belligerent attitude made him look greedy, out of touch and even a bully. Then they basically split up. Jason left for reasons that included James being a prick about him doing side-projects. Then James went into rehab for alcohol and 'other addictions'.[1]

Then they made a film about them having therapy. SERI-OUSLY, GUYS? You are making it very difficult to justify my still being a fan of yours. It's just not metal. Venom would never do that.

'Lay down your soul to the Gods Rock and Roll!'

'And . . . how does that make you feel, Cronos?'

'Sad.'

The film was called *Some Kind of Monster* and it is as embar-rassing as it is compulsive viewing. It shows what used to be my heroes[2] being petty and egotistical and at times really, really bad at making music. When Hetfield returned from rehab they made a genuinely terrible record – *St. Anger*. Terrible title, awful pro-duction (notoriously Lars decided his snare would sound good without the chain engaged), really bad lyrics. They don't play anything off it any more.

So what about now?

Their second-to-last album, *Death Magnetic*, was heralded by some as a return to form. Abandoning their long relationship with Bob Rock they instead worked with Rick Rubin, who not

---

1. That's got to be sex addiction, right? Cos he's apparently never done drugs. I mean, this is speculation but . . . I'm excellent at speculation.

2. . . . before I decided that elevating musicians I like to the status of heroes is a pretty lame basis for deciding heroes and now think more in terms of revolutionary anarchists and anyone who can drink more than me. Which is very few people. So, like, I should be your hero, right? RIGHT?! DRINK WITH ME! INDULGE MY ALCOHOLISM!

only has a tremendous reputation for returning 'legacy' artists to top form, but also produced *Reign in Blood* – Slayer's 1986 master-piece. Reviews were overwhelmingly positive. The album was their fifth to go straight to number one in the charts. At last it seemed Metallica were returning to what they do best.

But, in reality, it's not remotely up to the standard of their best albums. Occasional flourishes of their genius are hidden within self-indulgent arrangements and just Too. Many. Fucking. Riffs. It's the sound of millionaires who don't really listen to metal try-ing to make a metal album. The sound of pioneers following a formula. Like Isambard Kingdom Brunel making a Lego model of a bridge.

They are not making the music they are listening to. The same thing has happened to nearly all my favourite bands.

But it doesn't matter what Metallica do now. They will still always be metal gods. *Kill 'em All* alone is worthy of a signifi-cant mention in this history, and *Ride the Lightning* and *Master of Puppets* are two of the greatest albums ever made. *The Black Album* sustained heavy music through a distinctly dry period. Frankly, Metallica could record themselves taking a dump and release it and it still wouldn't diminish their standing in my eyes.[1]

The other reason it doesn't matter what Metallica do is . . . we still have Slayer.

The follow-up to *Reign in Blood*, 1988's *South of Heaven*, is a strikingly different approach. Realising that they'd 'done' fast, Slayer slowed down the pace and expanded their musical palette. The record is still brutal, but in a different way. *Seasons in the Abyss* carries on in a similar vein.

1994's *Divine Intervention* is fast once more. Kerry King once remarked that they seem to go fast every three albums. The

---

1. Oh no, wait, they did that already. And called it *Lulu*.

record has more of a hardcore influence, and the lyrics are more explicit than ever, heading much more into the territory covered by death metal. It also featured a photograph of a fan who has had SLAYER carved into his arm with a scalpel. This particular stunt had a big impact on my group of metal-obsessed friends and we subsequently all turned up to school with various half-hearted band-name-mutilations on our arms. *Divine Intervention* marks the point where people tend to divide on Slayer. Some, like me, reckon it's an underrated classic, some think it marks the start of them treading water. Whatever. Opinions, as Robin Williams once said, are like arseholes – everybody has one.[1] The band's own opinion of its records is clear from the songs they play live. The nerd-gasm that is the website setlist.fm. has archives of thousands of band's setlists and statistics on how many times bands play songs from each album. Slayer very clearly favour their output up to *Seasons*.

After their controversial but underrated album of punk covers, *Undisputed Attitude*, Slayer did what every band I love did – they went shit, releasing a nu-metal-inspired piece of shit that no one listens to any more. *Diabolus in Musica* is plodding and unoriginal. A few tracks stand out but it's mainly filler – a fact borne out by them never playing any of its tracks live.

Despite this view that their best days are behind them, in the sometimes harshly judgemental world of heavy metal Slayer have managed to remain incredibly popular without attracting too much of the negative attention most successful bands get. They remain incredibly well respected. The word that comes up time and time again in descriptions of Slayer is 'uncompromising'. In

1. Imagine how hairy Robin Williams's arsehole must have been?! Must have looked like a gunshot on a tarantula.

stark contrast to many of their contemporaries, Slayer have stuck
rigidly to their brutal guns and never wimped out once. As a
result, the later part of their discography is much, much less
interesting. It's a Catch-22 situation. Consistency produces
wildly different results to experimentation. It is a problem a lot of
metal bands face – boxing themselves into a corner by producing
the same sound over and over again. Most extreme metal
bands seem to perfect their sound around their third album and
then spend the rest of their career making music that keeps their
fans happy. New York death metal band Mortician have said in
interviews they intentionally keep their albums sounding the
same, hating bands who change. 'They should change their
name,' said frontman Will Rahmer, in an interview for *Terrorizer*
magazine.

Fear Factory are the most extreme example of this. They
boxed themselves into a corner with their 'future dystopia' concept. Cannibal Corpse, in contrast, have a very distinct sound but
they still manage to produce critically acclaimed records – their
2006 record *Kill* is considered among their very best.

Live, Slayer remain impeccable. Their live albums are some of
their very best – *Live Evil,*[1] *Decade of Aggression,* the home video
Live Intrusion and the *Reign in Blood* anniversary special *Still Reign-
ing* all totally destroy. But, in terms of albums, their glory days are
behind them.

The one thing that really strikes me about Slayer nowadays is
that they never seem that enthusiastic about being a band. They
have been hinting in interviews for years that they might soon
split up. For most of their career they seem not to have really
liked each other.

An odd aspect of their career is their rejection of the death

1. Not to be confused with the Miles Davis album.

metal they inspired. Kerry King, remember, was vehement in his criticism of 'Cookie Monster' vocals and the extremity of the bands who took the torch from Slayer. I find this weird. And almost suspicious. Is it possibly sour grapes that the band who at one point had made the most extreme heavy metal record of all time were relatively quickly overtaken in heaviness by people who took their lead? It means that Slayer are now somewhat isolated. Too heavy for trad metalheads, but purposefully cut off from what extreme metal developed into.

Slayer's story has a tragic turn. In May 2013 guitarist Jeff Hanneman died from 'complications arising from' a spider bite. In 2011 he was bitten by a spider in a friend's jacuzzi in LA. From this injury he contracted a flesh-eating disease. With a pretty amazing name (there is now a band in California called Necrotizing Fasciitis.) The disease crippled his arm and prevented him playing the guitar. After gruelling treatment involving skin grafts he was finally able to play once more and appeared on stage with Slayer at the Big Four show in Indio, California, on 23 April 2011. But it was too late. The psychological effect of not being able to play, of not being able to do the one thing that gave his life meaning was totally destructive . . . Slayer were dysfunctional band at best, their personalities never seemed to gel. Interviews state the other members barely heard from Jeff while he was in treatment. He had always been a big drinker, even having a custom guitar with the Heineken logo on it, altered to read 'Hanneman'. Isolated from the band, facing the prospect of never being able to play again, eff eventually died from cirrhosis of the liver, related to alcohol abuse. Depressed at not being in the band which was the only thing he had known since the age of seventeen, he basically drank himself to death.

Hanneman is sorely missed. Seeing Slayer without him is a strange and hollow experience. But MY GOD he went out metal. They are now admirably carrying on without him, with Dave Holt of Exodus installed on guitar, and they have released a perfectly decent record without Jeff. They'll never be the same, but Jeff's spirit lives on.

Slayer are ubiquitous, but they manage to maintain loyalty. Slayer fans feel like Slayer are theirs.

In their career they have mis-stepped, for sure. *Diabolus in Musica* sucks nu-metal balls. But they have always been committed to being heavy. In some ways they have pitched themselves against Metallica. Feeling somewhat the underdog, they have refused any commercial concessions and they remain at the top of the extreme metal tree. Uncompromising. Slayer.

Slayer's dalliance with nu-metal was only slight compared to what happened to the once-mighty Machine Head. Their second album, *The More Things Change*, grooves way more than their debut. The aggression of *Burn My Eyes* is replaced with a sonic heaviness born of production more than intent. The album seems self-conscious, an attempt to fill club dancefloors and sell units. It's okay, just slightly disappointing.

Then they went utterly terrible. *The Burning Red* has all rapping and that on it, and annoying discordant, Coal-Chamber-style riffs ... oh God. It's hard to tell whether it was a cynical attempt to cash in on the nu-metal thing or if it was a genuine attempt at experimentation. Either way it was dogshit.

However, like a phoenix rising from the flames, Machine Head have redeemed themselves with their last few albums. I was so excited by the return-to-form of the song 'Imperium' that I ran upstairs to wake up my girlfriend to tell her MACHINE

HEAD ARE GOOD AGAIN. She didn't get it. We're no longer together.

They now occupy a unique place in the affections of metalheads of a certain vintage. We have forgiven them their trespasses. As I've mentioned, *all* my favourite bands from the mid-nineties went shit. I take this as a life lesson. In much the same way parents give their children hamsters and gerbils and mayflies and other short-lived pets in order to teach them about death, so the bands who made me first fall in love with metal all went proper pony and I learned that genius is fleeting, inspiration is finite and metal bands generally have a solid five years in them before they begin to disappoint you. There are exceptions to the rule quite naturally, but on the whole they all go crap, at least for a bit. In some circles it's called the Cold Lake theorem. For others it's Roadrunner's law.

The night of Sepultura's Brixton Academy triumph, as I was making my way home and putting my six T-shirts back on to brace myself against the December cold, backstage a row erupted over the issue of their manager, Gloria Cavalera, who was married to Max. The other band members felt she was unfairly prioritising Max over the band as a whole. Which, remembering the balance of press coverage of the band at the time, seems like a fair complaint. They decided to fire her. Disgusted, Max left and Sepultura as we knew them were finished. Metal has never been the same.

Sepultura carried on with a new vocalist, Derrick Greene, and Max formed the terribly named Soulfly.[1] Both albums were hotly anticipated. Neither lived up to expectations. Hopes that

---

1. Soulfly is a terrible name. Ironically at this time he slagged off the name 'Sepultura' because apparently they once met Pelé and he thought it was a silly

Sepultura might revert to a more thrash metal style were dashed by an album that tries to pick up where *Roots* left off. Nothing they later produced lived up to the genius of their output in the mid-nineties.

Soulfly's debut is crammed with nu-metal guest stars, possibly indicating a lack of confidence in Max's ability to sell a record alone. There was enough of Sepultura's DNA in it to keep me trying, but, in common with most Sepultura fans, I've not listened to a Soulfly record in years.

Ho hum.

All my favourite bands made shit albums, some quicker than others. They all detached from their roots and became lazy, or commercial, or uninspired. Machine Head, Fear Factory, Pantera, Metallica, Slayer, Deicide, Sepultura. The only option was to look to the underground. And that is what saved me. Beneath the surface of metal, away from the bands pushed by big labels and publicists lies the beauty that is bands-who-don't-make-a-living-off-their-music. Bands whose commitment to direct artistic expression is unsullied by commercial considerations. That scene is healthier than it has ever been before, with the opportunities offered by the internet.

It's a cliché in heavy metal that the old albums are the best. If you want even more underground credibility, say the demos, or the band they were before they changed their name. It's a truism with all bands that in a live show no audience is enthused about the new stuff. Hence the relatively recent phenomenon of bands playing albums all the way through. Often it's a great idea. Metallica have done *The Black Album* and *Master Of Puppets*, Slayer cannily did *Reign in Blood* and even Public

---

name. Of course he fucking did. It's a metal name. It's like Lars disavowing thrash and then refusing even to say 'metal' in favour of 'hard rock'.

Enemy jumped on board. Nostalgia is big business and it's a fan-pleaser.[1]

As disappointing as it was to see my favourite bands slide into mediocrity, metal was about to explore new territory that was much, much worse.

1. Actually, if you're Faith No More or Satyricon, scratch that and just play your greatest hits, please.

13

An Honest and Open-Minded Reappraisal of Nu-Metal and Rap Metal

The mid- to late nineties were a strange time for heavy metal. The traditional, unalloyed forms were out of fashion. Metallica had cut their hair, seemingly abandoned metal in favour of alt-rock and headlined Lollapalooza. Carcass split, Napalm Death were making strange records, the major labels all dropped their death metal acquisitions. Entombed were playing rock'n'roll. Sepultura went experimental and then Max left – neither party would make a genuinely great record again. Pantera were mired in internal conflict and Phil Anselmo was addicted to heroin. The great hopes of Machine Head and Fear Factory never fully materialised. Maiden and Priest were playing to significantly smaller crowds with temporary frontmen and Saxon couldn't get arrested.

And as bad as this situation was, something about to dominate metal culture was far, far worse.

Nu-metal is the most maligned metal sub-genre of them all. And with good reason. It is, in the main, fucking appalling. It began to look dated almost immediately. Shallow, artificial, apolitical and gimmicky . . . It is the candy-floss of heavy metal, the strip-mall impulse purchase. It has all the artistic merit of a trip to M&Ms World.[1] It is a genre in a state of arrested development. A soundtrack to adolescence that fails entirely to translate into the adult world.

There has been no resurgence and no retro-resurgence and reappraisal by a new generation. It is a site people do not return to – an abandoned historical relic, like Chernobyl. Or your dad.

The combination of hip-hop and heavy metal had promising roots. In its early days the main progenitor of this genre mix was the once-legendary (and now somewhat maligned) producer Rick Rubin.[2,3] Stemming from hardcore punk roots, Rubin was infatuated with the hip hop scene that was emerging in New York. He formed Def Jam records with a college friend, Russell Simmons, and released several hip-hop singles, including 'Rock Hard' by hardcore-turned-hip-hop band the Beastie Boys.

In 1986 Rubin suggested a collaboration between faded hard rock veterans Aerosmith and up-and-coming hip-hop stars Run-D.M.C. on a version of Aerosmith's 'Walk This Way'. The track begins with the familiar stripped-down sound of early hip-hop; looped drums, scratching, then explodes with the guitar riff. The combination is so familiar now it's hard to recall how fresh the

1. Seriously, fuck M&Ms World. If you have ever been you are a fucking idiot and if you have ever taken your kids there you deserve to have your kids taken off you by social services.

2. Women who like both metal and hip-hop are 'Rubinesque'. And that, ladies and gentlemen, is the best joke in this whole book. I have peaked.

3. Maligned? Well – Slipknot slag him off, Slayer are annoyed at him for abandoning them for Metallica, and Metallica reckon he did very little to actually *produce Death Magnetic*, which is their sixth best album at best.

commercial success. It exposed a new (predominantly white) audience to Run-D.M.C. and hip-hop and entirely revived the fortunes
of Aerosmith in the process. The video shows explicitly what the
record was doing – metaphorically breaking down the wall between
the genres, the two bands initially compete in adjoining rehearsal
rooms and ultimately collaborate on stage.

The same year Def Jam signed Slayer and Rubin produced the
greatest album of all time. *Reign in Blood* is noted for its speed, but
what Rubin brought to the table was a stripping down of the
sound Slayer had used on their previous records, removing reverb
and creating something far harder and more immediate.

This signing led to another Rick Rubin-produced metal/hip-
hop crossover – Slayer's guitarist, Kerry King, laid down guitar
on the Beastie Boys' song 'No Sleep Till Brooklyn'. The title is a
nod to the classic live Motörhead album *No Sleep 'til Hammersmith*.
The video for the song is a bizarre have-your-cake-and-eat-it mix
of both ridicule and celebration of hard rock and metal. The
Beasties turn up for a gig and when asked, 'Where are your
instruments?', they hold up a record (cos, like, a DJ can be a
band, yo). The enraged promoter gives them what can only be
described as short shrift, smashing the precious vinyl over their
heads. Real bands play instruments, see? So our heroes enact a
fiendish scheme and turn up in disguise, with glam rock wigs
and guitars and play a show, ripping the piss out of all the glam
rock clichés and even machine-gunning the Marshall stacks.
Okay, so far so anti-metal. Then KERRY KING TURNS UP
AND PLAYS A SOLO. So . . . what is it, guys? Make your
minds up! You're either with us or against us! Are those Kerry's
amps? HE NEEDS THOSE AMPS! STOP MACHINE-GUN-
NING KERRY'S AMPS HE HAS SHOWS TO PLAY!

Another Def Jam signing was the politicised and aggressive
Public Enemy, easily the most metalhead-friendly hip-hop act

around. Public Enemy had grown out of the college radio scene in Long Island, New York. Their first album *Yo! Bum Rush the Show*[1] is a stripped-down, brutal-sounding record. Bleak and powerful, it's the sound of urban disenfranchisement.

By their second album, P. E. were expanding their sound with an increased use of sampling. *It Takes a Nation of Millions to Hold Us Back* opens (after a distinctly English-sounding introduction from Radio 1's Dave Pearce) with the sound of an air-raid siren and the austere pronouncements of Professor Griff. It is an astonishing sound, making all of its contemporaries sound dated in comparison. (It's amazing how flat and sparse old-school hip-hop sounds when compared not only to the modern sound but also to what P. E. were doing back then.) And it's fucking HEAVY. Especially compared to the weak, pansy-ass ballad shit that the glam metal bands were puking up all over MTV at that time. Aggressive, politically engaged, challenging authority – Public Enemy did with hip-hop what the best bands were doing in punk rock and metal.

Track two on that album is 'Bring the Noise'.[2] The song contains several unexpected references, including Sonny Bono and, rhyming, Yoko Ono. It also references the Big Four thrash metal band Anthrax. Public Enemy had a big impact on Anthrax, who in 1987 released a genuinely terrible song called 'I'm the Man' in which they rap. Badly. Chuck D had been impressed by the sight of their guitarist Scott Iain wearing a Public Enemy shirt in the video. This would later blossom into something huge. Later on

1. Which is impossible to say with any dignity in an English accent. I always feel like that English character in *Family Guy* when I say it.

2. I nearly typed that as 'Bring the Noize'. This is what happens when you spend all day researching Slade and their influence on heavy metal . . . In fact, I'm pretty sure a mash-up of 'Bring the Noise' and 'Cum on Feel the Noize' would be the best thing ever.

the same record the track 'She Watch Channel Zero' samples the bridge riff from Slayer's 'Angel of Death'; looped and combined with other noises it perfectly complements Public Enemy's hard edge.

An overlooked precursor to the rap-metal/nu-metal movement was another Rick Rubin product – the Beastie Boys. They had started out as a hardcore punk band, appearing on the *New York Thrash* compilation. They were a key element of the close relationship that existed early on between hardcore and hip-hop.

In common with Nirvana and Al Murray the Pub Landlord, the Beastie Boys accidentally cultivated an audience they hated. The song '(You've Got to) Fight for Your Right (to Party)' was supposed to be a satirical take on bullshit frat-boy culture, but in hilarious Alf Garnett style it ended up attracting exactly those people they were attempting to ridicule. It must suck to work hard at developing yourself as an artist in an underground scene and then find your explosion into the mainstream tarnished by the fact that your new-found audience is mainly made up of arse-holes. One such dickhead appeared on the Public Enemy track 'Incident at 66.6 FM' in a sample from a radio show in which the jock bell-end moaned about the aggressive militarised politicisation of P. E.'s stage show.

> I've seen these guys. I saw them warm up for the Beastie Boys last year. How were they? I thought it was one of the most appalling things I have ever seen. There were two gentlemen in cages on either side of the stage with, er, fake Uzis. It – it was unbelievable. And when I see somebody who's wearing one of their shirts, I think that they're scum too.

The cages in question were there for the dancing girls that the Beasties were 'ironically' exhibiting on stage. I assume the caller was down with that particular display of misogyny . . .

Adopting fake frat-boy personas as part of their pisstake, they became what they despised. Foreshadowing what would happen with nu-metal, the Beastie Boys took hip-hop to the white suburban masses. It was unthreatening and easy for middle-class white people to swallow. They went on to have an enormously successful career – the few times I've seen them their crowd has been noticeably white . . .

In 1991 Anthrax and Public Enemy collaborated on a new version of 'Bring the Noise'. The track is powered by a chugging riff provided by Anthrax, interspersed with the original electronic drum beats and samples. The mix is reminiscent of the wall-of-sound approach P. E. had on their first three albums and the rapping is shared between Chuck D and Scott Iain. For me this song was an absolute watershed. I was already a fan of Public Enemy and I recorded the video off the telly and watched it hundreds of times, learning the words and copying the headbanging in the video.[1]

This song began my inevitable descent into the world of heavy metal and it also seemed to herald the possibility of a new era of hip-hop/heavy metal crossover. That never quite happened.

After this period of metal and hip-hip being combined through collaboration, a few bands began to combine the two influences into something more coherent.

Faith No More paved the way, and a trend for hardcore punk/hip-hop crossover emerged with bands such as Biohazard, Dog Eat Dog, Downset and the actually-pretty-heavy Thumb from Germany.

White Zombie's extensive and dense use of sampling was a

---

1. Fun fact: Chuck D signed my patch denim jacket at a gig in 2012. He also wrote 'BRING THE NOISE!' Which made me very happy. Unfortunately it's since rubbed off and so I painted the Minor Threat logo over it.

callback to the pioneering work of production team The Bomb Squad on Public Enemy's best records. Rob Zombie's vocal style at times veers into something akin to rapping. Rob Zombie's later solo work combined electronic beats into a distinctly danceable style.

Rage Against the Machine soar high above everyone else in this field. Musically they are a callback to the classic rock riffs of seventies bands like Led Zeppelin. Innovative guitarist Tom Morello uses a battery of original methods to squeeze strange noises from his instrument in an attempt to sound like Terminator X of Public Enemy. Sliding his palm on the strings, using an Allen key, rapidly switching his pickup toggle switch – he makes his guitar sound like a helicopter, an air-raid siren and at times even like a guitar. Coming full circle, the musical three-quarters of RATM are now collaborating with Chuck D of Public Enemy and B-Real of Cypress Hill on a project called Prophets of Rage.

Combining rap with rock music soon became commonplace. Then came Korn.

At the time my metalhead friends and I thought the first Korn album was a breath of fresh air. Released in 1994, it contained loads of the elements we already dug in metal – downtuned guitars like the death metal we loved, an emotional truth in the lyrics and a vocal performance which spoke directly to our suburban teenage alienation (as it would to literally every other suburban teenager who thought they were alienated . . .).

Korn's subject matter in early records was rooted in childhood trauma. In contrast with most metal, which has a persona of toughness, of projecting inner strength and anger directed outwards, Jonathan Davis showed his weakness. His was a persona of the bullied child having had enough and finally lashing out. In the song 'Faget' he takes the homophobic insult he grew up hearing and turns it into a desperate expression of rage. In 'Daddy' he ends the track crying inconsolably.

This was an absolute watershed in rock music – later it would be taken even further in the emo movement, which fetishised alienation, self-harm, post-traumatic stress disorder and depression/anxiety. Goth and industrial music did this to a degree, but with a pathology rooted in adulthood – addiction, heroin and adult fuck-ups.

Musically, Korn blend their influences into a coherent whole. The hip-hop elements are infused in the rhythm section in the manner of the Beastie Boys, rather than imposed on top of the music like the mash-ups of Anthrax/Public Enemy and Aerosmith/Run-D.M.C. Later nu-metal would exhibit an uneasy oil-and-water mix. The guitars are downtuned and the bass and drums lock together in a powerful groove. Though exhibiting some remnants of rap, Davis's vocals are aggressive, expressive and fucking weird. He does the most bizarre raging scat vocal.

My flirtation with Korn only lasted as long as the tail-end of puberty. I still have a soft spot for them – I admire anyone who sticks to their guns as much as they have, and there will always be a fresh market of disenfranchised suburban teenagers who need music.

After the success of *Korn*, the album's producer, Ross Robinson, became the most sought-after producer in mainstream metal for the best part of a decade, the familiar label goldrush began and hundreds of similar bands were signed. It turns out we had been wrong. That album wasn't a breath of fresh air. It was a pocket of fresh air being pushed along the music industry's colon in front of a massive load of shit.[1] Anyone with a DJ, a quirky hairstyle or a shopping-centre kook appeal was snapped up. Roadrunner – formerly a reliable label for metal that had broken Sepultura, Machine Head and Fear Factory – began to chase

1. It was a fart.

trends and sign any old shit with turntables and wacky hair. Like fucking Coal Chamber. Coal Chamber were a distinctly forget-table, cartoonish band, taking all the childish aspects of Korn and throwing away the real emotion and aggression. Try to find a picture of Coal Chamber where one of them isn't doing a broken-doll I-SO-KRAZY pose. You won't find one. They took an ice cream van to their gigs to hand out free ice creams. That's like the opposite of metal.

Limp Bizkit[1] were a much more testosterone-driven band, adding a lot more hip-hop and a great deal more self-confident swagger to their mix. They were signed after touring with Korn and, basically, they suck,[2] but they got HUGE. If you think that name is bad, you're right. Fred Durst says he wanted a name that would repel people.[3]

Then we had a real deluge. Puddle of Mudd, Mudvayne, Papa Roach, Creed. Nu-metal is clearly influenced by the early days of the internet. Bands whose titles are like usernames (Sum 41, Primer 55, Linea 77, Factory 81, Project 86) are joined by bands whose names resemble things my cat spells out when he walks across my keyboard: (Hed) PE., P. O.D., AqME, Sw1tched, 4 Lyn. The wackiness makes my teeth itch.

Nu-metal began to infect older, good bands. Sepultura used Korn's producer, Ross Robinson, on their tribal-meets-death-metal album *Roots*. The album was an enormous success, but disquiet

1. Korn, with their weirdly spelled and nonsensical name, started a trend for KERAZY band names.

2. An argument I had with a Limp Bizkit fan at Reading Festival still baffles me to this day. 'Are you going to see Limp Bizkit?' 'No. I don't like them.' 'Well, you obviously haven't heard them.' 'Yeah, I have. I've heard their whole album.' 'No. You can't have heard it.'

3. 'Then what's the music for?' asked Jez, the drummer in my band.

over the departure from their – ironically – extreme metal roots was expressed by old-school Sepultura fans.

The worst thing nu-metal ever did was ruin Machine Head. Whether as a result of record label pressure or simply due to them going out of their fucking minds, Machine Head followed up their flawless post-thrash debut, *Burn My Eyes*, with a series of records that increasingly took the hip-hop-infused chug of nu-metal and ruined everything that was good about them. *The Burning Red* is Machine Head's *Cold Lake*. They have redeemed themselves in recent years with an injection of Judas Priest-like dual-guitar old-school metal, but they have never quite recaptured the genius of that first record.

Then in 2000 came Linkin Park. Rumours abounded that they were a full-on manufactured boy band, cynically put together to capitalise on the mainstream pop-metal market. They certainly sound like it. It has been suggested that the terrible name was suggested by their record label, so they'd be next to Limp Bizkit in CD racks. The music is soulless and sounds like it was made by a committee. Everything about them is designed to be marketable. They have a policy of not swearing. Fuck that. I'll take that from Jerry Seinfeld but not from a metal band. Unsurprisingly they have sold tens of millions of records. The frontman has his own line of clothes, in conjunction with Porsche. Make of that what you will.

It wasn't all bad. Unlike glam metal, these bands could all play their instruments and had a degree of musical ambition. And within the foetid swamp were some real diamonds.[1]

Deftones got lumped in with nu-metal but in reality are more

1. Swamp diamonds. Or something. Shut up. It's my metaphor and I'll mix it how I want.

like a new-wave band who just discovered their brother's thrash records. Their take on post-metal is dreamy, soaring, infused with eighties pop as much as hip-hop. It is a seamless blend of influences, decades more mature and leagues ahead of their wacky-image, stick-a-rapper-on-it contemporaries.

System of a Down are great musicians and interesting song-writers (and the only mainstream band to attempt to raise awareness of the Armenian genocide).

Er . . . that's it. I can't think of any other nu-metal bands that weren't shit.

Oh. And then there's Slipknot.

It's my opinion that you come of age as a metalhead when you find a band that makes you feel too old. And because of the rap-idly shifting nature of heavy metal trends that happens really young. For me that band was Slipknot. I was about twenty when they really broke. At that point I was listening to hardcore bands like Converge and Cave In and Kiss It Goodbye and rapidly descending into my love of black metal through the likes of Emperor, Darkthrone and Marduk. The unadorned, this-is-us nature of hardcore and the otherwordly atmospheres of black metal made Slipknot seem silly. Contrived. More like a musical product fine-tuned for maximum consumer appeal than an expression of self. With their masks and boiler suits and anonym-ity it looked overwhelmingly to my eyes like a gimmick, a Fisher-Price my-first-metal-band.

In early interviews they talk the talk, full of rage and hate and boasting about how they've been working out how to kill people and get away with it. It almost sounds convincing. But all of this 'BEING IN THIS BAND IS SO INTENSE, MAN' swagger belies the fact that there was a music industry juggernaut behind them – their PR budget was enormous. And the complicity of the music press to preserve their image and play along with the anonymity and the imposed nicknames reminded me directly of the way in which the Spice Girls had been marketed as 'Baby Spice', 'Sports Spice', 'Scared Spice', 'Patriotic Spice' and 'Skeletor'.

The symbiotic, often sycophantic attitude of the metal press to the bands it fawns over makes me yearn for the days when *NME* would slag bands off at the drop of a hat. Metal is a relatively small world and the magazines have learned over the years that the big bands are their bread and butter. *Metal Hammer* needs Slipknot way, way more than Slipknot need *Metal Hammer*.

All of which is fine. There absolutely is a place for beginner-metal. For music for fourteen-year-olds. Fourteen-year-olds are way better served listening to Slipknot or Bring Me the Horizon or Motionless in White than Ed Sheeran or Justin Bieber or fucking Nicki Minaj.

Slipknot remain an important band for a whole generation. They are possibly the heaviest band to have achieved such a stadium-dominating, festival-headlining level of success. And that is notable and a worthy accolade. Their mainstreaming of heaviness has paved the way for thousands more commercially minded bands to be able to include real extremity as part of their package.

Nu-metal couldn't last. As its audience moved beyond puberty and the new millennium made its so-nineties-it-hurts image look anachronistic, it withered and died. Nu-metal's appeal was uniquely suburban, painfully white. It was music destined to be scrawled on school bags – ultimately, music to be outgrown.

But, then again, maybe I'm wrong. Maybe the grass-roots authenticity or occult atmosphere I enjoy in my favourite bands are just as a much an artificial construction as the DayGlo mall-angst of nu-metal. Certainly black metal is extremely image-led and made by a large number of artists who still live with their parents. In their bedrooms. As rebellious as Bathory, Death and Obituary sound, they all enjoyed levels of parental support that would have got them bullied at my school.

The fundamental truth, though, is that nu-metal was never a progression within metal, it was a departure from it. A side-turning into a dead end. Which is fine. All musical genres find their boundaries, and nu-metal represents an outer limit. And not in a good way.

Of course, nu-metal was eventually replaced in the affections of teenagers-in-stripey-tights-who-hang-out-near-fountains by an even more shallow sub-culture – emo. But, you know what? I'm not even going to dignify that shit with an entry in the book. Fuck 'em. There's other stuff to cover and I have a deadline.

14

Metalcore and the Return
of Good Music

The decline of mainstream metal into nu-metal and general crappiness didn't last. Metal was reinvigorated at the turn of the millennium, despite Fear Factory making every metal band hide in underground bunkers in case the millennium bug hit and the computers took over and turned us all into cyborg slaves.[1] This injection of energy came from hardcore punk.

Ever since Discharge, the boundary between metal and punk has been porous. Influence flowed both ways, whether acknowledged or not; after punk pushed metal back towards the street for its image and lyrical focus, metal in turn began to show its influence within punk. Black Flag never denied their debt to Black Sabbath. The crossover movement, which combined hardcore and thrash never really went away, and the thin bridge between the two movements widened and became a motorway. Bands like Agnostic Front, Cro-Mags, Suicidal Tendencies, Carnivore, Cryptic Slaughter, D.R.I. etc. utilised metal elements all through the 1980s.

In the early nineties, hardcore bands were increasingly leaning towards a metal sound. The boldest use of metallic sounds in

---

1. And Linkin Park making music that sounded like it had been made by computers in order to turn us all into cyborg slaves.

hardcore stemmed from the vegan straightedge movement, a culture that can seem pretty baffling to the bacon-sandwich-and-beer-orientated metalhead.[1]

Straightedge began with the seminal hardcore band Minor Threat. Initially, it was simply a statement of how Ian MacKaye didn't fit in with the world around him, particularly the punk scene with its focus on booze, drugs and promiscuous sex. The song 'Out of Step' contains lyrics expressing his alienation ('I don't drink / I don't fuck'). On the song 'Straightedge' he introduces a note of superiority, justifying his decisions against the peer pressure and mockery of his choices, writing that he's got 'better things to do' than drugs.

The symbol for straightedge was a cross drawn in thick marker pen on the back of the hand. It stemmed from MacKaye's previous band, the Teen Idles, having crosses drawn on their hands to signify they were under drinking age whilst on tour.[2] It was introduced to the Washington DC scene as a way to facilitate all-ages shows in licensed venues and became a badge of honour. The YCS 1006 Swatch watch, which depicts a bold X on the face, became the must-have straightedge accessory.

Considering the rest of the band didn't share MacKaye's abstinence, it was hardly a political mission statement, but nonetheless the concept of straightedge wrenched itself from these fragile, introspective beginnings and became a proselytising and angry movement. Bands such as Youth of Today and Cro-Mags

1. I was once told that ordering a vegetarian pizza was the opposite of rock and roll. I asked the prick in question if he'd ever heard of Black Sabbath, and their vegan-since-the-sixties bassist and lyricist, Geezer Butler. (He had . . .)

2. . . . and seriously, America, you need to fucking lighten up with your drinking restrictions. It's easier to buy a fucking rocket launcher than it is to buy a beer in some places.

began to suggest starting fights and SSD went round knocking beers out of people's hands. While straightedge offers a useful positive alternative to the peer-pressured habit of drinking, it also attracts self-important dickheads. Ho-hum. At one point Ian MacKaye was criticised for drinking a Coke because, like, caffeine is a drug, and we don't do drugs. Have you got that, Ian?

Starting with Youth of Today in the second half of the eighties, straightedge bands began advocating animals rights, vegetarianism and veganism. Which is great.[1] Good work. Then the hardline movement came along and it went kind of Nazi. There's even a band called Vegan Reich. They were not just militant vegans, but railed against what they perceived as 'deviant sexual acts' and were also anti-abortion. Happily they got loads of shit for their views and were very short-lived.

A slightly more balanced take on vegan straightedge came from a band who strived for a harder, more metallic edge – Earth Crisis, though the lyrics of their 1993 song 'Firestorm' are pretty full on, advocating as it does a violent purge of drug dealers.

Reversal of Man, a powerviolence/screamo band (and one of my favourites) wrote a song called 'Get the Kid with the Sideburns' which parodies 'Firestorm' to tell the story of an altercation the two bands once had.

Earth Crisis's main focus, though, was on animal rights. They are the only band I've ever heard use the phrase '*REJECT THE ANTHROPOCENTRIC FALSEHOOD*'. And it's to their credit.

1. Due to my being a comedian and being vegan and my favourite genre being black metal, many people have assumed that I am responsible for the parody creation that is 'Vegan Black Metal Chef'. Let me state for the record that not only am I not Vegan Black Metal Chef, but that I take black metal very, very seriously and I would never produce anything so utterly un-grim in connection with the sacred name of black metal. Seriously, fuck that guy.

Their second full-length, *Gomorrah's Season Ends*, is a brutal, dense, suffocating record with the depressive atmosphere of the slaughterhouse. Sadly they got infected by nu-metal and went shit.

Earth Crisis inspired a much more heavy metal sound in hardcore and soon the distinction between the two started to crumble.

In Boston, at the same time that Earth Crisis were getting started, Converge began playing hardcore covers and 'leftover Slayer riffs'. These humble beginnings spawned the single most inventive band in all of hardcore. Entirely in their own genre, they developed into the most arresting, emotionally affecting, brutal, complex band I have ever seen live. And I have seen them a lot. They produce in me an emotional response I only otherwise get from Jimi Hendrix.

Their early singles exhibit a fresh take on metallic hardcore, with a wrenching and somewhat disturbing emotional punch. Their first album was an extremely limited release, followed by an EP that was later re-released with bonus tracks, making it something more like a full-length. Their second proper full-length, 1998's *When Forever Comes Crashing*, is my personal favourite. It is a record of extraordinary ferocity and emotion. Co-produced by Today is the Day's Steve Austin, it is reminiscent of that band's style, with its dense sound, multi-layered vocals and experimental noise fragments. As with many of my favourite albums, it is a document of a band in transition, straining against their limits and seeking new sounds.

The real breakthrough came with 2001's *Jane Doe*. Recorded by the guitarist Kurt Ballou in his own God City Studios, it is heavier, more dense and less weird than *WFCC*. The biggest change was the addition of Ben Koller on drums – they finally left behind the limitations of hardcore and embraced a fully extreme metallic style with machine-gun snares and incredibly tight fills. When I had the chance to interview them in 2012, Jacob Bannon and Kurt Ballou told me they felt it was the first record in which they really found their way. Since then they have risen to universal critical acclaim and commercial success all without remotely compromising their sound or their DIY approach.

Inseparable from the history of Converge is fellow Massachusetts[1] band Cave In. The band began in a similar vein to Converge, and the two have exchanged members and collaborated a great deal. After their incredible *Until Your Heart Stops*, Cave In veered into space-rock for the enormous-sounding *Jupiter*, a record influenced more by Radiohead's *OK Computer* than by Slayer or Black Flag. Sadly, they then made a bold break for commercial success and signed with RCA, a venture that didn't work out, mainly because it involved giving up everything that had been good about them.

This brief period between 1996 and 2001 produced a startling number of inventive, musically ambitious hardcore bands. Most were underground, touring and recording on a small scale while holding down day jobs or studying at college. A disproportionate amount of these emerging metallic hardcore bands begin with 'C' – including Catharsis, who spawned an entire anarchist movement, CrimethInc., Culture from Florida and the British counterpart Canvas from Leeds.

Belgium was also a hotbed, giving us Arkangel, Congress and the excellent Liar.

Morning Again and Culture channelled the sound of Belgian metalcore and swapped members. Culture in particular struck a balance with righteous choruses and verbose lyrics. Their main

---

1. I had to look up how to spell Massachusetts. Look at it. Looks weird, doesn't it?

influence was Sepultura.[1] Their final record – the *Heteronome* EP – is a pinnacle of vegan straightedge anger.

There were signs of a break into the mainstream. Vision of Disorder became a big noise in the metal press, as did Will Haven. Both fully crossed over into the metal mainstream for a while, though like most underground bands they ultimately crashed and burned under the stress of the music industry. It's useful to think of these bands as early Devonian animals, trying to survive on the land when they have evolved in the sea. They look so full of promise, landing on the beach, but most of them flap about, flounder and suffocate. Hatebreed were one of the few that grew lungs and stayed the distance. Initially way hardcore, they opened up to a considerably more commercial metal sound and now headline festivals.

Meanwhile plenty of bands in this expanding scene had no interest in commerciality. Kiss It Goodbye were heavier than most, their dense, emotional, bleak sound reminiscent of Black Flag. Only much more pissed off.

San Diego spawned the short-lived but hugely influential Swing Kids, members of whom would then don insect costumes and adopt bizzaro keyboards and make schizoid grindcore as The Locust. Similar were Melt-Banana, who tethered grindcore with Japanese pop sounds. Controlled chaos was the order of the day, with Botch's *We are the Romans*[2] and the stand-out Dillinger

1. Cool! Mine too! No wonder I like you so much!

2. My old hardcore band SunStarvedDay supported Botch in London. There is a video of it on the internet – you'll see me in the process of re-growing my hair after shaving it all off. Which had been a mistake. I have a very pointy face and a shaved head makes me look like a racist. The show was pretty good, although we were plagued by constant line-up changes and a drummer who had anger management issues and no sense of rhythm. A powerful combination.

Escape Plan, whose *Under the Running Board* EP showed promise and album *Calculating Infinity* fulfilled it. Dillinger are known for their blistering live performances, although for me there seemed something contrived, almost rehearsed about their jumping-off stuff. As impressive as it is to be able to play very technical music while repeatedly jumping off your amplifier, it made me crave something more emotionally connected and authentic. At the Reading Festival in 2002 I watched their new frontman, Greg Puciato, do a poo and throw it in the crowd.

Dillinger Escape Plan's complex playing style earned the genre title 'mathcore'. It was ultimately this that led me back into the path of *true metal* – the 'math' end of hardcore for me lacked atmosphere. It lacked the magic I felt when I first listened to Deicide and Slayer. The spookiness, the evocation of something other, something alien. Dillinger's live show just looked like some college kids jumping off stuff. Dillinger have gone on to prove themselves as one of the most inventive bands around. But for me this live show was a revelation that what I wanted out of music was to pass through a gateway into another world. And only metal could do that for me.

Eventually all this blistering inventiveness and extreme heaviness trickled into the mainstream and a slew of low-carb bands emerged with their eyes on the cover of *Kerrang!* magazine. In the 2000s metalcore became the dominant sound of heavy metal. Bands such as Killswitch Engage, Hatebreed and Trivium. Bring Me the Horizon had enormous success, leading to the standard format for band names in this genre becoming 'Verb the Noun', with bands such as: Behold . . . the Arctopus, Beneath the Sky, Betraying the Martyrs, Bleed the Sky, Capture the Crown, Come the Dawn, Crown the Empire, Design the Skyline, Desire the Fire, Destroy the Runner, Embrace the End, Escape the Fate, Haste the Day, Horse the Band and Poison the Well!

The form was inevitably watered down and then polished up for mass consumption. The new normal within mainstream metal is an extension of metalcore. It is awful. Drums are so processed they entirely lose their live feel. Guitars are thick and vocals inevitably flip between heavy and clean.

The band that typifies this new approach is Trivium, who, I must confess, I fucking hate. I apologise if you like them. It's never nice to suddenly come across a stinging criticism of something you hold dear. So, let me attempt to be fair, and to objectively work out what it is that I feel they represent, and thus why they get right up my nose. Cos they do. They get right up my nose.

Number one – the music. To my ears it lacks passion. True brutality tends to stem from a shit life. Trivium sound to me like some suburban guys trying to get angry about something. There's no darkness, no vigour, no snot. Number two – the production. The modern metal production style makes everyone sound the same. Number three – they are poseurs. Matt Heafy bangs on and on about how he loves black metal. He wears an Emperor shirt in one of their videos. He made a patch denim with all extreme metal bands on it. This is fucking bullshit.

Claiming underground credibility when you are making music that is exactly the opposite of credibly underground is a peculiar trait. Trivium have from the start been a corporate rock band, chasing the dollar. There is nothing black metal about them. I remember the same thing happening with Slipknot. They played crappy nu-metal with blastbeats which I hated and people kept trying to persuade me that I should like them because 'they all used to be in death metal bands'. Unfortunately that argument just makes things worse. That's like a meat-eater trying to placate a vegan's animal-rights righteousness by saying 'Well, I used to be vegetarian.' That's just saying, 'I actually know better.'

The rise of mainstream metalcore bands coincided with a general swell in the quantity of popular metal coming out of the United States. Called the New Wave of American Heavy Metal, which as a term is pretty hard to define, it includes a wide range of bands from different corners of the metal world. Lamb of God are possibly the stand-out in terms of popularity. Musically they play a version of the chuggy post-thrash style popularised by the likes of Machine Head and Pantera.

Mastodon grew like a plant cutting out of the extreme, endlessly experimental Today is the Day, whose 1999 album *In The Eyes of God* emerged from the same melting pot as Converge's *Jane Doe* and Dillinger Escape Plan's *Calculating Infinity*. Today is the Day is basically the sole work of the guitarist and vocalist Steve Austin (not the wrestler), the genius who produced Converge's sublime *When Forever Comes Crashing*. Changing his backing bands between albums, on *In the Eyes of God* he put together the drummer Brann Dailor and bassist Bill Kelliher. After Steve moved on to new musicians these two hooked up with Troy Sanders and Brent Hinds to form Mastodon, a band who would grow exponentially, going on to sell a huge prehistoric beast's worth of records and headline festivals with their splendid mash-up of every rock band you've ever heard.

The next genre to emerge was Deathcore, or, as I prefer to call it, 'visible tattoo core', which takes the worst of hardcore and the worst of death metal and produces a bullshit, triggered-drums hyper-clean, poseur, clean-cut mash-up that is less good than either of its influences. They have short hair and get tattoos on their hands and necks before they get them done on their arms and *fuck off it's just fucking shit listen to Dismember instead*. Ahem.

Nearly every mainstream metal band today contains elements of this combination of metal and hardcore. Modern mainstream metal (MMM) is a magpie-mix of cherry-picked elements:

heavy/clean vocals, hardcore-inspired riffs, Judas Priest melodic leads. Metalcore is the new standard, and while bands like Kills-witch Engage and Bring Me the Horizon aren't my cup of tea, it is pleasing that at the top of the metal tree are bands who are relatively gimmick-free and a bit heavy.[1]

But beneath the surface lies metal in a more pure, distilled form, as young people with internet access try to replicate and build on the genre-stratified metal forms of the past. There's nothing new under the sun.

1. Well, heavy-ish.

15

Trouble in the Sorting Office: the 'Post' Explosion

People bloody love labels. Especially metalheads. Most metalheads are geeks and we find enormous satisfaction in picking apart the minutiae of genre labels.[1] Of course, the negative part of this is the tendency to mansplain – to wear knowledge heavily and to patronise other people with it. This poses the very real danger of Being Found Out when the knowledge being boast-shared is bullshit.

I once spent an hour arguing against someone's claim that Napalm Death were 'grind' and that 'grindcore' came later as a mix of what Napalm did and 'hardcore'. The dickhead in question argued vehemently that 'grindcore' was a mixed genre and something utterly different to 'early grind'. Without the modern recourse to Wikipedia the argument was left at a draw as he refused to believe my counter-claim that (a) it was always called grindcore and that 'grind' is just the short form, that (b) it was Napalm Death themselves who coined the term grindcore, and (c) he was a bell-end who'd benefit enormously from shutting his cake-hole.

Throughout the nineties, metal experienced colossal genre inflation. What started off as 'heavy metal' then became thrash/

---

1. We're like zoologists or some shit.

speed/death/black/power/doom metal, then each of those genres multiplied to give us a baffling and massively unhelpful
pantheon of metal genres.

As well the explosion of death metal into a million sub-genres
as seen earlier, black metal became *first-wave/second-wave black
metal, symphonic black metal, bestial black metal* (or *war metal*),
*National Socialist black metal, red and anarchist black metal, Viking
black metal, blackgaze* . . .

As for tracing the history of metal, through the nineties our
narrative becomes increasingly complex.[1] Not only do we see this
huge increase in sub-genres, but there is a concurrent increase in
the number of bands. Like bacteria. As the number of people
creating heavy metal music increases exponentially, so does the
complexity of the history. Movements, trends and subcultures
become much less distinct and the influences of each sub-category
merge and interconnect.

The bands that influenced the more experimental types of
heavy metal in the nineties came from all over. Our narrative is
no longer linear. Hip-hop, industrial, folk, noise, jazz . . . all of
these began to pollute and enhance the pure metal sound. The
beginning of this tendency is obvious in the bands that were big
between 1992 and '96 – Sepultura, Machine Head, Pantera –
bands who were taking elements from tons of different places
and mashing them up into a satisfying whole.[2] The biggest pol-
lutant was hardcore punk. And out of that came metalcore.

Then the posts arrived. Thousands of posts, delivered by post
by the postman. Put in front of all the genre names. It started
with post-punk, then post-rock. Pantera and Machine Head were
post-thrash. Then we went fully post-metal.

1. Like the *Matrix* films. Or a really hard sum.

2. Like your dad's.

The trouble with post-genre names is that they never fully escape the weight of the genre they are supposed to be post. The prefix tends to get added pretty freely, without a great deal of accuracy or consideration.[1] Post-metal could have been the name for any progression on from Black Sabbath. Judas Priest could have claimed the name if they'd wanted. But they were too metal to be post-metal. Of all the genres we cover in this book, post-metal is the hardest to pin down.

So what the hell does post-metal sound like? Well, it sounds a bit like post-rock.[2] It is heavily dependent on effects pedals (see 'Shoegaze') and has long, epic, building structures more akin to classical music than anything by Tank or Praying Mantis. But the term is a very loose one, and is often applied to anything that's a bit metal but also experimental.

The inspiration for post-metal comes from combining traditional metal forms with the more experimental end of non-metal genres.

Melvins came out of Seattle and predated and influenced grunge, as well as just about every other genre from doom to grindcore. Their style is a combination of Black Sabbath with punk and a range of more experimental elements, and their frontman, Buzz Osbourne, has massive hair like Shane Embury of Napalm Death. They've released twenty-four records in thirty years, and their influence can be heard throughout extreme music.

But the inspiration for nearly every post-metal band can be traced back to one source: Neurosis. The influence of Neurosis on heavy metal is as immense as their music. Like Venom in the early

---

1. Back in the nineties my mates and I invented the genre 'ManPat' and then suggested that the style of punk we were playing in our various different bands had moved beyond that scene, meaning we were more PostManPat than anything else. It think it got into a few interviews.

2. I hope that helps.

eighties, they blew the doors off what people considered possible. They were a game-changer. A watershed. A turning point. A sea-change. A pivotal moment. Their masterpiece *Through Silver in Blood* had a galvanising effect on the ambitions of those who heard it. While punk had made prog rock seem po-faced, Neurosis made every other metal band seem like they weren't being remotely serious enough. What's the point talking about corrupt governments and social inequality when the UNIVERSE ITSELF IS BEING RENT IN TWO and THE STARS ARE FALLING OUT OF THE SKY?![1]

Neurosis were oblique and complex, but always remained somehow accessible. They tapped into something primal. I've listened to them while camping in woods, hiking across wind-blasted cliffs, and in a ski-lift ascending bleak mountains and it works really well with the natural landscape. As someone who suffers from gender dysphoria, I can say the video of them playing 'Locust Star' at Ozzfest is one of the few things that makes me feel happy to be male. Theirs is a masculinity I can admire. A funnelling of testosterone and rage into something so ferocious it becomes beautiful, like a storm. Or a wolf on a T-shirt.

Neurosis employed a visual artist to complement their live shows, projecting epic montages on a huge screen. They also paved the way for the full beard to really make a comeback. This is often overlooked and undervalued. Metal had lived under the twin tyrannies of the razor and the goatee for too long. Sadly the advent of the hipster has demeaned this entirely. In the wake of Neurosis, a million bands used effects pedals, projections and epic, slow time-signatures. One such band was Isis[2] (who were

1. Although that might be a metaphor.
2. Who were so popular in underground metal circles that the jihadist militant group is named after them.

dismissed as Neurosis clones until Neurosis signed them to their Tribes of Neurot record label . . .). Isis's frontman, Aaron Turner, also founded Hydra Head Records, who oversaw releases from most of the seminal experimental metallic hardcore bands of the nineties and 2000s – Botch, Cave In, Coalesce, Neurosis, etc. Sadly it's now defunct, though still trading old releases (you should support them and labels like them, you know). Weirdly, Isis began to sell loads more T-shirts when the Islamist group started getting in the news. Presumably it reminded people they like the band. 'Oh yeah, I remember Isis. I must buy a T-shirt.'

Other bands in this scene include the short-lived Battle of Mice, who put out one devastating record which narrated the break-up of two of the people in the band. Like Abba![1] Many post-metal bands forgo vocals in favour of complex instrumentals. Bands such as Pelican,[2] Russian Circles, and Red Sparrows. A good rule of thumb as to whether a band is post-something or other is if loads of hipsters like them. Or my mate Al, for that matter.[3]

Other post-bands come from very different scenes. Associated with alt-rock and even nu-metal, TOOL are from a different planet. Massively aided by the fact that their guitarist, Adam Jones, is also a film effects technician who used to work for Stan Winston and thus they could make the absolute fucking best music videos of all time. Their stage shows are psychedelic, almost spiritual experiences, and the band exhibit enormous occult leanings. They're difficult and spiky and massively take the piss.

1. Metalheads love Abba, by the way. That is a fact.

2. The wonderful thing about Pelican: their rider holds more than their belly can.

3. I'm not saying he's a hipster but he has a beard and he lives in Brooklyn now and he lectures on magick.

Godflesh demonstrate the principle that the founding figures in musical movements rarely stay in those movements for long. Justin Broadrick was in the first incarnation of Napalm Death but quickly grew bored of grindcore and went off on his own brutal, electronic/noise direction.

Then there's Godspeed You! Black Emperor. Not a metal band but a keystone for all who heard them (including the people who did the music for the film *28 Days Later* which helped popularise them). They came out of the same sort of squatter/anarcho scene as the mighty Catharsis and that sensibility courses through them, much like the anarchist black metal solo project Panopticon.

Ultimately, post-metal is a broad term for a relatively small clutch of bands. While it suggests everything-that-comes-after-metal, metal will never die and so there is no after. And far from looking to the future, metal continues to feed off its past.

16

The End of the Line:
Retro Metal and the
Revival Movement

The most merciful thing in the world I think is the inability of the human mind to correlate all of its contents. We live on a placid island of ignorance in the midst of black seas of infinity and it was not meant that we should voyage far. The sciences, each straining in its own direction have hitherto harmed us little, but some day the piecing together of dissociated knowledge will uncover such terrifying vistas of reality, and of our frightful position therein that we shall either go mad from the revelation or flee from the deadly light into the peace and safety of a new dark age. – H. P. Lovecraft, 'The Call of Cthulhu'*

In the early 2000s, heavy metal went massively retro. All of a sudden it stopped pursuing the new and revisited old movements. Thrash, doom, power metal, traditional heavy metal, occult rock . . . everything got dug up and revived. In doing so, these movements projected a coherence onto genres that they had previously lacked. Like a UKIP supporter, metal began to find inspiration from a past that never quite existed.

So what's the explanation for heavy metal's sudden U-turn into its back catalogue? Up until the late nineties, metal pushed itself relentlessly forward. Experiment after development, constantly craving novelty, always trying to be heavier, more melodic, harder, faster, slower, more textured. It expanded out in all directions in search of new sounds. It craved the extreme, then it polished it and packaged it for mass acceptance. It was restless and forward-looking. As we've already seen, after the founding of the basic heavy metal template it then found thrash, speed, black, death, doom, grind, industrial, gothic . . . Always pushing forward.

Each movement was a reaction to the last, some spinning off from the current and forming ox-bow lakes – little micro-climates of metal sub-category, like thrash stepping off the escalator before the inevitable march towards death (metal), and the expansion and development of doom as a genre in itself being a self-conscious return to Sabbath's influence after the speed-rush of thrash and grindcore.

Then nu-metal happened and suddenly it felt as if the genre was in retreat, flailing its arms and shouting 'RUN AWAY' like the knights in *Monty Python and the Holy Grail*[1] Terrified of the discovery, like a Lovecraftian scholar it shrank back into the peaceful, reassuring nostalgia of the past. The retro movement was born.

To be truthful, metal has always had an eye on its own history. We celebrate our progenitors as much as any other movement. We revere the old. Just look at the cliché of 'the first album was better'. Everything is better with the benefit of hindsight. In the nineties I wished I had been around for the eighties. Writing this in 2017, the nineties seem like halcyon days, and yet there are more and better bands now than there were when I was a teenager.

---

1. Metal and *Monty Python* go hand in hand. More than once I've joined in with a rousing chorus of 'The Bruces' Philosophers Song' in queues for gigs.

There is a theory that every musical movement will eventually map its own boundaries. If you push heavy metal any further
out from its core it ceases to be heavy metal and becomes something else. It is entirely possible that the sudden interest in
revisiting the past came from metal having fully explored its territory and thus innovation was no longer required. Imagine a
stone dropped in the middle of a large pond. The waves emanate
out from the centre – finding new territory, then they rebound
off the edge, revisiting the parts they've already covered but in
new ways. Then they combine, increase and decrease, creating
endless new patterns. If you want something truly new, you won't
find it recent metal. Instead you find *refinement*, cross-pollination.
New combinations of old sounds.

And this is not a negative thing. At all. It's not even remotely
limiting. The alphabet didn't occur all at once. New letters were
added one at a time. We no longer feel the need to add to it. Those
twenty-six letters do everything we could possibly want them to
do – from *Moby Dick* to the Chilcot Inquiry to all the lyrics on *Ooh
Crikey, It's . . . Lawnmower Deth*. Similarly, the elements of heavy
metal that were created between 1970 and 1996 provide the raw
materials for endless permutations, infinite combinations. Hence
the rise of such genres as 'blackened thrash' and 'death/doom'.

The other factor that led to this revivalist attitude was the
internet. By the end of the 1990s most homes had an internet
connection. Suddenly information on bands was way easier to
access.[1] Newsgroups and websites allowed like-minded headbangers to communicate in unprecedented ways, like a broadband

1. Although photographs of them took FUCKING AGES to download, line
by line . . . and they were in black-and-white, and you had to pick them up
from Boots. And they'd have those little stickers on them criticising your
photographic skills . . .

version of the old tape-trading network. Whereas we used to have to scrape around for mentions of bands' influences in magazines, suddenly an encyclopaedia of knowledge was at our fingertips. A comprehensive knowledge of metal's history was no longer only the province of geeks and record collectors – it was available to all. And those old bands proved to be really, really fucking good. The focus shifted from what was current and novel to what was best from the past: Bathory, Venom, Diamond Head, Discharge, Von – all the bands who we'd heard name-checked or covered but that weren't readily available were open to all. Obscurity was no longer a thing.

This explains both the thrash/old school and death/doom revival movements and it also explains the massive rise in bands re-forming. Refused and Carcass are bigger now than they were at their creative prime.

And then there's the image revival. The internet also gives access to pictures and shopping and so it's now much easier to accurately dress like a metalhead from 1981. And, my God, people really do that. It's like cosplay or some shit. There's moustaches and everything.

There is a thin line between revivalist bands and novelty or pastiche. The Darkness were an early mainstream example. The only time I've ever been accurately heckled on the street was when people saw my (then) bright red hair and sang 'I Believe in a Thing Called Love' at me. To which my reply was simply, 'Yep. I do like that song.' The Darkness were ludicrous, but no more so than the bands they revered. I think theirs was an honest tribute. Which is more than can be said for current glam novelty act Steel Panther, who seem to me to be massively taking the piss. Maybe black metal has removed my sense of humour about the ludicrous.

The first band that really struck me as visually embodying a retro approach was Municipal Waste, a neo-thrash band from

Richmond, Virginia. Reading about them in the pages of *Terrorizer* magazine around 2005, I thought they seemed a bit fake, their anachronistic image looked contrived. But then I saw them live, supporting the peerless New York hardcore band Sick of It All and I was massively, massively impressed. They seemed to take all their influences and mash them up into something really satisfying. Standing on the shoulders of giants, for sure, but standing on the shoulders of A LOT of giants. Plus they have Dave Witte from Discordance Axis on drums and that man is a stone cold legend.[1] Then when I went to see Municipal Waste headlining a show I was even more blown away by the support act, Toxic Holocaust, who do thrash revival in a much more underground kind of way. Tons more bands joined this thrash revival, with a healthy number coming from the UK – Evile, SSS, Kremated, and the superb Send More Paramedics. The movement never reached the scale that thrash did in the eighties, but the bands persist and their influence lingers.

After the thrash revival came a tide of backward-looking bands.[2] Nostalgic occult-rockers Ghost have become bigger than anyone expected. Initially enjoying a small underground buzz, partly due to their being Fenriz's *band of the week* on his MySpace page, they play Blue Öyster Cult meets occult-rock and they do it really well. At least, they do on their excellent first album. I've gone off them a bit. They have this whole anonymity thing going, which was fun for a while. Frankly it's good to see a band that don't trade solely on good looks and over-production get

1. That's pretty much the metal equivalent of getting Leonardo da Vinci doing cartoons for *Viz*. NB. Don't get me wrong – I really fucking love *Viz*. So having Leonardo drawing for them would be totally sick. NB. I mean sick as in good.

2. Which isn't a criticism, by the way. I'm just as nostalgic as you are, trust me.

big. I wish them all the best. Though for nefarious reasons I have their *Metal Hammer* Golden God award in my flat. They are welcome to come and get it but ONLY if they promise that there will be another Repugnant album . . .

Occult-rock in general has seen a massive resurgence (parallel to a wider revival of interest in the occult in general), with bands like The Devil's Blood, In Solitude, and Blood Ceremony. A whole new scene is vastly overshadowing its brief popularity in the seventies.

Black metal has always looked to its roots, but the 2010s have seen a massive swell of bands who hark back to the glory days of the early eighties when extreme metal sub-genres were all one big mush of noise. My particular favourite black/thrash/speed metal retro band is Dungeon, who are from London. Part of me hopes there's another band of the same name in some other part of the world so they'll be forced to call themselves Dungeon (London). Haha. That would be funny.[1]

None of this is to say that new sounds aren't possible. There are still bands making extraordinary and fresh music, whether the hammer-dulcimer-based black metal of The Botanist or the experimental drone of Sunn O))), but the old school still dominates the underground and to my ageing ears that is entirely a Good Thing!

1. Particularly if they covered 'London Dungeon' by the Misfits. Hahaha. In a dungeon. In London.

17

The State of Metal Today

Was metal all better in the past? Have the glory days gone? With Lemmy dead, Black Sabbath retired and two different versions of Entombed knocking about things might seem bleak.

There is no doubt that most mainstream metal today is utter dogshit. But, then, most mainstream *anything* is utter dogshit. The bands who headline the big metal festivals are generally legacy bands whose best albums are twenty or thirty years behind them. I just listened to a 'best metal songs 2017' playlist and it was depressing. The metal music industry is so corporate and capitalistic that it shovels the shiniest, most over-produced crap to the front. Bands who will be as short-lived as the one-hit-wonders you see on re-runs of *Top of the Pops*. It's depressing to watch bands playing that music industry game while the music industry is in the process of dying. Betting on a race long since finished. High-gloss metal is dead. The only metal worth playing comes from the soul, not from a focus group. So fuck that.

However, look beneath the surface and things look much, much healthier. Heavy metal's nostalgia constantly harks back to perceived Golden Ages – whether the nineties for black metal, the mid-eighties for thrash, or the seventies for traditional heavy metal. The truth is there has never been a better time to be a

metalhead than right now. A quick survey of the metal that was
most popular in the eighties suggests it was far from the halcyon
age we now look back upon. It was metal's underground that
made the eighties glorious. And the metal underground today is
bigger, better, healthier, stronger, more vibrant and more heavy
than it has ever been.

The single biggest effect on heavy metal since its birth
has been from the internet. The way recorded music is consumed
has changed so radically in such a short space of time that it has
left people of my generation feeling old before our time. A
few years ago I was performing comedy in an arts centre just
outside Newcastle. An Iron Maiden T-shirt caught my eye,
worn by a teenage girl in the front row. We had a pleasant chat
about metal and I asked what her other favourite bands were.
She told me her very favourite band was Sepultura. This
was awesome! *They were my favourite band when I was sixteen! I
have a Sepultura tattoo!* After asking 'Where were you when I
was your age?'[1] I asked which was her favourite Sepultura
album.

She replied, 'I don't really have one. I listen to them on
YouTube.'

After that my memory is hazy. I recall a ringing in my ears
and three days later I woke up in hospital. While recovering from
the shock in a convalescent home for nineties metalheads, I began
to reflect on the fact that there had been a fundamental shift in
the way in which people consume music. For a start, people used
to actually buy it. When Sepultura's *Roots* came out in 1996 it was
the culmination of months of expectation. On the day of release
my metalhead mates and I jumped on the bus from school to our

---

1.   ... and then reflecting upon the fact that she would have been a toddler
and thus not really my type ...

local independent record shop[1] to buy it on CD.[2] I took it home and listened to it non-stop for the next month. I read every word in the booklet.

But my obsession with Sepultura didn't stretch to listening to all of their recorded output. For a start, my mate Alex told me their first EP and album were unlistenable garbage ('they sound like they were recorded in a tin bath') and I had no real clue where to buy them.

The modern Sepultura fan, while dealing with the fact that they haven't made a genuinely brilliant record since *Roots*, has access to their entire recorded output, including rarities and demos, at the click of a button.

Hard-copy music does still sell. Just yesterday I opened my latest purchase from Bandcamp – the doomy black metal album *Moving Monoliths* by Wilt. It was recommended by Austin Lunn of Panopticon in a column on the website No Clean Singing. I listened to his recommendations through links to streaming tracks, bought the album on Bandcamp, downloaded the digital version and stuck it on my phone, then received the hard copy through the post, along with a patch. People bemoan the drop in record sales, and they're right. It is hugely important to support bands

1. Hot Rocks in Sutton. It was fucking awesome. A little treasure trove of heavy metal and alternative rock. The guy who worked there, Fat Matt, was a strange bloke – not unlike the Comic Book Guy in *The Simpsons*. I was always baffled by the fact that he loved Sepultura but didn't like Pantera. To my sixteen-year-old sensibilities these two bands were the Yin and Yang of extreme metal and if you liked one you surely must like the other. Many years later he proved himself to be more metal than I had given him credit for – he was killed when a helicopter crashed on him.

2. Though as I write, I'm listening to that album on Spotify, because it's the early hours of the morning and I am using headphones and it's easier to listen to music on my laptop.

by shelling out for their records and their merchandise. The music consumer is now like a mini-patron, helping their favourite bands stay on the road.

The tape-trading network that was the scaffold for the death and black metal underground is now something everyone can access. It can be overwhelming – Lunn's end-of-year recommendations consist of more records than the average person buys in a year.

It's not just distribution that is facilitated by technology. The availability of affordable recording equipment and the ease of digital recording mean that a band on a meagre budget can make records with very little outlay, then upload them to the internet and share with their friends, who can then in turn link to it on social media. It's so easy to get songs out there. Once it seemed that everyone in an extreme metal band pretty much knew each other, nowadays there are more new bands than it is possible to keep up with; more thrash metal albums are released every year now than in the whole of the eighties.

This is true broadcasting. The lack of funnelling through record labels, PR, radio stations and corporate record shops has meant a vast democratisation of the entire music industry. It's an expansion of the underground model. It is more meritocratic. People are less influenced by the trend-setters and taste-makers, because they can simply find better music. It may be hard for a young reader to fully comprehend, but we often used to have to buy a record in order to find out whether it was any good. And that's not good when CDs cost £16 a pop. (According to the Bank of England's online inflation calculator, £16 in 1996 is worth nearly £27.56 in 2017.)

What is the impact of this? More great bands to listen to means that individual bands will no longer get as massive. Theoretically it's just as possible for new bands to become massive, if their music is good enough, but, realistically, there will never be another Metallica. Some people see this as a problem, bemoaning the lack of future festival headliners. I think it is brilliant. Metal is best in clubs, not in stadiums. The big weekend festivals should change their model – have one massive headline band, and then invest the rest of the money in smaller stages for a more diverse range of other acts. Download could have a dedicated black and death metal stage for the price of one headliner.

The music industry has been painfully slow to roll with the changes – a pathetic dinosaur still essentially staring in incomprehension as the meteor falls from the sky. Once again, it is ALWAYS the metal underground that is the coal face, the bleeding edge of the subculture. For years the underground has embraced the possibilities of the digital format, from MySpace (remember MySpace? Remember Geocities websites? Remember spangles? How come you don't see white dog poo? Remember Coal Chamber?) to Bandcamp, Soundcloud and Spotify.

Another impact of freely available music is a reduction in concentration span. One of the major advantages of cassette tapes was the lack of random access – you just started it where you'd left off. As a result albums and mix tapes got listened to more evenly. Records and CDs favour the beginnings of albums, and MP3s lead to the universal experience of listening to someone dj-ing at a party and skipping tracks halfway through. Being spoiled for choice means many people give albums less time to grow, and fewer listens in general. Personally, though, I find that a really good record will still get played to death.

In total contrast to the often repeated and seldom challenged statement that it was all better back in the day, there has never been a better time to be a metalhead. Every genre has had a renaissance! Whatever your particular favourite type of metal there are amazing bands out there right now making really, really

fucking good versions of it. The internet provides an embarrassment of riches. And you can listen to it for free. Anyone in doubt
about the quality of new music being released all the time simply
needs to look at the end-of-year best-album lists produced by the
dozens of online metal publications. Oh look, there's a hundred
albums I haven't listened to that are really fucking good.

Metal is still a relatively young culture. It is still developing,
still exploring. Most of the old bands are still playing live, and
more bands than ever before are making amazingly high-quality
music. Sure, we'll never see Motörhead again, and Sabbath have
just shut up shop, but their records are still on our shelves, like
time capsules of moments when metal was perfect. And while
new discoveries await the curious explorer,

in your record collection,
it's all happening now.

Epilogue

The Future of Heavy Metal

The history of heavy metal is a rich patchwork of scenes and golden years. It is easy to look back and to pine for the past. Nostalgia is big business and many great bands had their peak many years ago. But the metal scene today is healthier than it has ever been, with more bands playing more gigs and digital technology allowing recording and direct distribution in a way that was unthinkable for most of metal's history. Most of the bands I have mentioned in this book are still together and touring, and new bands are playing old styles just as well as any of the originators of those styles. The flame of heavy metal will never die.

So what does the future hold?

To extrapolate from the past what will happen in the future is a difficult task. It takes deep analysis of patterns, a wide knowledge of history, a recognition that cause and effect are rarely neatly linear.

In 1970, Black Sabbath could never have foreseen that they were starting a whole new genre and that they would fill arenas nearly fifty years later. In 1982 no one could have predicted that nu-metal would happen, with bands wearing tracksuits and employing turntables in their stage performances. Happily for you, dear reader, I am not just an historian,[1] I am also a practitioner of black magic. In order to formulate an accurate idea of

---

1. Or is that 'a historian'?

the paths heavy metal will take in the future I began with the simplest tool – a ouija board made out of letters cut from an issue of *Kerrang!* magazine. Alas, the spirits I spoke to were all those of dead fourteen-year-olds with terrible taste in music.

'What's that, spirit? Green Day are your favourite ever band and you think Asking Alexandria are dreamy? Is there anyone else up there we could talk to? Like, maybe, your mum or dad?'

It was clear that a sacrifice was necessary. I considered my record collection. The first pressings and seventies gatefold vinyl. The box sets. The entire Darkthrone discography. Then I thought 'fuck that' and made a sandwich and then threw it away. Sacrifice complete. Now for the ritual of divination. I tried tarot cards but the hippy, new-age vibe was not metal enough. A friend suggested reading tea leaves and I suggested she fuck off. But then I struck upon the ultimate heavy metal divination method – the ancient Scandinavian tradition of runes.

I cast the runes while listening to the song 'Runestone to My Memory' by Amon Amarth. But I got distracted by changing the lyric to 'Rhinestone to my mammary' and imagining the frontman, Johan Hegg, with a Dolly Parton cleavage. And, trust me, once you've got that image in your head it will not fucking budge.

I was at a loss. So I drank a bottle of Jack Daniel's, ate a handful of weed and waited until the spirit of Lemmy, or Dio, or that bloke out of Slipknot got in touch.

The rest is as dictated to me by those spirits. Every word is true.

2018 – The second edition of this book is published. It becomes a surprise runaway success, read by everyone from dedicated metalheads to those in academia, to figures in popular culture. Kim Kardashian is photographed reading it, and as a result her fans all buy a copy. *A History of Heavy Metal* becomes the must-have accessory for everyone on social media. Suddenly an entire legion of dickhead pop culture clones begin to actually listen to the bands whose T-shirts they are given to wear by their stylists. Sales of heavy metal records immediately spike, leading to a renaissance in the worldwide popularity of heavy metal not seen since the glory days of the 1980s. Saxon, Lamb of God and Exodus become stadium-filling bands.

2019 – Fenriz makes the fictional band Creme Brulee from *The League of Gentlemen* his band of the week. Due to overwhelming pressure from the newly reinvigorated worldwide metal scene the actors who portray Creme Brulee are forced to form a real band. Their shows become the surprise success story of the year, smashing records worldwide for ticket sales and audience attendance. They become the best-selling live band of all time, selling more tickets than peak Led Zeppelin. A grumpy Led Zeppelin humbly ask to open for them. Mötley Crüe re-re-re-form and drummer Tommy Lee exceeds his upside-down and rollercoaster drums by having a drum kit that tunnels through the centre of the earth. Talk of the heavy metal bubble being about to burst comes to nothing. Beyoncé and her ilk are knocked from the top of the international music charts in favour of Nile, Cradle of Filth and, sadly, Trivium. The massive increase in arena-touring metal bands puts a strain on the hospitality industry and band-proof hotels are developed in response. Drone technology is installed in televisions, allowing them to automatically fly back into hotel windows. Axl Rose announces a new Guns N' Roses album, due to come out in 2020.

2020 – No sign of the Guns N' Roses album. Bruce Dickinson trains as an astronaut so that Iron Maiden can play the first ever gig on the moon, having become far too big for any normal-sized show to hold them. They play a twenty-four-hour set, which repeats six times so that every quarter of the globe can watch the show through special telescopes, the sound being blasted through speakers the size of Belgium. Over 99 per cent of the population watches the show and Maiden become more famous than the sun.

During a television address, the US President Donald Trump splits into two separate but identical entities, one of which always tells the truth, the other always tells lies. Two contradictory statements are made – the first suggesting there is nothing to worry about, the second stoking fear and paranoia that he has been replaced by hostile aliens. 'I fully intend to continue to serve this country and do the best job I can,' he said, adding, 'Screw you lot, I'm in this for myself. Every inch of power and every dollar I can grab. Fuck America and fuck the human race.'

Emergency legislation is put in place to accommodate this 'dual' presidency. During a charity drive for/against disabled children five weeks later the two Donalds split open again, revealing themselves to have been made up of highly intelligent lizards with unrealistic English dialects. (Like Russell Brand's.) A lizard spokeswoman for the gestalt Trump is quoted as saying, 'Strike a light! Apples and pears! I've ownly bleedin gawn an been all lizards!'

The constitution is further updated. Taking advantage of the new political landscape, Manowar launch a campaign to become the next president under the slogan 'Make America Metal Again'.

2021 – Still no new Guns N' Roses album. Despite the gestalt lizards-Trump doing well in pre-election polling, Manowar win by a landslide. Their first move in office is to declare war against False Metal. Resources are shifted from the fight against global terrorism and the undefined concept of 'False Metal' is declared illegal and un-American. Linkin Park are immediately arrested and sent to Guantánamo Bay. A new McCarthy-ite era dawns as the whole of America becomes paranoid about un-metal 'poseurs' under the bed. Civil unrest breaks out across the nation as 'band shirt justification vigilantes' terrorise anyone unable to answer questions about obscure albums. 'Name the producer' becomes a slogan of civil war.

The twenty-first-century poet Gerhard Heintz writes:

> *First they came for the hair metal bands, and I did not speak out,*
> *For I am not a hair metal band,*
> *Then they came for the nu-metal bands, and I did not speak out,*
> *For I've never really like nu-metal apart from the first Korn album,*
> *And even that has a lot of filler,*
> *Then they came for the bands that have short hair or use keyboards,*
> *And I did not speak out because I have long hair,*
> *And I don't like music with keyboards in,*
> *Except maybe Emperor.*
> *Then they came for me, and there was no one left to speak out for me.*

In order to maximise economies of scale, Steel Panther buy Colombia.

Several bands are forced at gunpoint to reform their classic line-ups. Sepultura are first. An ailing Bill Ward plays with an ailing rest-of-Black-Sabbath. Darkthrone are made to play live.

Meshuggah record an album with such complex time signatures they get trapped inside the music. The album is never released for fear of opening a black hole. Guns N' Roses announce that their new album is nearly ready.

2022 – Varg Vikernes launches an attack on a mosque. His rifle jams and he is beaten to death by Muslim shoes. The clip goes viral.

America annexes Finland and declares it the fifty-first state.

2023 – Dream Theater publish an album entirely in musical notation and physically disappear up their own arses. Guns N' Roses say they've scrapped what they've written so far and started again, it's sounding great and it will be out next year.

2024 – Still no Guns N' Roses album. After four years of totalitarian heavy metal rule, the inevitable backlash begins. Metal is seen as deeply uncool – the music of the elites. Rebellious Christian groups in Norway begin to burn down heavy metal venues and rehearsal rooms. Manowar win a second term, but are impeached after being photographed with their nipples covered up.

2025 – Metal is outlawed in Europe. Rob Halford is imprisoned. Europe are also imprisoned. Guns N' Roses say their album is ready, but the political situation makes it too dangerous to release it this year. Next year for sure, though.

2026 – The First Metal War. Manowar increase the scope of their offensive and declare war on irony. Anti-metal forces coalesce and begin the fightback. French Nationalist band Peste Noire immediately surrender.

Anti-metal forces develop an irony bomb and aim it at metal, in general.

The band Cancer is the first to die. Of cancer. Flotsam and Jetsam drown off the coast of New York, and wash up three days later. The few surviving ex-members of Rainbow are chopped up and made into skittles. The less said about the way Sodom died, the better . . .

It soon occurred to the anti-metal side that far from being ironic, these deaths are actually *fitting*, which is actually sort of the opposite of ironic. Initial thoughts are that the anti-metal forces simply didn't really understand what irony was. They are fundamentally wrong being anti-metal, after all. However, it is soon revealed that the Forces of Metal had launched an attack on the irony bomb software, re-coding it so that it fundamentally misunderstood what irony was. It was nicknamed the Alanis Morissette virus. After the malware is removed, the irony bomb is redeployed, and the ironic casualties on the metal side really begin to mount. Life of Agony are despatched quickly and painlessly. Dark Funeral are buried at midday in the Sahara Desert. Overkill are taken out with a single shot to the head. Nuclear Assault die of natural causes.

The anti-metal forces strongly resemble fascism, which makes all the NSBM bands really conflicted. Soon enough, they're all rounded up and executed as 'bad examples' of fascism.

2027 – The war goes nuclear. Which secretly delights all the thrash and crust bands. The survival rate for metalheads is considerably higher than the general population for a number of reasons: most metalheads have at least one survivalist friend, nearly all own at least one gas mask. It also transpires that Manowar's administration had built nuclear bunkers in all the metal bars and rehearsal rooms – worldwide.

2036 – In the wastelands of the post-nuclear earth, the metalheads emerge blinking into the drab sunlight. Into a world populated entirely by people who love heavy metal. Guns N' Roses say they're really sorry but their album got destroyed in the war.

2044 – Headbanging well into his nineties, Cannibal Corpse's vocalist, George 'Corpsegrinder' Fischer, suffers the indignity of headbanging his head clean off. It is retrieved by security in the gap between stage and crowd, put on ice and reattached an hour later. Fischer immediately writes his first set of lyrics ever based on a real-life experience. Still no sign of that Guns N' Roses album.

2047 – Black Sabbath are cloned. An anniversary tour is booked for 2070.

2078 – The cloned Black Sabbath massively fall out and become addicted to futuristic drugs. Sharon Osbourne is hastily cloned to provide cloned Ozzy with a successful solo career.

2081 – The ghoulishly preserved Metallica commence a hundred-year anniversary tour, which will last fifteen years. They ask Guns N' Roses to tour with them, but they're too busy working on the new album.

2130 – The last ever hard-copy, real-life piece of recorded music is released, mainly as a novelty item for collectors.

5078 – As people live increasingly in computer simulations, it becomes possible to go on the internet in other alternative dimensions. A world in which Lars, not Cliff, died in the coach crash shows Metallica making pretty much the same artistic decisions but without any of the success their highly driven drummer gave them. The near-infinite amount of music once available becomes a literally infinite amount of music. Most of it is rubbish and the good stuff is mainly bands' first albums . . .

Millions of years in the future, the universe expands so far that it suffers heat death. The bonds between every particle no longer effective, light and heat and time all cease. Finally there is silence.

Just before the final star goes out, in the very last twinkling of the universe, as time itself dies and all that is, was and ever will be cascades into infinite nothing . . .

. . . Guns N' Roses' new album finally surfaces.

And then a new big bang starts the whole thing once more.

Humans evolve on a new earth, begin bashing rocks with sticks and . . . well.

You can just go back to the start of the book and read it again . . .

Index